ENRICH
PUBLISHING

HUMANITY

The Next 50 and 500 Years

LEE Wai-choi

ENRICH
PUBLISHING

Published by

Enrich Publishing Ltd.
A Member of Enrich Culture Group
Unit A, 17/F, 78 Hung To Road
Kwun Tong, Kowloon,
Hong Kong

Copyright © 2023 by Enrich Publishing Ltd.

By Eddy LEE Wai-choi

English translation from the 2020 Chinese edition by POON Chiu-keung
Edited by Glenn Griffith and Penny Ho
Cover image by Getty Images
Book design by Joyce Leung

ISBN 978-988-8853-04-5

Published in Hong Kong.

Contents

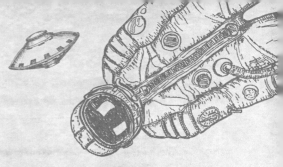

Acknowledgement

I would like to express my heartfelt thanks to Ms. Annie Chen, without whose encouragement and support this book would not have seen the light of day. It was she who proposed the idea of producing an English edition of my 2020 Chinese book on this subject. Ms. Chen not only sponsored the translation costs but also funded a portion of the production costs for this English edition. For her generous support I will forever be grateful.

The Chinese edition of this book was published in 2020. For this English edition, I have updated the contents to reflect the state of affairs up to mid-2023. Additionally, I have incorporated new materials to reinforce my arguments and further clarified some of my explanations. As such, this is not a mere translation of my original Chinese book, but a thoroughly revised edition for English-speaking readers. I hope you find it a rewarding and worthwhile read.

Preface

The book in your hand has been more than half a century in the making.

I have always wanted to write this book, but from the day I first decided on the project to the completion of the manuscript, events important or otherwise in life have intervened, including the writing and publication of close to forty other books.

Looking back, all that time taken - and the knowledge and life experience acquired - has worked out better not worse. A monumental project of this magnitude meant that being over-prepared is not nearly enough.

It all began with a book named *What Man May Be - The Human Side of Science*. It was a book written in 1956 by the American science writer George R. Harrison. The book I read was a Chinese translation published in Taiwan, and the Chinese title adopted was literally "The Future of Mankind."

I was in grade 6 when I saw this book in a bookstore by chance. I grew up in a family of limited means and pocket money was a luxury. But a book on the future of mankind was just too good to miss, so without sparing a thought I parted with my treasured saving of HK$ 2 (*which works out about to be around 40 cents in US currency at that time*) and bought it. (This is the second book I bought for myself. The first one was *The Story of Electricity* bought together by me and two school friends each contributing HK$ 60 cents each.)

I bought the book in grade 6 and finished reading it shortly after I started high school. The influence it has on me could not be over-exaggerated, and for which I could not thank the writer Mr Harrison as well as the translator Mr Yi enough. Not only did it ignite my lifelong passion in science, it also impressed me deeply about the inseparable connection between science and the human world.

While I treasure the book very much, I was also somewhat disappointed. This is because according to the Chinese title, I expected to find a prediction of the future of humankind, but that was virtually non-existent. I should have known from the subtitle of the book '*the Human Side of Science*,' but as I was reading the Chinese translation, I missed that initially. For a long time, I felt cheated.

From that day on, I have been searching for books that really tried to forecast the future. Over the past several decades I have read many books but have yet to find a single one that is truly satisfying. The better ones are *Profiles of the Future* by Arthur C. Clarke (1962) and *The Next Ten Thousand Years* by Adrian Berry (1974). These are projections on the far future. For the near future, the most notable work is Alvin Toffler's *The Future Shock* (1970), and its sequels *The Third Wave* (1980) and *Power Shift* (1990), all of which I devoured feverishly. They whetted my appetite, but I was yearning for something more. And there are the poorer ones: the series of "mega-trends" book written by John Naisbitt, which I found to be a waste of time, and George Friedman's The *Next 100 Years* (2009) and *The Next Decade* (2011), which I found to be highly unimaginative. The latest disappointment was the 2016 work *Homo Deus: A Brief History of Tomorrow* by Israeli historian Yuval Noah Harari. In my view, one would be better served by reading Al Gore's *The Future* (2013), Martin Rees' *On the Future* (2018), and Stephen Baxter's *Deep Future* (2001) for glimpses into the near-term, medium-term, and far future.

If there isn't one, how about writing one myself? And so, after several decades of thinking and a solid year of hard work, I wrote the book I had always wanted. I shall leave it to you to decide how good it is.

A quick read of the table of contents shows how much emphasis I place on the argument that 'to foretell the future one must know the present, and to know the present one must know the past.' This book begins with a look back on history starting with the Agriculture Revolution. For a better and complete understanding of the story of humankind, however, I would in this Preface give you an even more long-term perspective by going all the way back to the very beginning of it all:

* 13.8 billion years ago: the Big Bang, which gave rise to all space, time and matter we now know of (though scientists are still trying hard to make sense of the true nature of "dark matter" and "dark energy");

* 10 billion years ago: our Milky Way galaxy formed;

* 4.6 billion years ago: Solar System, with our Earth in it, formed;

* 3.9 billion years ago: origin of life on Earth (initially along the coastal regions);

* 3.5 billion years ago: photosynthesis arose (first in a lifeform called cyanobacteria);

* 2.5 to 2 billion years ago: amount of free oxygen increasing significantly in the atmosphere, the ozone layer was formed, and most life transitioned from anaerobic to aerobic;

* 540 million years ago: the Cambrian Explosion, when multicellular organisms of all shapes and sizes appeared, mainly in the ocean;

* 450 million years ago: appearance of vertebrates on land;

* 240 million years ago: rise of the dinosaurs;

* 65 million years ago: mass extinction caused by an asteroid impact led to the eventual demise of the dinosaurs, and mammals began to take over;

* 55 million years ago: rise of the primate, which includes species such as the modern-day lemurs, monkeys, apes, and humans, and their ancestors;

* 30 million years ago: monkey and ape lineages split;

* 20 million years ago: ancestor of the gibbons and Hominidae primates (such as orang-utans, gorillas, chimpanzees, bonobos, humans, and their direct ancestors) became separate taxonomical families;

Hereafter we would focus on the history in connection with the origin of humankind:

* 16 million years ago: the ancestor of modern orang-utans split from the family of Hominidae;

* 9 million years ago: the ancestor of modern gorillas split from the family of Hominidae;

* 6.3 million years ago: the common ancestor to the chimpanzee and bonobo apes split from the ancestor of humankind;

* 4 million years ago: Australopithecus, a distant ancestor of modern humans, developed an erect posture (bipedal locomotion);

* 2 million years ago: *Homo habilis*, a kind of ancient humans, began to fashion stone tools on a regular basis;

* 1.5 million to 500 thousand years ago: diaspora of *Homo erectus* (a kind of ancient humans) began, spreading into parts of Eurasia. *Homo erectus* had a brain size of over 1000 ml compared to 1350 ml of modern humans and 450 ml of a gorilla. An example is 'Peking man' who thrived 500 thousand years ago and had mastered the use of fire.

* 300 thousand years ago: archaic *Homo sapiens* (such as *Homo heidelbergensis*) emerged in East Africa;

* 200 thousand years ago: modern *Homo sapiens* emerged in Africa, world diaspora began;

* 70 thousand years ago, the last great wave of emigration from East Africa, considered to consist of the direct ancestors of all modern humans;

* 200 to 40 thousand years ago: *Homo neanderthalensis or Homo sapiens neaderthalensis* (Neandertal Man) thrived;

* 40 thousand years ago: *Homo neanderthalensis* crowded out by modern *Homo sapiens*;

* 12,500 years ago: Agriculture Revolution began.

Just to show how incredibly brief human history is in cosmic terms, scientists have devised a calendar in which the entire history of the Universe is compressed into a single year. On this Cosmic Calendar, the Universe was born in the Big Bang at 0h 0m 0s on January 1, with 24h 0m 0s December 31 being the here and now.

Now let's look at the various mileposts in this cosmic calendar. The most ancient stars and galaxies formed in about mid January. Our Milky Way galaxy was a latecomer, formed only on May 11. Our Solar System came even later, not until September 1, with our Earth forming at about the same time.

The oldest life forms on Earth appeared on September 21. Photosynthesis began on October 12, filling the atmosphere with oxygen, but not significantly until October 29.

Most people would find it hard to believe, but multi-cellular life did not appear until very late in the Cosmic Year. By the time the Cambrian explosion happened it was already mid- December. Fishes became a dominant aquatic animal on December 18. Amphibians appeared on December 22, followed by the reptiles one day later.

Along the way, dinosaurs ruled the Earth for about 150 million years, but they were a Christmas event, lasting just those five days from December 25 to 30 on the Cosmic Calendar. Unfortunately for the dinosaurs, an asteroid impact on December 30 doomed them to eventual and almost total oblivion (with birds being their distant descendants).

New Year's Eve on the Cosmic Calendar was an eventful day, with the various ancestral species of apes coming on stage. By the time the ancestors of humankind appeared, it was already past 2 o'clock in the afternoon.

Humans did not acquire the necessary skills to mass produce stone tools until 10:30 pm on New Year's Eve. When the first fire was lit by humans it was 11:44 pm. When humans became the first farmers at 11:59:32 pm, midnight was less than about half a minute away.

Someone has come up with this analogy: if the distance between the tips of the middle fingers of our outstretched arms was the length of cosmic history, scraping off the very tip of the middle finger nail on one side, and the entirety of human history would be gone.

With this in mind, we are now ready to embark on a journey beginning with the Agricultural Revolution up to the present. We will then examine the current state of the human world, after which we will attempt to map out the future path of human development in the next 50 and 500 years.

I have an invitation for you my Dear Reader. After reading through chapters 1 to 7, please pause for a while, and try to contemplate what the world will look like in 50 and 500 years' time. Continue reading, and try to answer the questions one by one as posed in the rest of the book. By doing so, I hope you would be able to come up with the best educated guess of what is in store for our race, and also come to an understanding of what are the most urgent tasks lying ahead of us.

One last plead. Please try to preserve this book or better still, ask your kids to be custodians of this book until 2070. It would be an interesting exercise for you (if you are still around) and for your kids to compare the fears and aspirations of this author (who most definitely would not be around anymore) with the reality at that time. Thank you!

Eddy LEE Wai-choi
10th August 2023

1

The Ascent of Civilization:
Blessings and Curse

1.1 From Nature to Culture:
Memetic Evolution

You may be wondering why a book on the future of humankind begins with a review of history. Well, as the Chinese saying goes, "Past events not forgotten are the teachers preparing us for the future." [#] For an individual, a nation, or the entire human race, it pays to know one's past. Without an adequate understanding of the past, there is no way one can make sense fully of the present, let alone forecasting the future. Just as a long jump athlete needs to make a long approach run, and an archer needs to draw back the string, we need to take a long hard look at our past to power ourselves up for that leap of imagination into the future.

American-Spanish philosopher George Santayana (1863-1952) once said, "Those who cannot remember the past are condemned to repeat it." American historian Howard Zinn (1922-2010) described the indispensable nature of history in a different way, "If you don't know history it is as if you were born yesterday. And if you were born yesterday, anybody up there in a position of power can tell you anything, and you have no way of checking up on it." Needless to say, the first thing a new conqueror does is to destroy the culture and erase the history of those he subjugated, for that would be the safest bet against any future insurgence.

In the Preface I gave a quick rundown of the origin and evolution of humankind. Here we will focus our discussion on the 'civilised phase' of human history over the past 10,000 years.

Anthropologists who study human behaviour and culture draw a distinction between 'culture' and 'civilisation.' Culture refers to traits, habits and practices acquired through learning versus those inherited biologically as in the case of ants and bees. In the restricted context of the human species, culture refers to particularities exhibited in different groups of humans, such as in food preference and taboos (Europeans prefer bread while Asians rice; no pork for Muslims and no beef for Hindus etc.) and burial

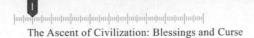

rites (ground burial for all except Tibetans who practise *jhator*, sky burial). Civilisation on the other hand is more on the commonalities between different cultures, such as the Agriculture Revolution, social stratification, male dominance, warfare, use of writing and metal, and religion in society.

The distinction drawn between culture and civilisation is by no means clear cut. Another distinction is in terms of the level of development, so much so that there is the Mayan "civilisation" in ancient Central America but only an Inuit "culture" in the North Polar region. Yet another distinction is time. Civilisation refers to what happened in the human world in the past five to six thousand years. Not so for cultures which could have lasted much longer. Hence the study of human culture rather than human civilisation 50,000 years ago.

In his book *The Philosophy of Civilization* (1949), Albert Schweitzer offers a succinct summary on the nature of civilisation: "Civilization is then twofold in its nature: it realizes itself in the supremacy of reason, first, over the forces of Nature, and secondly, over the dispositions of men."

As with many things in research, the understanding of culture and civilisation changes over time. Culture used to be associated only with the human societies past and present, such as the Maori culture in New Zealand, the Yangshao culture in China 6,000 years ago in the New Stone Age, the 60,000 year continuous culture of the Australian Aborigines, the Acheulean culture of the *Homo erectus* dating back a million years ago, and the oldest culture on record, the Oldowan culture of the stone age Homo habilis which thrived more than two million years before present.

In recent times, the concept of culture has been broadened thanks to scientists studying animal behaviour. Japanese macaques, or snow monkeys as they are more popularly known, are a representative example of *behaviour culture* in animals. One troop has been observed to wash sweet potatoes clean of mud and sand before eating, the practice having been imitated and adopted by the whole troop after one monkey tried it. Another troop was observed to be dropping handful of wheat grains and sand in water, so that the grains float and the heavier sand particles sink to the bottom, after which the monkeys scooped up the grain to eat. Such learned behaviour remained in the group practising it, and has not been seen to have passed on to other groups.

Māori village, late 1800s

Chimpanzees in the wild are not as easy to observe as Japanese macaques. Still, field study over many years have revealed that chimpanzee troops also possess skills which require learning, in other words, skills passed on culturally, and not biologically via genes. Such skills include the use of thin branches that are trimmed of leaves to fish for ants (a delicacy to chimpanzees) from tree holes. Such learned behaviour, which varies from troop to troop, would also fit the criteria of cultural traits.

Richard Dawkins, British biologist, and proponent of the idea of the "Selfish Gene," also introduced the word and concept of *meme* to the world. Human behaviour, Dawkins contended, are influenced just as much by cultural as by genetic factors. And just as biological information is transmitted between organisms by genes, so cultural information, such as learned habits and practices, and the underlying concept and ideas, are transmitted between organisms or groups of organisms by *memes*. While Dawkins introduced the concept to explain the evolution of human behaviour, such reference had since been broadened to include some other higher animals.

According to this view, genetic evolution, which has directed the evolution of life for 99.9% of the time since life first appeared on Earth, was supplemented by *memetic evolution* when hominids emerged some 2 million years ago. Just as the Cambrian Explosion 500 million years ago heralded in a new age of genetic evolution, the Agriculture Revolution 10,000 years ago ushered in a new age of cultural evolution: the rise of civilisations.

1.2 Agricultural Revolution and **the Rise of Civilization**

The Agricultural Revolution, which began about 12,000 years ago, is arguably the most significant evolutionary milestone in the history of humanity, after toolmaking, fire, and language.

To say that a rise in human intelligence brought forth the Agricultural Revolution is probably correct but is an incomplete assessment. Paleoanthropology studies show that the Cro-Magnon and Neanderthal Men who lived 40,000 to 50,000 years ago possessed larger brains than modern *Homo sapiens*. Yet these two ancient humans did not develop agriculture.

The missing piece is provided by paleoclimatology. It turned out that in the past several million years, our Earth has gone through several ice ages. The last ice age began about 120,000 years ago and reached its peak around 22,000 years ago. Needless to say, agriculture in the frigid weather and frozen landscape simply was not an option open to humans. It was not until warmer weather returned toward the end of the last ice age, around 12,000 years ago, that cultivation of wild plants for their seeds and tubers appeared in various parts of the world. In other words, intelligence aside, there must also exist the right environment for breakthrough, in this case the Agricultural Revolution, to occur.

Scientists once believed Mesopotamia, a historical region of Western Asia, was the only place in the world where agriculture originated. (This region is situated within the Tigris-Euphrates River system being parts of nowadays Iraq and Syria.) Agriculture elsewhere in the world all derived from here. Research over the past several decades have shown this to be otherwise: agriculture also arose independently in the North China plain, the Ethiopian Highlands, Western Africa, and the Sahel, south of the Sahara Desert. In the New World, the Mayan and Inca civilisations, in Central and South America respectively, also developed agriculture independent of Mesopotamia.

Agriculture in ancient Egypt, ancient India and amongst First Nation North Americans are indeed offshoots of those centres of development. Latest research also showed that agriculture on New Guinea is also indigenous.

Developments in the New World (North and South America) is of particular interest. The global sea level was much lower 13,000 years ago, so that what is now the Bering Strait, which separates the continental landmasses of Asia and North America, was dry land back then. Humans entered the New World via this land bridge, and in a relatively short time of less than 10,000 years, they migrated all the way to the very southern tip of South America. No contact whatsoever took place between the humans in the New World and the Old, until 1492 when Christopher Columbus landed somewhere in the Bahamas. This state of isolation has offered an unprecedented opportunity to anthropologists to study cultural development in isolation. (Vikings from northern Europe landed on the northeastern Canadian seaboard in the tenth century and set up a small colony which did not last long. They only had minimal contact with the indigenous people.)

When the Maya and Inca civilisations were discovered in the early 16th century, the Spanish Conquistadores marvelled at the magnitude of their engineering in architecture, urban planning and hydrology. Missionaries were amazed by their complex social hierarchy, and their elaborate rites and rituals. (The Mayan calendar was at least on par if not ahead of its European counterpart.) What was most surprising was that neither of these advanced civilisations, while adept in crafting exquisite gold ornaments, used metal tools or weapons. What is more, the Inca Empire had no written language. Tying knots with a rope was the sole means of record.

However, the Mayan and Inca civilisations are the exception than the rule in a global perspective. Metal tools and a written language are still considered important milestones in the evolution of human civilisation, as we shall see later.

Broadly speaking, the Agricultural Revolution encompasses plant cultivation and animal husbandry. Both involved the domestication of plants and animals growing in the wild. Let's now examine how these processes had influenced the human world.

Success in the cultivation and harvest of domesticated plants led to sizable surplus of food crops, freeing up labour to work on other tasks such as making tools, weaving cloth, building shelters and other structures, and then on to wine making, food preparation, storytelling, educating children, trading, and commerce, observing nature to foretell omens, etc. Social division of labour marked the first steps toward civilisation.

Adam Smith (1723-1790), widely regarded as the father of modern economics, explained the importance of the division of labour in the very first page of his seminal work *The Wealth of Nations*, published in 1776. Smith made use of the case of a pin factory to illustrate the importance of division of labour. Assuming one skilled craftsman can make 20 pins a day. With ten unskilled but suitably trained craftsmen, each working on one step in the fabrication of a pin, they may produce as many as thousands of pins a day. Put simply, division of labour increases productivity immensely.

With crop production leading to food surplus and the rise of the leisure/ruling class, the Agricultural Revolution gave rise to heightened division of labour and social hierarchy. On the other hand, domesticating wild animals also led to a steady supply of edible meat (high quality proteins) as well as muscle power. Draught animals such as the horse, donkey, oxen/water buffalo and camel (and llama in South America) multiplied the pulling and load carrying power of humans, making possible long distance travel by people and of goods, enabling material and cultural exchange between hitherto isolated communities. Tribes turned into kingdoms and even empires, with the accompanying warfare and cultural diffusion across vast distances.

Needless to say, the above scenario did not always eventuate. The diaspora of *Homo sapiens* and the end of the last ice age led to the emergence of advanced civilisations in some parts of the world, while humans in other regions, notably the Aboriginal Australians who first set foot on that continent some 60,000 years ago, the indigenous peoples along the Amazon, and the Inuit inhabiting the north polar region, have remained very much unchanged over time.

It used to be argued that difference in the intelligence and diligence of races gave rise to drastically different outcomes in human societies around the world. Research over the past decades has shown, however, that it is where these ancient peoples chose to make their home which has a decisive influence on their subsequent development. In other words, given two equally vegetated and habitable areas, there still exist significant differences in the number of plant and animal species which can be domesticated for the purpose of agriculture. One example is the zebra in Africa, which has resisted domestication into a draught and ride animal. It is no exaggeration to say where early migrating humans made their homes determined their subsequent fate for the next hundreds of generations. (Imagine this extreme case, where an early people had chosen to inhabit an area with lethally high ambient radioactivity. To their descendants' dismay generation after generation died from an unknown illness, until their modern day descendants found out it was cancer caused by exposure to radiation.)

A Yanomami baby removed from its own people living in the Amazon jungle and raised in New York becomes a typical New Yorker, and might even make a mark on Wall Street. Likewise, a baby born in New York but raised by the Yanomami in the Amazon jungle becomes a Yanomami hunter or warrior. Trying to explain the diversity in human societies by attributing it to differences in genetic makeup is just not good enough.

The British historian Arnold Joseph Toynbee is credited as the first to examine comprehensively the rise and fall of civilisations. In his seminal work *A Study of History*, published between 1934 and 1961, he examined the development of 23 (later expanded to 26) civilisations, in which he put forth his theory of 'Challenge and Response'. Toynbee argued that the rise and blooming of civilised societies is the result of human response to various challenges posed by the environment. A society whose people are too well provided for by Nature, such as those on lush and fertile South Pacific islands, face so few challenges that civilisation remains relatively unsophisticated. On the other hand, peoples having to constantly tackle the severe challenges posed by a harsh environment, such as desert dwelling Aboriginal Australians and indigenous peoples inhabiting the densely forested mountains of New Guinea, will have no spare energy to develop a sophisticated civilisation.

Toynbee's theory is widely regarded as a kind of 'environmental determinism,' and in the last hundred years or so has been roundly criticised by many historians. Not only that, his critics also pointed out the weakness in the theory, that 'challenge and response' is a circular argument in the nature of a tautology. Given the difficulty in quantifying 'environmental challenge' in the first place, it would be easy to say that a civilisation did not make it because there was just too much, or too little, challenge, or, conversely, a civilisation prospered because the challenge happened to be just the right amount. A theory that explains everything explains nothing.

Such are the criticisms levelled against Toynbee's theory which I find rather unfair. Toynbee, far from being a pure 'environmental determinist,' placed almost equal emphasis on the power of the human will, or subjective agency. Toynbee pointed out that more often human societies were propelled forward by the effort of an elite few, possessing extraordinary foresight and courage. Civilisation moves forward thanks to this 'creative minority.'

Put it another way, it is the same nurture vs. nature conundrum in the interpretation of history. Be it 'Man makes the Times' or 'Times makes the Man,' the truth is always somewhere in between. It is where to draw the line that is the eternal problem.

In his 1997 book *Guns, Germs and Steel* the American zoologist Jared Diamond elevated this debate to a new level. He put forward a comprehensive and cogent argument, based on a large volume of scientific research worldwide on the origin of the Agriculture Revolution, that the natural environment, in particular the existence or otherwise of *domesticable* plants and animals, poses a decisive influence on the rise of civilisation. Diamond's argument has helped to advance Toynbee's theory of the rise of civilisation, as well as giving 'environmentalism' a substantial scientific basis.

In his book Diamond also made this penetrating observation, that the Eurasian landmass straddling a big east-west expanse has proven conducive to the interaction between human societies inhabiting the same climatic zone. Such interaction has over the centuries led to cultural exchange and racial intermingling, catalysing the rise and prosperity of many civilisations. On the contrary, Africa and the Americas, with a north-south expanse much bigger than east-west, thereby creating massive latitudinal variation in climate and ecology, has impeded the growth of civilisation and empires.

That is the origin of the Agricultural Revolution in theory. How did it influence the course of human civilisation? In one word: ascendancy, as in the following list:

1. Most human societies became sedentary, having no further need to migrate in step with animals and plants due to seasonal change. The few that remained hunter-gatherers, and those remaining nomadic so their domestic animals could move around and graze, found themselves more and more often in conflict over natural resources with sedentary societies. Such conflict between human societies became a main theme in civilisation.

2. Food surplus led to bigger and bigger populations and the rise of villages, towns and subsequently cities.

3. Writing and arithmetic were invented, initially as a means to record harvest and its distribution and storage, land demarcation, and taxation by the authority.

4. Formulation of codes and rules on how people and societies should interact with each other, leading to the promulgation of laws and legal codes, such as the Code of Hammurabi which dates back to 3800 years ago.

5. The creative arts became more and more sophisticated, for example, the architecture and sculptures of the Babylon empire, and the epic poem Gilgamesh composed more than 3000 years ago.

6. The rise of philosophy and religions, the earliest example in writing being the Rig Veda written in ancient India some 4000 years ago, and the Zoroastrian doctrines from the Persian empire, nowadays Iran.

7. Beginnings of the scientific quest. Eratosthenes in ancient Greece, some 2300 years ago, came up with the diameter of the Earth by inference.

But history is paradoxical. The Agricultural Revolution was a blessing to early human societies. It also proved to be a curse to humankind in many respects, as we shall see in the next chapter.

1.3 the Agricultural
Trap

While the Agricultural Revolution and the ascent of civilization is undoubtedly a milestone in human history to be celebrated, it also turns out to be, paradoxically, a curse to human societies through the ages. Here are some of its adverse impacts:

1. Massive destruction of the natural environment, with countless species driven to a niche existence, or worse, to extinction, at the expense of vastly expanded populations of domesticated plants and animals.

2. Occurrence of large scale armed conflicts, triggered by the fight over accumulation of sizable surpluses from agriculture and the resulting wealth, or disputes over resource rich territory. Come the Age of Metals, and later the invention of gunpowder, and of dynamite in the 20th century, modern warfare became massively bloody and lethal. It is no exaggeration to say that warfare is humankind's 'original sin.'

3. Oppression on an unprecedented scale. People captured in tribal conflicts ended up as slaves, eventually slavery becoming institutionalised, which did not end until recent times: in North America, only after the Civil War ended in 1865, a mere century and a half ago.

   Slavery aside, human civilisation became characterised by the 'class society,' one in which a minority (more often than not the rich and powerful, such as nobility, land owners, capitalists, etc.) has control over the bulk of society's resources (land, cattle, machinery, capital, information/knowledge), and directing the majority at their behest in exchange for a living. Needless to say, the new social order has since become the tool of oppression and exploitation worldwide.

4. Male domination, yet another depraved development in which the oppression and subjugation of women was institutionalised. While basic gender equality is the

norm in hunter-gatherer societies, the agriculture revolution brought women a fate for the worse. A sedentary lifestyle, land acquisition and ownership, the pursuit of higher productivity through more and more intensive labour, the accumulation and personalising of and disputes over wealth all contributed to the decline of women's status in society. As an example, women in late dynastic China were viewed as nothing more than men's appendage, as evidenced in the sayings such as "follow the father at home, follow the husband when married, follow the son in old age," and "it is a woman's virtue not to be learned." One half of humanity is thus dispossessed of its character, creativity, and uniqueness, thanks to the agriculture revolution.

5. The scourge of famine, which seemingly is a paradox, given that revolution in agriculture is widely applauded to have made substantial food surplus possible. The fact is that increased food production meant more mouths could be fed, hence a higher birth rate. Moreover, the number of boys born meant more men to work the field and therefore more crops harvested (this, of course, is why sons became that much valued over daughters), hence every tribe wanted more men. The result was a surplus of population and a running match between birth rate and food production.

One lesser known fact is that a woman stops ovulating for as long as she is lactating and breastfeeding her children. In a hunter-gatherer society, women could be lactating for as long as five or six years, and so five or six thriving offspring was considered many. However, in the agrarian society, grains could be ground into powder, cooked, and fed to toddlers, weaning them off mother's breast, making the mother susceptible to impregnation. Needless to say, the birth rate shot up, and parents with a dozen offspring became commonplace. Now, should there be an untimely and unfortunate natural disaster or plague of locust, destroying ripening crop in the fields, a famine would be in the making. In a human world of hunter-gatherer tribes, with a much sparser population overall, tribes had plenty of room to move out of harm's way when bad times set in. This was no longer an option to an agrarian society.

6. Epidemics, resulting from humans and their domesticated animals living in close proximity. Aside from the lack of hygiene, research also showed that many new and emerging diseases occurred when pathogens originally residing in animals migrated successfully to a new host: the human body.

Another broad and lasting impact on human societies was the increasing crime rate. In a hunter-gatherer tribe with a few dozen members, any wrongdoing would be known if not witnessed by the others. In a well-developed agrarian society, the much larger population meant that there could be people we have never met in the community, making it easier for criminals to hide among these strangers after committing crimes such as theft, fraud, rape or murder, evading punishment physical and emotional.

One seemingly insignificant impact of the Agricultural Revolution, testament to it being more of a curse than a blessing to humankind, is the worsening state of our dental health. Anthropologists have found from the skulls of ancient humans that the condition of the human denture have worsened since the adoption of agriculture and grains became our staple food. Starch in the grain, broken down by saliva in the mouth, became sugar which rots our teeth. Toothache was the new bane in an early agricultural society.

It could even be said that, of the Four Horsemen of the Apocalypse representing Famine, Plague, War, and Death featured prominently in the Bible, the first three are borne of humankind's adoption of agriculture.

It has been said that rather than a glorious achievement, the adoption of agriculture is like falling into a trap, from which it would be very difficult for humankind to escape. Similarly, the Industrial Revolution which began in England in the 18th century created another trap, as we shall come to discuss later, and the Technology Revolution which came after it yet another, so much so that a pessimistic view was taken of technology and civilisation turning back on us.

But such is the nature of all things, a duality which resides in everything, symbolised by the Greek god Janus bearing two faces turned to opposite directions, and the Yin-Yang symbol of Daoism in Chinese philosophy. Before we discuss further how technology has turned back on us, let's take a look at another two-faced human invention: money.

1.4 ▶ Money makes the World

Of all the memes ever created by the human mind, the one which has the most profound influence on the course of history in the past 3000 to 4000 years has to be money.

Division of labour gave rise to civilisation. It also gave rise to money. The two are inseparable.

Division of labour exists in the animal kingdom. Social insects like ants and bees have long since made it an art form. Higher mammals like the wolf and dolphin, when hunting in packs, also practise division of roles. But these pale in comparison with the complex and highly adaptable divisions of human labour, especially after the adoption and practice of agriculture. In a sufficiently advanced agricultural society, those who found themselves not having to be involved all the time in food production, turned their attention to developing other skills and tasks, such as making tools (becoming the earliest stonemasons, carpenters, and blacksmiths), defending the tribe/village/town (the first soldiers), teaching children (the first teachers) and fortune telling (shamans and priests). To ensure the livelihood of these people with their specialised skills, a medium for exchanging skill for food was required. What better medium of exchange than money, or more precisely, a currency?

The use of money, or currency, also helps to make an exchange economy over and above that of the primitive barter economy so much easier. Let's say I am exchanging your fish with my pheasant. How do you and I decide on an exchange rate for my pheasant and your fish (2 fish or 10 fish for one pheasant)? And, for that matter, someone else's pheasants or fish? Bearing in mind both pheasants and fish come in all shapes and sizes, and fish of great variety can be fresh or stale etc. Using money, or a currency, as the common medium of exchange makes life so much easier for everyone. With this, the concept of *price* was born. Let everyone who has something to sell set a price. Buyer and seller can then decide, after taking into account various factors such as personal preference, quality, supply and demand etc., how much they are willing to pay for a piece of goods. This is the beginning of modern economics as we know it. It is true that it took a long time before economic activities became entirely measured in dollar and cents. But as early as the Warring States period in the history of China, in about 260 BCE, Guan Zhong, the chancellor of the state of Qi and credited to be the first Chinese economics expert, was already managing what was largely a currency economy. Wang Mang, who usurped the throne from the Western Han ruling family, established a new dynasty which lasted barely 14 years (9 to 23 CE). A failed currency reform, among other policies, was widely attributed to be a major cause of his downfall.

It can even be argued that in a society, when the division of labour reaches a certain degree of complexity and sophistication, money is something that begs to be invented. Writing as a human invention occurred in a similar way, but its influence on human societies is not as far reaching. The reality is that for a long time, beginning with the widespread use of money until the appearance of welfare states several decades ago, people who did not know how to read or write, which made up the majority in a population, could still get by in a community. In contrast, anyone who found themselves penniless, begging was the only means to get paid and survive. Civilisation, so it was said half-jokingly, is when 'people starved because they have no food' became 'people starved because they have no money'.

In almost any textbook on economics, *money* is defined as:

a. a medium of exchange;

b. storage of value;

c. a unit of accounting.

These definitions are correct but not complete. Two additional definitions, from an anthropology perspective, must be added. They are 'the claim to real wealth' (or 'purchasing power' in more conventional terminology) and 'a measure of indebtedness'.

Is money wealth, and wealth money? To most people they are interchangeable. Or they don't care. Strictly though, the two are not equivalent. Wealth - physical not spiritual of course - encompasses a whole lot more than money, and the measure of wealth likewise diverse. One of environmentalists' favourite quotes come from the Cree, a North American First Nation people: " Only when the last tree has been cut down, the last fish been caught, and the last stream poisoned, will we realize we cannot eat money."

But isn't it just common sense that when all goes well, money is wealth? What would you rather have: tons of grain and crops in storage, hundreds of metres of the finest silk and satin, dozens of cattle, and pig? Or the equivalent value of all these *in cash*? No doubt you would prefer the latter. Money, and money alone, possesses the much sought after flexibility, or in professional jargon, the *liquidity*. Even Aladdin, with his fabled cave filled with treasures of all kinds, would be delighted if he had a less cumbersome means to pay for his extravagant lifestyle than having to pay with chunks of gold or silver or gemstones from his treasure trove.

One other characteristic of money which makes it far superior than physical goods is its 'use-by date', or "shelf-life". Unlike grains and timber in storage which can rot, and farm animals which must be fed, cleansed, and tended to when they are sick, and slaughtered by a certain age so as not to lose their value, money has a long or near eternal shelf-life. (This is especially true in times of very low rate of inflation.) What is more, money in cash form does not take up as much storage space as physical goods. These days, we hardly feel the cash in our wallet. It is either spent, or has gone digital!

Money has thus reigned supreme among all forms of "wealth", and the pursuit of money has therefore become one of the main themes of human endeavour in the past millennia. It is true that a prerequisite for money to operate as a claim to real, or physical, wealth is a market economy, but unless a total civilizational collapse has occurred, a money-based market economy is always to be found whenever society persists.

There is no better venue to witness the true nature and power of money as a claim to physical wealth than at an auction, where items going under the hammer could be heirlooms, artwork, antiques, or foreclosed properties. Another more common example yet attracting much less attention, let alone concern, is the sell-off of valuable natural assets such as lumbering and mining rights by a poor country, more often than not as a result of a mismanaged economy or a corrupt government or both, to foreign, usually multinational, corporations. The Sri Lankan government sold off large stretches of seaside land on the southern coastline to foreign interests, in a bid to salvage the economy post 2008 global financial crisis. What used to be beautiful sandy beaches for the enjoyment by all Sri Lankans became five-star hotels and seaside resorts accessible only by the privileged wealthy few. As these coastlines have been privatised, traditional fishing communities are deprived of their livelihood. Disenfranchised and expropriated, many found themselves becoming cheap itinerant labour in big cities living in squalor conditions.

Let's now look at a hypothetical scenario. Two Third Way countries with their economies based on the export of cash crops such as coffee are in dire straits owing to extensive crop failure, either because of adverse weather or a blight. Suppose the first country has foreign currency reserve enough to procure food from the international market to feed its people (say, until the next harvest), while the second country's reserve is only enough to procure food to feed half of its population. The upshot is that half of the population in the second country will starve to death. An alternative scenario is a virulent epidemic breaking out in both countries, and the second country could only afford medicine to cure half of its infected population, condemning the other half to death from infection. In both cases, the "claim to real wealth" (food in the first scenario and medicine in the second) translate directly into "right for life".

Often, when confronted with the power of money, people retort with something like, "but money can't buy you love!" True, but a billionaire can buy and surround himself (let's assume for the sake of this illustration it's a he) with an illusion of love, when he could offer a mansion to a newly crowned Miss Beauty Pageant, a leading movie role for a budding starlet, or the directorship of a start up for an ambitious young entrepreneur. Of course, "money can't buy everything", such as true immortality or the resurrection of a loved one. Who ever said it can? But what money already can buy, apart from our mundane needs and occasional indulgences, is a whole lot more than you and I can ever dream of, including employing hitmen to eliminate whoever you dislike or stood in your way.

As a matter of fact, the temptation of money is so irresistible there are people who have no compunction to kill for it. In the 2014 Hong Kong Cantonese movie *Overheard 3*, a crime thriller centred on factional wars over property developing rights in the New Territories in rural Hong Kong, actor Louis Koo who played the role of the head antagonist's driver, had this to say to Joe, the other main accessory to the crime of eliminating one's competitor by assassination, played by actor Daniel Wu, "We all know there is no limit to the depth of depravity that people can descend in pursuit of money."

To both historians and sociologists, money is the embodiment of contradiction. First, a currency economy is the foundation of complex social undertakings involving high levels of planning and organisation. Without this foundation, it is almost impossible to imagine such achievements as the building of the Grand Canals in China, or the St Peters Basilica in Rome; the Ming Dynasty maritime expeditions led by Admiral Zheng He, or Ferdinand Magellan's voyage around the world, all the way through the invention of the steam locomotive, ocean liners, airplanes, to humankind landing on the Moon. It is no exaggeration to say that money provides the wings through which the ascent of civilization could soar.

From the sociological perspective, it was money which had help break through if not entirely breaking down the rigid class barrier in feudal societies. What used to be the privilege of the rich, acquired usually by being born into royalty or nobility, eventually became accessible to all those who had the money to spend. And in a world where 'money is the measure of all things'; people have since stopped questioning how or from where the big spender got his money. Anyone who spends like a king lives the life of a king. No questions asked. In this way, money has become the Great Equalizer, removing disparity in life and lifestyle when before it was determined by birth and class.

The paradox is that while one disparity was removed, money, or the pursuit and use of it, has erected another more disadvantageous and sometimes detrimental disparity. As the few became filthily wealthy over time, by hook or by crook, and acquiring influence, status and power in the process, the majority found themselves having less and less of the same, and more and more marginalized and disenfranchised. Thus, the Agricultural Revolution and the currency economy together created yet another curse to humanity: poverty. In gatherer-hunter societies, systemic poverty was unheard of. In agricultural, and later industrial societies, poverty of the masses amidst affluence of the few has become a norm. The Great Equalizer that was money now becomes the Great Stratifier, creating a new class order, with those born into different classes experiencing vastly different life choices and trajectories. The Janus-face of money as both a liberator and an oppressor is the hallmark of modern civilization.

The Irish poet and playwright Oscar Wilde once said, "Nowadays people know the price of everything and the value of nothing." When human and social values are distorted and profit trumps everything else, pricing everything, even everyone (an everyday practice in actuarial science), has become commonplace. Kindness, generosity, and human dignity are inevitable casualties under this onslaught. In the latter half of this book, we will examine some revolutionary ideas to counteract this dehumanizing trend.

Next, we return to the other additional definition of money, the one that is seldom mentioned, if at all, in a regular textbook on economics. For that we need to go back and examine the development of the finance market in 17th century northern Europe. These include the establishment of the first modern banking system based on the fractional reserve system, and joint-stock companies and the stock market which still form the backbone of our modern economy. Together these pushed the money game to a new and dizzying height. Soon thereafter, and in the name of 'risk management', derivatives such as futures, options, and many others with names just as complicated as their working, burst onto the investment scene. The dazzling world of High Finance was born.

Today, notwithstanding the bitter lessons of the 2008 global financial crisis, young people across the world still aspire to become a successful finance professional, and many in fact have made this their career goal.

Turn the pages of any textbook on modern finance, and you find passages which read like "the social function of modern finance is the effective channelling of capital through the market to areas of highest productivity/growth." Or "matching innovation to funds, and capital to creativity." Never will you find this short, simple definition: Finance is a Game of Debt.

Finance is a form of debt exactly because money itself is a form of debt. True, we have just been introduced to money as a claim to wealth, but at a deeper level money is a debt. Just think about this: no matter how, or how much, a value we ascribe to money, let's say in this case hard currency, i.e., coins, made of precious metals, it cannot help you when you are starving or freezing. They are at best a symbol, representing the quantity of indebtedness. This true nature of money was cast into high relief by the invention of paper money.

Simply put, all paper money, i.e., bank notes, is in fact an IOU (I owe you), an acknowledgment of indebtedness, which had since become recognized and accepted for circulation and exchange in a society. Money, or currency, has grown to such complexity that economists categorise them as M1, M2, M3, etc, and with the market and trading going digital money has, or is going to, become a series of ones and noughts in a computer. Yet the nature of money as a form of indebtedness remains. Nowadays, out of the massive fiscal reserve of a country, a sizable portion under the heading of foreign exchange reserve is held in U.S. Treasury Bonds, which is essentially an IOU from the U.S. government. If this is not debt, what is?

The bank note is a Chinese invention. The *Huizu*, issued by the imperial government, first came into use in 12th century Song dynasty in China. The concept soon spread to Europe, and later the rest of the world. Bank notes carry a face value set against a standard, usually a reserve of gold (gold standard) or silver (silver standard) or other precious metals, and giving the bearer of such notes the right (in principle at least) to exchange for a corresponding value of gold or silver. With the U.S.A. emerging as the major victor of World War 2, it championed a new global financial order under the rules of the Bretton Woods Agreement of 1944, in which the price of gold was set at US$35 an ounce, and that the currency of several other major countries would be pegged to the value of the U.S. dollar, effectively linking these other major currencies to a gold standard, but via the greenback, and crowning it as the world currency of choice in the process. Giving it due credit, this new order did help world finance recover quickly from wartime chaos.

This state of affairs lasted only until 1971. U.S. president Richard Nixon, for a whole host of reasons, of which a massive deficit brought about by the prolonged war efforts in Vietnam was just one of many, decided to unpeg the U.S. dollar from gold, dismantling the global financial order established by his predecessors less than three decades before. Decoupled from the gold standard, currencies worldwide became standard-less "fiat" money.

What difference has this made in the world of finance? As long as a currency was standard based, be it gold, silver, platinum, or other recognized and accepted precious metal or commodity, the total value of currency issued by a government cannot in theory exceed the value of its precious metal or commodity reserve at the time. With this standard gone, there is nothing to stop a government from printing bank notes non-stop, just to fulfil ever increasing financial needs. Of course, to most countries without currency sovereignty this would be financial suicide as unlimited currency issue leads to runaway inflation and a consequent credit crisis.

Unfortunately, history has shown time and again that there were governments reckless enough to do so, to the detriment of itself and the people whose interest it was supposed to serve. The world at large is now at risk of living this fate, as the American dollar hegemony tightens its grip on not only the finance but people's lives around the world. Americans would rather not give up their lifestyle of abundance or their country's prosperity. And their government is all too happy to oblige them by switching on the printing press to issue more greenbacks. The euphemistic 'quantitative easing' these days does not even require a printing press. All that is needed is a few more taps on the accounting computer's '0' key, with some fiscal sleight of hand to help pull off the trick.

And it is not just America playing the quantitative easing game. Many countries joined in as a consequence of the 2008 global financial crisis, including China. The then Chinese premier Wen Jiabao simply made an announcement, and just like magic there was suddenly an additional 4 trillion RMB/Chinese Yuan available to 'save the market'! Where did this additional amount of currency come from; you may ask? It cannot be clearer: they were created out of thin air, and bank notes being IOUs, issuing more money means incurring more and more debt. Human civilisation has become one of indebtedness: borrowing money has become the modus operandum from the governing of countries, operation of corporations, to the maintenance of personal livelihood. While countries, corporations and individuals have been driven to ruin by such indebtedness (the PIIGS countries being the prime examples in recent times), this has not lessened the lure of this modus operandum in modern societies. Witness the mind-boggling array of credit cards and personal loans available to consumers, and the burgeoning student debt crisis in the States, and we could see how pervasive this trend is. It is anybody's guess as to what will become of our financial future.

Henry Ford, the American industrialist, and founder of the Ford Motor company, once said, "It is well enough that people of the nation do not understand our banking and monetary system, for if they did, I believe there would be a revolution before tomorrow morning."

In 2011, British anthropologist and activist David Graeber (1961-2020) published *Debt: the First 5000 Years*, in which he dissected and examined the intricate interplay of money and debt from an anthropology and historical perspective. Several other books dealt with debt as a manipulative political tool, such as American political scientist Susan George's 1988 work *A Fate Worse than Debt*, American economist Joseph E. Stiglitz's 2002 book *Globalization and its Discontents*, and American author John Perkins' 2004 book *Confessions of an Economic Hit Man*. Together they portrayed a world in which Western powers have made use of foreign debt in the past decades to entrench the exploitation of and political influence on Third World countries even after they had been freed from their colonial shackles. These books are indispensable to anyone trying to make sense of the wide-ranging issue of money and debt.

On a more fundamental level, Karl Marx highlighted the illusion behind 'the fetishism of money'. When we say we do not have the 'necessary resources' to do something, what we have in mind is invariably 'money resource'. This ignores the fact that the real resources are the materials and energy provided by Mother Nature, and the talents, skills and labour of people. Money is just a tool to coordinate the utilization of these resources, and should not become a barrier to our efforts in solving various social problems.

Coming in from a non-Marxian perspective, the Modern Monetary Theory (MMT) championed by some heterodox economists in the last several decades also highlighted the 'coupon' nature of money i.e. money should be treated as coupons that facilitate the running of the economy. As such, nations with currency sovereignty should not be afraid of large-scale 'deficit spending', especially when this could help to solve pressing social problems. "Not enough money" is just an excuse for inaction.

Be that as it may, the compound interest accruing to any borrowed money is still the main driving force in the relentless race of profit-maximization and capital expansion, the never-ending quest for a growing economy, and ultimately to the depletion of all natural resources and the destruction of the natural environment. The simple logic is that corporate profits must grow at a rate not less than the lending rate of banks, for otherwise the corporations will eventually become insolvent. Compound growth is hence a necessity rather than a luxury for big business. Some scholars like Margrit Kennedy had called for the creation and promotion of interest and inflation-free money to get us out of the rut. Unfortunately, this has never been taken up seriously by mainstream economists.

From the compound growth perspective, it is no exaggeration to say that if we cannot control money, money will be humankind's undoing.

1.5 ▶ The Great Axial Age and the First Enlightenment

The great paradox of the human condition is that the rise of civilisation also brought about conflicts and killings on an ever-increasing scale. Like a riddle wrapped in a mystery inside an enigma, it also provided, intriguingly, a setting for those fortunate few, assured of wellbeing either by status or wealth, to embark on unprecedented intellectual quests sparked by the impacts of the great turmoils of their times.

One such example is Siddhārtha Gautama (Pali: Siddhattha Gotama), born of nobility in ancient northern India (nowadays Nepal) around the 6th and 5th century BCE. Pondering on the mystery of life and death and the scourge of human suffering, he came to attain a state of "enlightenment" transcending pain and pleasure. As such, he became Buddha, the Enlightened One, and founded Buddhism. Earlier still in ancient Persia, another great thinker called Zoroaster founded a religion bearing his name (Zoroastrianism), and preached the doctrines of "good thoughts, good words and good deeds" as a way to a good life, although its subsequent influence and spread is far beneath that of Buddhism. In the Spring-Autumn Period of China, roughly contemporaneous with the rise of Buddhism, Confucius established the Confucian school of thought, and Laozi (Lao Tse) the school of Daoism (Taoism), both of which have exerted great influence on the development of Chinese culture. Shortly afterwards, Socrates, Plato and Aristotle of ancient Greece/Macedonia laid the foundation of Western thoughts. All these giants of the human mind all lived, so it happened, around the 8th to the 3rd century BCE, a period of ancient history which the German philosopher Karl Jaspers (1883-1969) called the Axial Age.

There is no evidence to date that these ancient thinkers had somehow influenced each other across vast distances. Yet one after another they made their mark on human intellectual, and spiritual, advancement. As introductions and analyses of their stories and insights abound, there is no need for me to go into their philosophies in any detail. Suffice it to say that taken together, they represented the first flowering of the human mind, with the comprehensive examination of the human condition from various perspectives.

While different cultures placed different emphases on the mystery of Life and the Universe, deep down they all have the same fundamental questions to ask:

1. Where did the Universe and everything therein come from?

2. What is the nature of space, time, and matter?

3. What is human nature? Are we inherently good, or inherently evil?

4. What is the relationship between the physical and the mental realms?

5. What is the nature of reality? How could it be differentiated from illusion?

6. What is the purpose in life? What about its meaning and value?

7. How should we live in harmony with one another?

8. What is the difference between the sacred and the profane?

9. Is there life after death? Will we go to heaven, hell or be reincarnated endlessly?

10. Whence lies the paths to immortality, spirituality and transcendence?

Irrespective of the answers offered, the questions themselves already put humankind well beyond the level of his fellow creatures on Earth. In short, this is humanity's First Enlightenment.

For these ancient sages, their places in history are more than assured. Their actual influence on the course of history, though, is a different matter. Take the example of the ideals propounded by Confucius, or the Buddha. More than twenty-five centuries have passed, but humanity in general is none the wiser. Or better. True, countless people have benefited from the teachings of these ancient sages. Jesus has made people felt loved, and saved from damnation. The Buddha has awakened and inspired many, and as many if not more made a better man by the ideals of Confucius. (Although I would not have a clue as to how many did attain Nirvana, or became a true Superior

Man.) Yet humanity as a whole persisted in fighting with and killing off each other notwithstanding their exhortations.

The Western world has not given the teachings of Jesus (He who said among other things "Love thy Enemy") a better reception either. Countless wars were fought on the excuse of religion. While the Crusades could be understood as ethnic, cultural, and geopolitical clashes fuelled by religious fervour, the Thirty Years' War pitching Protestants against Catholics among culturally homogeneous Europeans could only be understood as the result of pure religious bigotry. And let us not forget the African American slaves, who were not freed until around 150 years ago: all their masters were purportedly devout Christian, yet they all played a part, without qualm, in the institutionalised human trafficking of Africans which was the Atlantic slave trade. Numerous books and movies have exposed the horrors of slavery. The 2013 movie *12 Years A Slave* is as good as any if we want to have a glimpse of the brutalities and atrocities committed.

On a different level, Jesus once said, "It is easier for a camel to go through the eye of a needle, than for a rich man to enter into the kingdom of God." (Matt. 19:24.) And yet throughout the ages, the super-rich of the day - however devout - care not for the Kingdom of God but the Kingdom of Gold.

In a nutshell, people do not practise what they preach. Confucius' Ideal World of Great Unity (*Da Tong*) is as out of reach now as when he was preaching his political theories which fell on deaf ears.

What is more, both Buddha and Jesus exhorted against the worship of idols, and advocated a simple lifestyle. (Clutter-free, tiny house, back to basics, wabi sabi, hygge...) Since their death, however, believers have been trying to out-compete each other by erecting more and more colossal and lavish temples and cathedrals, with idols covered with gold and gems. Were they alive today, both Jesus and the Buddha would be horrified and greatly saddened by this demonstration of vanity over the discipline of the human heart.

But all is not lost. In about the 6th century BCE, in the ancient Greek city state of Athens, proto-democracy was born, in which political decisions were freely deliberated by citizens. This, together with the spirit of rational inquiry of early Greek philosophers, would become the seed for humanity's Second Enlightenment some 2000 years later.

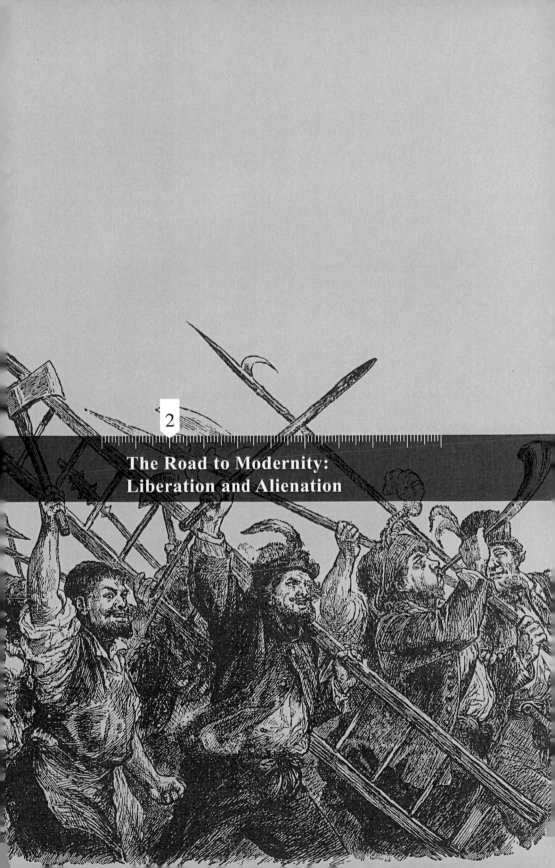

2

The Road to Modernity:
Liberation and Alienation

2.1 Rise of the West and Global Domination

American anthropologist Elman Service (1915-1996) proposed a classification of humankind's social evolution, in which political organisation went through four stages: the *band* in hunter-gatherer society, the *tribe* in garden farming society, the *chiefdom* led by a ruling hierarchy with the *chief* as the head together with priests and warriors, and, finally, the *state*, for agricultural society ruled by a king and bureaucrats. Historical records in writing only began to appear when this fourth stage was reached.

The earliest civilisations to enter stage four, namely the formation of a *state*, were the Sumerians in ancient Mesopotamia, Egypt, and the ancient Chinese civilisation along the Yellow River. Thereafter, vast, and powerful empires appeared one after another on the map of the world: Persia, Han, Tang, Alexander the Great, the Mongols, Byzantine, Arab, Mogul, Inca, Ottoman, and Britain, with the last two coming to an end only in the last century.

Civilisations and empires differ in their lifespans. The ancient Chinese civilisation persisted until today, being made up of imperial dynasties of various durations. Zhou was the longest lasting at nearly 800 years, while the Sui was only 38 years, and Qin shorter still at 14. The shortest lasting empire would have to be that of Alexander the Great, which, from his first expedition of conquest until he died, was just 11 years. The Mongols once ruled a vast empire straddling two continents but lasted only 160 years. The longest lasting was the Roman Empire, at 1,500 years. The Ottoman Empire came in second, lasting 624 years.

German journalist and popular history writer C W Ceram (1915-1972) once wrote, "If we humans want to feel humility, there is no need to look at the starred infinity above. It suffices to turn our gaze upon the cultures that existed thousands of years before us, achieved greatness before us, and perished before us." Many such cultures and civilisations have since vanished, the most famous of which are the civilizations of

44

ancient Egypt and that in the Indus Valley of northern India, and the Khmer Empire in southeast Asia. Lesser known are the various civilizations south of the Sahara Desert. Even along the Mediterranean coast, civilizations such as the Minoan, Mycenaean, Trojan, and Etruscan had come and gone well before the Classical Greek period. Some scholars thought one of them is the origin of the "Atlantis" legend. In the Americas, the Aztec Empire was preceded by the Mayan civilization, and the Inca Empire by various cultures including the oldest Caral-Supe civilization. Some vanished civilizations only came to light in the latter part of the twentieth century. One example is Sanxingdui (Three Stars Mound) Culture (c. 2000BCE) in present day Sichuan, China. One wonders if there are still lost civilizations waiting to be excavated.

Fast forward to 1500 CE, a little over 500 years in the past. If we loosely group China, India, and the Arab world as the East, with Europe and much later the United States as the West, then the East had been markedly more advanced and powerful than the West from antiquity up to 1500 CE, and would continue to be so for another century or two. Research has shown that, up to the year 1750, imperial China and India together made up close to 60% of the global GDP, with the West contributing less than 18%.

Owing to limitations to long-distance travel, however, such prosperity and power only led to regional supremacy, with imperial China dominating the Far East and India southern Asia. A global hegemony did not arise. Imperial Ming China launched a series of seven maritime expeditions, from 1405 to 1433, under the command of a Muslim general Zheng He, with one voyage reaching the west coast of Africa. Yet China did not seize any land or claim any colonies, and the places visited were barely affected politically and economically.

And yet, at the same time, the seeds for a rise of the West had already been sown. Using the year 1500 as the starting point, it was only 47 years before, in 1453, that Constantinople, the capital of the Byzantium Empire, was finally sacked by the Turks, marking an end to the eastern Roman Empire and causing the repatriation of countless scholars and valuable works of art and literature, in particular the works of Aristotle, to western European, thus propelling the rise of the Renaissance. Half a century before 1500, German inventor Johannes Gutenberg (c. 1400-1468) and his mechanical movable-type printing press brought about the printing revolution, enabling the preservation and dissemination of ancient Greek texts since rediscovered, as well as manuscripts of early Renaissance humanists such as Petrarch (Francesco

Petrarca, 1304-1374) and the later Italian polymath Leonardo da Vinci (1452-1519). The Mazarin or 42-line Bible, the first text to roll off Gutenberg's metal movable-type printing press, remains better known as the Gutenberg Bible to this day.

Eight years before 1500, something happened that was to bring a vastly bigger impact to peoples outside of Europe. In 1492 Italian explorer Christopher Columbus (1451-1506) landed in the Bahamas, geographically part of North America. From then on, vast areas of "virgin" land, natural resources including precious metals such as gold and platinum, and crops such as sugar cane, not to mention an almost endless supply of near zero-cost human labour in the form of enslaved indigenous population, helped built the power and might that is Europe today.

What happened after 1500? Forty-three years later, the Scientific Revolution began with the publication in 1543 of Polish astronomer Nicolaus Copernicus' *De revolutionibus orbium coelestium* (*On the Revolutions of the Heavenly Spheres*), which revolutionised the Western world just as much as Columbus's landing in the Bahamas. Subsequent breakthroughs included Italian astronomer Galileo Galilea (1564-1642) and his celestial observations with his self-built telescope in 1609, English philosopher Francis Bacon (1561-1626) and his promulgation of the Scientific Method (1620), English scientist Robert Hooke (1635-1703) and his discovery of cells with the microscope (1665), and Isaac Newton's formulation of mechanics, optics, and the Laws of Gravity in 1687, among others. By the 17th century, knowledge of the Europeans has pulled ahead in leaps and bounds compared with any other peoples in the world.

Karl Marx in his theory of dialectical materialism identified science as the primary force behind any advances in production. The Great Leap Forward in knowledge described above led to explosive growth in many areas of craftsmanship and manufacturing. In particular, the invention and improvement of the steam engine in the 18th century, the electrification of everyday life by the end of the 19th century and the subsequent discovery and adoption of petroleum as the fossil fuel of choice in the 20th century, changed the West forever. European nations, armed to the teeth with iron ships and invincible guns, came to lord over the rest of the world. Europe, whose combined population made up less than a fifth of the world's, became the masters of the globe. British economist Eric Jones called this the European Miracle. American historian Kenneth Pomeranz called it the Great Divergence.

While it might be a matter of national pride to whatever European state that happened to dominate the world, it is unmitigated tragedy to the peoples unfortunate enough to be subjugated as colonial subjects, be it by the Spanish, Portuguese, Dutch, French, English or American. The military might of the West, augmented by their superior - relative to the East, that is - social, political, and economic institutions, overwhelmed, and in some cases supplanted, native practices and culture. As of the year 1500, imperial China led the world in agriculture (paddy rice cultivation in the south with three harvests annually), craftsmanship and technology (metallurgy, ceramics, textiles, etc.), architecture (Forbidden Palace in Beijing, etc.), the arts (literature and painting, etc.), economic management (Rural Credit Scheme, Price Adjustment and Stabilization Act etc.), financial services (the first paper currency and money houses), public administration (neighbourhood gentry, standardized civil service examination, meritocratic scholar-bureaucrat system etc.), the laws (the Ming Laws), medicine (herbal medicine, moxibustion and acupuncture, acupressure, etc.), and education (e.g. the Four Great Academies). Four hundred years later, by the beginning of the 20th century, 'modern' science (to China as well as the world over) was Western science, 'modern' architecture was Western architecture, 'modern' medicine was Western medicine, 'modern' finance was Western finance, 'modern' laws was Western laws, 'modern' education was Western education… In short, nearly all historic achievements such as the academies, imperial examinations, the apparatus of governance, and money houses were obliterated like sand castles in a tsunami. Quite a few commentators have said that 'modernisation' is essentially 'Westernisation' by a different word. One may not entirely agree with this view, but the worldwide adoption of the Gregorian calendar is sufficient proof.

By 1900, the combined GDP of the West made up 75% of the world total, with China accounting for less than 10%.

China, of course, is not the only country so affected. Every single nation and person outside the European sphere has been deeply affected as well. And it was against this background that the ideologies of white supremacy and racism gained ascendency. These are the self-rationalizations through which Christian love and the evils of colonialism in general, and the Black Slave trade in particular, was purportedly reconciled. Austrian anthropologist Eric R. Wolf (1923-1999), in his 1982 work *Europe and the People Without History*, profoundly pointed out that in the eyes of European colonialists, only their own history matters. The rest are all peoples without history. While Europeans were busy claiming their colonies and subjugating those peoples in the process, they boasted they were civilising these lesser peoples. A few even shamelessly claimed, with hands on their hearts, that all these coloured peoples around the world are the White Man's Burden.

Students educated in a Western-styled curriculum will learn about the so-called Golden Age of Discovery, described as an important landmark in the development of human civilisation. To countless nations across the surface of this planet, however, it marked the start of a 500-year long nightmare from which they are yet to be getting out of.

The peoples of Africa and the First Nation peoples of the Americas were the hardest hit. Massive waves of Africans ended up as Black Slaves sold across the Atlantic to the New World. The North American natives, called Indians just because of Columbus' wishful thinking and mistaking the Bahamas for India, as well as the peoples making up the Aztec and Inca civilisations in present day Mexico and South America, faced an even more horrible fate - genocide. Armada after armada, European nations swept across both the western as well as the eastern hemisphere: the Portuguese took possession of Malacca (*Melaka*) in 1511, Macau (*Macao*) in 1557; the Spanish took possession of Cebu in the Philippines in 1565; the Dutch took possession of *Formosa* (present day Taiwan) in 1624; the British formally colonized Ceylon (present day Sri Lanka) in 1815, took over from the Dutch the Malay Peninsula in 1824, made Hong Kong its colony in 1842, and annexed India in 1858. The continent of Australia, far away in the Southern Ocean from all this, did not escape the same fate, with the majority of its indigenous peoples almost wiped out.

The United States is a late comer in conquests and colonies, but did not want to be left behind. The Monroe Doctrine, announced in 1823 by its president of the same name, purportedly opposed European colonialism in the western hemisphere and proclaimed that foreign intervention in the affairs of the Americas would be regarded as potential acts of hostility against the U.S. Thereafter, vast areas of present day southern United States was ceded to the U.S as a result of the Mexican-American War. U.S. annexed Hawaii in 1898, and took control of the Philippines from the Spanish in the same year.

At the dawn of the 20th century, with the European scramble for Africa coming to an end and imperial China having become a quasi-colony, the division of the world by the Western powers was complete.

48

Do not think for one moment that by now this is all water under the bridge. Western dominance is still alive and kicking. True, after the two World Wars fought in the last century, peoples in formers colonies around the world have risen up in fights for independence. Viewed on a broad historical canvass, these valiant - and almost invariably bloody - efforts should be applauded and the results celebrated. The reality remains, however, that while political independence is gained, economic and financial independence are still, for many such former colonies, a distant dream. They are trapped so deeply in menageries of money which the West had devised that the latter no longer need to resort to naked aggression. Simply put, old-styled colonial dominance is superseded by neo-colonialism. This is not helped by the corrupt dictators which came to rule such newly-liberated countries from time to time.

In his famous World-Systems Theory, American sociologist and historian Immanuel Wallerstein (1930-2019) argued that the modern world order is one in which affluent Western countries make up the Core, monopolising knowledge, technology, capital, means of production, talents, as well as making and enforcing rules of the game worldwide, and with the rest of the world as Semi-periphery and Periphery, supplying cheap labour - sometimes even human lives - and valuable raw materials such as food, fuel, timber, minerals, to generate income in order to exchange for merchandise exported by the Core at a much inflated price. This two-way trade is in no way balanced or equitable. This is the case both with historic and neo-colonialist exploits.

Such an unequal relationship is undoubtedly an upshot of the West having gone through the Scientific Revolution and thus coming into possession of advanced technology. But on the other hand, it is also due to the destruction wrought by the West to their colonial subjects' native economy. In simple words, the subsistence economy (particularly in food production) practised almost universally by indigenous peoples across the globe was wiped out by Western colonial masters, who imposed their economic order in the form of monocultures: vast tracts of arable land devoted to a single cash crop, such as wheat, corn, soya, cotton, sugar cane, tobacco, coffee, rubber, banana…etc. to maximise revenue for their colonial masters. Of course, there is also the large scale extraction of valuable minerals and precious metals such as gold, silver, copper, iron, bauxite for aluminium, tin, manganese, and also crude oil, coal, and diamond. The result is that these countries, even after gaining independence, are still heavily dependent on the export of such raw materials for their economic well-being, and hence subject to the impacts - often calamitous - of the fluctuations of the international market prices of such commodities.

Researchers specialising in the Third World countries have put forward the paradoxical concept of a 'Resource Curse', in which the more endowed a Third World country is with natural resources, the more it is plundered by powerful nations (to be precise by trans-national corporations operating from these powerful nations), and hence the more tragic its destiny in terms of corruption, poverty, chaos, conflict and war. The Congo region in central Africa is the prime example of such a tragic fate. (The movie *Blood Diamond* (2006) is an attempt to depict such a situation in Sierra Leone.)

By now we should understand better the deep historical root of the Anti-Globalisation and Global Justice movements. Founders of these movements have pointed out that in the past decades, aided by revolutions in communications, computers, transport and logistics, the overwhelming wave of Globalisation, lauded by the mainstream economists in the West as the panacea for prosperity, is simply the entrenchment of the international division of labour under Neo-Imperialism.

The first major anti-globalisation protest took place in Seattle in 1999. Apart from looking up the relevant literature, those interested might want to watch the 2007 movie *Battle in Seattle*, which is based on this event. For those who would like to understand better the harm neo-colonialism has brought to Third World countries, the documentary *The End of Poverty?* (2008) is highly recommended. The situation as depicted has actually worsened because of the adverse impacts of the 2008 financial crisis and the COVID-19 pandemic.

The Second
Enlightenment

It would seem to readers that this author holds a highly negative view on the Ascent of the West, but it just shows once again the complexity and paradoxical nature of civilisation's progress. On the one hand, the ascent of the West did cause immense suffering to many peoples, but on the other, it also represented a quantum leap amounting to a Second Enlightenment for humankind.

Fact is, the Renaissance, which occurred in the period from the 14th to 17th centuries, is not only something worth celebrating in Europe, but for all humanity. Derived from it are humanism, scientific revolution, rationalism, romanticism, liberty, the Enlightenment, democratic institutions, civil rights movements, etc. Together they transformed the world into what we now know.

Of course, there are also the more problematic impacts of Industrial Revolution and capitalism, two other powerful forces of change shaping the modern world, to which I will come back in latter chapters. Here, we shall examine briefly the Second Enlightenment.

Firstly, humanism took the Middle Age theocracy head on. In a theocratic society, man is either God's servant or His subject. This mundane world is simply a way-station, at which place, through devotion and faith, we might move on to Heaven and eternal life. Renaissance humanist could not refute such arguments, but by erecting a 'anthropo-centric' way of thinking as an alternative to a 'theocentric' thinking, they argued for living a good life on Earth, instead spending our whole live in pursuit of an eternal life in Heaven. The subject of a good life in the mortal world is Man, the source of all morality and values, and of creativity and imagination. Man's ascension is not dependent on grace or salvation from any outside agency, but only through his own endeavour and self-actualisation. (This is also the view of the Buddhists and Confucians.) Dignity, duty, and choice form the core of humanism. That famous and popular quote from ancient Greek philosopher Protagoras, 'Man is the measure of all things' was given a new vitality and importance.

The Renaissance once again revealed to Europeans the Greek civilisation in all its glory. Moreover, ancient Greek democracy - albeit restricted to adult male citizens of Athens only, all females, foreigners and slaves not entitled - led to the awakening of democracy in 17th century Europe.

The new wave of humanism was followed closely by the Earth-shattering Scientific Revolution, widely regarded as a blossoming of the ancient Greek spirit of rational inquiry. Calling the Scientific Revolution 'Earth shattering' is not exaggerating, as the Revolution opened with the Heliocentric Theory of 1543 which dethroned our Earth from the centre of the Universe. The long-held idea of an eternally unchanging and perfect celestial realm was replaced bit by bit with a fascinating and ever-changing - sometimes violently - dynamic universe, with the Earth, the home planet for all humanity, relegated to merely one tiny body among countless ones in an unimaginably vast expanse of space. Courageous were the first ones supporting this revolutionary view: Giordano Bruno (1548-1600), Italian philosopher and himself a monk, put forward views including the theory of multiple worlds, and was found guilty of heresy by the Church in 1600 and burned alive at the stake.

Yet, once the door to truth is opened, it can never be shut again. Published in 1687, Newton's Law of Universal Gravitation showed that laws of nature on the ground - as in the fabled apple falling on his head - applied just as well in the heavens, for example in the motion of celestial bodies such as the Moon around the Earth and the Earth around the Sun. Such universality - that's why Newton chose to name his Law of Gravitation 'Universal' - and the fact that we humans can know beyond our earthly bounds elevated our relationship with nature to a whole new level. Thereafter, Darwin's Theory of Evolution in 1859 broke the barrier between Man and other animals, thus relegating us to simply being a part of - instead of over and above that of - nature.

On a personal level, we all subscribe to the truism of "achieving maturity through understanding." The truth is that this applies equally to the human species as a whole. Viewed in this light, science is a powerfully humanising force, instead of a dehumanising one as deemed by some humanists. The way science has contributed to the spiritual growth of humankind has been underestimated and even totally neglected by many scholars of the humanities. (Later we shall see how dehumanising effects could arise when technology - the application of science - is misused or abused.)

Science comprises the three overlapping domains of scientific spirit, scientific method, and scientific knowledge, oftentimes without any clear dividing line between them. Simply put, scientific spirit is the aspiration for truth, an attitude of persevering to get to the very bottom of things. Driving it is this belief - more strictly speaking an assumption - that things in the Universe obey certain laws and can be understood. Further, it requires the inquiring mind to be open and humble. If one knows, one knows, but if one doesn't then one doesn't. (A famous saying of Confucius.) Same with right and wrong, valid, and invalid. One should not gloss over one's errors. And assertions should be judged on objective validity rather than on the character or status of the speaker.

At its core, the scientific method means strict adherence to facts and to logic. In more concrete terms, it is a methodology which has evolved over long practice, a method of inquiry which combines:

• a sceptical attitude and an open mind (a rather strange combination)

• theory and practice

• inductive as well as deductive reasoning

• graphical thinking and abstract thinking…etc.

Living in the modern would, it is not easy to fully realise how revolutionary this methodological innovation was. But from then on, attributing anything to demons and spirits, tradition, authority, intuition, ignorance, and the mass, became unacceptable means of knowing.

One could very well say that the emergence of the scientific spirit and method is one of the most celebrated milestones in the course of Memetic Evolution on Earth.

Humanism and the Scientific Revolution were followed by romanticism and the Enlightenment, the former requiring us to respect the individual, his values (versus going along with the mass), and his inner feelings (versus the demands of traditional mores), while the latter combining the best of all described above, and in the belief that Man, armed with reason, kindness and ethics, is capable of defeating falsehood, evil, and ugliness. The belief is that after prolonged striving, no matter how circuitous and torturous, he has in his capacity a chance to establish "heaven on earth."

Summing up the above developments, the Enlightenment is without doubt a grand voyage in the liberation of the human mind and spirit, for it releases us from the shackles of traditional culture of rituals, mores and biases. True, there had been scholars who, in their critique of the zest to undo anything traditional, triggered a so-called Counter Enlightenment. But on the whole, Enlightenment values have since been adopted universally, and the rights and freedom of the individual, the rule of law and democracy, both in spirit and enshrined by institution, brought about the modern world as we know it. If the Axial Age which we have discussed previously was the First Enlightenment, then that which arose in 17th century Europe is the Second Enlightenment of humanity.

Democracy as an institution was heralded in England. True, the *Magna Carta* of 1215 only served the feudal nobility not the common folks, for it was merely an instrument employed by the nobility to counter-act the absolute power of the monarch. This was nonetheless a victory for it led to the establishment of a parliament with authority, thereby making it an important beginning in humanity's pursuit of democracy.

The Glorious Revolution of 1688, instigated by the new social class of the bourgeoisie, managed to gain recognition for civil rights against the backdrop of monarchical authority. The Bill of Rights passed in 1689 stipulated that people have the following inalienable civil and political rights:

• the monarch shall not interfere with the law;

• the monarch shall not maintain a standing army in times of peace and without the prior consent of the parliament;

• the monarch shall not impose or levy any tax without the consent of the parliament;

• citizens have the right to petition the monarch;

• citizens have the right to carry arms in self-protection;

• citizens have the right to participate in the election of parliamentarians;

• the monarch shall not interfere with the freedom of speech in the parliament;

• citizens shall not be subject to torture or undue punishment;

• citizens shall not be subject to a fine without being tried and convicted;

• the monarch shall call parliament into session at regular times.

Thus began the constitutional monarchy movement, and thereafter democracy in the West has gone through the following milestones:

1. English philosopher John Locke (1632-1704) published his *Two Treatises of Government* in 1689, in which he put forward clearly the concept of the Natural Rights of men;

2. French philosopher Charles Montesquieu in his *The Spirit of the Laws/ De l'esprit des lois* (1748) enunciated the concept of Separation of Power (*Trias Politica*);

3. The American *Declaration of Independence* in 1776, followed by the United States Constitution in 1789, with subsequent amendments in the form of the United States Bill of Rights of 1791;

4. Monarchy overthrown in the French Revolution 1789-1799;

5. American Civil War 1861-1865 and the abolishment of slavery in the United States;

6. English philosopher John Stuart Mill (1806-1873) published *On Liberty* in 1859;

7. Universal suffrage of parliamentarians and head of state expanded, and subsequently included women.

Each of the above developments, on its own, was undoubtedly limited by its historical context. And yet what emerges is a set of core values transcending their historical origins. Just look at the opening paragraph of the American Declaration of Independence, and you will realise what a great leap forward it is in political thinking:

"We hold these truths to be self-evident, that all men are created equal, that they are endowed by their Creator with certain unalienable Rights, that among these are Life,

Liberty and the pursuit of Happiness.—That to secure these rights, Governments are instituted among Men, deriving their just powers from the consent of the governed,— That whenever any Form of Government becomes destructive of these ends, it is the Right of the People to alter or to abolish it, and to institute new Government..."

The first non-Western country to adopt constitutional monarchy - a democratic system while retaining a monarch - was Japan. The Meiji Restoration from 1868 to the end of the century succeeded in transforming Japan into a modern nationalist constitutional state.

Note that in a transformation such as the one described above, regardless of whether the monarchy is preserved - as in Britain, Japan, Thailand, Spain, and some Nordic countries, or abolished, as in the case of France, China, Russia, and Turkey - hereditary monarchy as traditionally practised is gone for good. The monarchs of Britain, Thailand and Japan are just titular heads of state. Thus, humanity's political organisation - or in a slightly abstract description the relationship between the one and the many - entered a brand new phase.

However, it must be pointed out that democratic progress achieved in a country did not reduce the keen competition among nations. Put plainly, apart from the traditional geopolitical vying for power and influence, the logic of imperialist capitalism dictates that the global scramble for land and natural resources must persist, democracy or not. "Democratic nations do not go to war" is groundless naivety. And yet at the dawn of the 20th century, many people, including well-learned academics who should know better, truly believe that the advances of the Victorian Era would continue and ensure prosperity and peace for all in the new century. Yet just the first-half of the new century saw not one but two devastating World Wars - and the building up of a huge arsenal of nuclear weapons to kill us all many times over. These historic events dulled the beacon of the Enlightenment, and almost destroyed people's faith in our ability to create a better future.

The United Nations, established after World War II under the auspices of the United States, ratified the Universal Declaration of Human Rights at its General Assembly in 1948, and for the first time in history proclaimed the rights entitled to and enjoyable by all in the world. In 1966, the United Nations General Assembly adopted two international treaties to later become the International Covenant on Economic, Social and Cultural Rights, and the International Covenant on Civil and Political Rights, in a move to further highlight the rights of the individual. No matter how little they practised what they preached, the majority of countries have by now signed and ratified these Covenants (one notable exception is the People's Republic of China on the latter Covenant, which it signed in 1998 but never ratify), which is a clear indicator of the universality of the values enshrined in these documents, and of their core value status in modern civilisation.

In summary, these values include:

• Rights of the individual: freedom of the person, protection on private property and privacy; no searching of private premises without a court warrant; no arrest without a warrant; no interrogation by torture, etc;

• Rule of law: independence and separation of the legislative, judicial, and administrative functions of government; equality before the law, etc;

• Constitutional freedoms: freedoms of speech, publication, association, and protests;

• Freedom of belief: *free to choose* whatever religious faith;

• Right of political participation: the right to participate in political activity; formation of political parties, and the right of being nominated and elected;

• Constitutional democracy: direct democracy (e.g., referendum) and representative democracy; universal suffrage regardless of race, religion, gender, political or sexual orientation (including those serving a sentence in prison).

It is true that there has always been critics of democracy. Those with an emphasis on efficiency would say democracy is less than efficient. Some say it is chaotic. Elitists say it has been hijacked by populism…But nothing is ever perfect. Churchill famously said, "Democracy is the worst form of government - except for all the others that have been tried." A simpler way of putting it across would be "If not because of despotism, democracy is the worst form of government."

Despite all its shortcomings, the main reasons in support of democracy include:

1. It allows succession of political power without chaos or bloodshed;

2. It allows the collective will of the people to be better manifested, and its demands met in a relatively effective way;

3. It allows the people to supervise and criticise the government in its daily operations;

4. It allows major policy failures to be corrected, the ultimate means being the voting for a change in government;

5. It allows the people to replace leaders who have become incompetent, unresponsive, and/or despotic;

6. It allows for a more equitable balance of interest between different social groups, especially when it comes to protecting the rights of the vulnerable.

In my view, the spirit of democracy, coupled with the establishment and functioning of such institutions, is one of the greatest achievements of humankind's civilisation (memetic evolution) worthy of our highest respect.

After the overthrown of monarchy in 1911, Chinese intellectuals in the early days of the Republic of China wanted to bring Mr De (meaning Democracy) and Mr Sai (meaning Science) to China. To most people, the two seemingly belong to separate and distinct domains. Yet if we go back to our discussion previously, it is clear the two stems from the same root. A scientific spirit requires a free, independent, and critical mind, and an open and embracing attitude. Scientific quest respects fact, reason, and others' views, is receptive of criticism, accepts the fact when mistakes are exposed, and is ready to make any correction that is necessary. Come to think of it, aren't these qualities also exactly those behind the spirit of democracy, one that say no to arbitrariness and imperiousness and insists on openness and inclusion?

"Can democracy fill your stomach?" This seemingly silly question has attracted a lot of comments online, one of which is rather interesting: "Democracy doesn't really put food on your dining table, but it does guarantee the food on your dining table are safe to eat; and if you got sick from improperly processed food, democracy also guarantees you or your family the chance to sue the supplier; and even if you fail in the lawsuit, democracy guarantees you'll not be beaten up because you want justice, or worse still, end up being prosecuted for inciting social unrest."

Many Westerners, especially Americans, seem to think that non-Westerners are inherently opposed to democracy, and that the anti-West sentiment spreading across the globe is a result of the West imposing democratic institutions on them. American Chinese writer Amy Chua's 2003 book *World on Fire: How Exporting Free Market Democracy Breeds Ethnic Hatred and Global Instability* is a typical example. Such a conclusion is of course erroneous. The fact is, as a result of nationalist movements in the last century, many newly-formed countries embraced the freedoms and democratic institutions which had come from the West. In the global reality dominated by neo-colonialism and an American hegemony, however, these institutions, although democratic in spirit, are no match to the logic of 'pro-' or 'anti-American' stance. Simply put, any democratic but "anti-imperialist/US" regime will be overthrown by the CIA, and any despotic regime that are "pro-US" will be propped up and sustained. And dictators on both sides make use of this rift to impose their will on the people.

Anyone who cares to study post-war history would find many such examples. Note that among other things, the definition of pro and anti-America entails the willingness of a government to allow American (and other Western countries) to have control (via their banks and corporations) over their resources, industries, and finance. One typical example is Chile, when the socialist Allende government was overthrown, with covert military involvement, in a *coup* in 1973, mainly because Allende wanted to nationalize copper production in Chile. On the contrary, the ultra-conservative and repressive Saudi Arabia ruling regime is fully supported by the US, to the extent that the widely condemned murder (and dismemberment) of the dissident journalist Jamal Khashoggi in 2018 at the Saudi consulate in Istanbul was eventually glossed over by the US government.

In the first few decades after the end of World War II, the Cold War became a convenient excuse for such political manipulation and military interference. Now that the Cold War is well and truly dead, there is no further excuse. As recently as 2011, the Arab Spring initially brought hope of an impending democratisation to many countries in the Arab world, but subsequent events have shown otherwise. Much as democracy is sought after by the people, it is always subject to America's "national interest" of maintaining a status quo.

In short, the wave of anti-American and anti-West sentiment across the globe arose not because of any opposition to democracy. It is a response to the political bullying under Western hegemony and neo-colonial exploitation. For the governments of these Western countries, however, it is anathema to put it in these terms to one's citizens. Therefore, these governments, as well as the media in these countries, resort to perpetuating the myth that non-Westerners are alien to Western values, and that is because of the latter's very different cultural tradition, religious beliefs, emotional and mental disposition, and genetic makeup etc. Sadly, such myths have been co-opted by dictators and authoritarian regimes in developing countries themselves to suppress demands for democracy and political participation. Over time, many people in many countries got brainwashed into believing that Western-styled democracy is not compatible with the state of our nation, that democracy is a sham, that democracy will end up in chaos....

Just as Buddha's profound wisdom and compassion is no longer something Indian, and Confucius' ideal of righteous harmony is no longer something Chinese, the so called Western-styled democracy, together with values on human rights, freedom, rule of law, and all that the Enlightenment gave rise, is no longer something Western, but universal and belong to all humankind. Not practising what is preached does not alter this fact.

It is true that Mencius (273-289 BCE), the greatest Confucian thinker after Confucius, once said: "Those who labour mentally rule, those who laboured physically are ruled." While this could be interpreted as a defence for the feudal nobility class at the time, from a broader historical perspective, it was merely an objective description of social reality. Social animals always have a leader, so that they as a group does not become overwhelmed and eliminated by another group. When it comes to human society, it is true that in any community there are people keen on becoming leaders as well as those, often forming the majority, happy and willing to be led. Leaders work with the mind, as they are required to also think for and about others, while those who follow the leader would devote their time and energy on their livelihood and leave the rest to the leader. The majority of people would gladly accept such an arrangement. The crucial question is: how does one become the leader? Hereditary? By consultation? Selection by voting, or on merit? And what about a leader that subsequently turned arrogant, imperious, or incompetent? An enlightened monarch turned tyrant? A democratic system is the answer, derived from centuries of practice to these problems.

True, any country that boast democratic institutions without a democratic spirit will not see true democracy take root and thrive. In other words, a country keen on democratising itself must improve the quality of education as well as its

administration. The often seen excuse that 'people are not ready' is no reason to stall or even suppress democracy. Democratisation is never plain sailing, and there is no magic path to take. What we can, and should, do is to take solid and well thought out steps towards democracy, instead of just window-dressing. The acid test is to see if the government succeeds or fails in offering and protecting freedom of political expression, and in nurturing and facilitating a widely participated public sphere and a civil society, or, as the philosopher Karl Popper would call it, an Open Society. Repression of free speech, always labelling it as a threat to national security, is a sure sign of "false democracy."

In fact, democracy will always be work-in-progress, an ongoing experiment, and with changing times - such as the impact of Big Data has on personal privacy - democratic institutions will need to adjust and adapt.

Today, whether it be a newly-formed country or an age-old democracy, things are not looking good. Democracy is facing daunting challenges. In the quest to know the future of humanity, the future of democracy is a most important topic.

2.3 Industrial Revolution and the Rise of Capitalism

If the Enlightenment is the liberation of human thought, then the Industrial Revolution and the subsequent rise of capitalism is an even more amazing liberation of human productivity.

Steam engine, the weaving loom, milling machines, locomotive, steamboats, telegraph, automobile, aeroplanes, electrification, electronic revolution, chemical synthesis (esp fertilizer and plastics), the factory system, the assembly line, mechanization, automation, computerization, industrialised agriculture, communications satellites, television, optic fibre, Internet & World Wide Web.... All these developments brought about an explosive increase in productivity, changing the face of human society and the destiny of many. In terms of the three-sector model of economic activity, people working in primary sector, namely those engaged in food production - agriculture - as well as extraction of raw materials such as timber and minerals, decreased drastically, at the same as those engaged in the secondary sector, namely manufacturing, and tertiary sector, namely service industries, rapidly increased. People's daily life also vastly improved, with living conditions greatly enhanced by modern conveniences such as clean tap water, the flushing toilet, gas and electric lighting and cooking, air-conditioning, and various forms of personal and public transportation. People also began to enjoy a much richer cultural life: public education, publishing, literature, music, drama, movie, sports, leisure...etc. Average human lifespan lengthened as a result of improvement in public hygiene, and advances in medical science.

The Industrial Revolution was to a large extent an energy revolution. In the past, muscle power and draught animals were the main forms of energy, supplemented with fuels such as wood. True, coal in its various forms had been used as a fuel for thousands of years, but it was not until the Industrial Revolution, when the steam engine was invented, improved, and widely adopted, that the face of civilisation really changed. England found itself in the enviable situation of possessing not only the

62

hardware and knowhow but also a vast reserve of shallow-layered coal. Understand that coal is nothing but a compact form of stored energy, energy which had come from the Sun over billions of years. Once this stored energy was released, England's productivity, and the ability to change nature, took off exponentially, making England the pioneer of the Industrial Revolution.

Strictly speaking, if capitalism is defined as any economic activity in pursuit of a profit, versus simple subsistence, then capitalism preceded the Industrial Revolution by a long time. There was mercantile capitalism, in which trading generated profit; financial capitalism, in which money lending was profit making; and agrarian capitalism, in which profit is derived by buying and selling of land, livestock and produce. In the past, however, these activities made up an insignificant part of the traditional self-subsistence economy. The Industrial Revolution changed this entirely. With the rise of industrial capitalism, capitalism emerged to become the one institution dominating people's lives.

The Industrial Revolution brought about some far-reaching changes, including:

• A rapid rise in world population, which was 1 billion in 1804, 2 billion in 1927, over 6 billion in 2000, and standing at 80 billion at the time of writing;

• Migration from rural to urban living. The United Nations reported in 2000 the ratio of rural to urban population stood at 1:1, with 8 out of 10, or more, living in cities in developed countries;

• A shrinking rural, and almost invariably farming, population spelled the demise of a self-sufficient economy, at the same time as a market economy, one that depended on uninterrupted flow and trade of goods and service for daily necessities, rapidly expanded.

Basically, human society has become a market society. We have seen in the previous chapter that centuries of Western colonisation has devastated many non-Western self-sufficient economies. But even in the West, due to a high degree of regional division of labour, many European countries require sustained trade and commerce to keep their economies ticking. Needless to say, this inter-dependence has become exacerbated under the relentless waves of globalisation, starting from the 16th century onwards. Fourteen centuries ago, the Tang Dynasty of imperial China would not be waging a trade war with Persia, and even if it did, only a handful would be affected. (Traded commodities would be luxury goods like tea, silk, and porcelain.) But today, a trade war between China and the U.S. would be headline news, with economic ramifications throughout the world.

In the past, the rural hometown, with its self-sufficient economy, was a safe haven, a place for imperial bureaucrats to return to it in retirement, or, for those unfortunate ones fleeing a war or disaster, to seek refuge and reprieve. With the demise of rural communities with their self-sufficient economies, such human stories have vanished from the pages of history.

- Closely connected with self-sufficient economy is self-directed labour, also known as self-employed labour, which was the case throughout history in the thousands of years preceding the Industrial Revolution. Thereafter, and as a result of land enclosure (more to follow), people who lost their land moved to the cities to find work, and ended up as employed labour, or wage labour, earning a living by offering their time and toil in exchange for a wage with which to buy daily necessities in the market. Note that in 95% of human existence, this arrangement was the exception rather than the rule, and was extremely rare. It has only become commonplace, or even the accepted norm, in the most recent 5% (about 200 to 300 years) of our existence. And so, 'starving from lack of food' becomes 'starving from lack of a job.' The majority of us has forgotten that unemployment, especially in times of recessions, is a unique phenomenon of modern civilisation. Humankind has never run out of work in its millions of years of existence, and it has never 'needed a job.' The fact, of course, is that what we need is a salary, not a job. This is a big turning point in the human condition.

These developments brought to the fore the crucial role capitalism plays in the human condition and the future of humankind. Throughout the years, there has been many books exploring the human predicament (recent examples being Israeli historian Yuval Noah Harari's two bestsellers, *Sapiens: A Brief History of Humankind* (2011/15) and *Homo Deus: A Brief History of Tomorrow* (2015/16)), yet without a full consideration of capitalism's crucial influence, most of these works smacks of irrelevance and missing the point.

To understand capitalism, one must first understand the nature of profit. It is incorrect to think that profit is invariably an outcome of a market economy. Long ago, even in ancient times, people traded essentials and luxuries, as well as skills and labour, through a system of exchange known as bartering. Such face-to-face transaction with payment in kind resulting in equal mutual benefit to the parties in trade did not generate any profit, even after the invention and adoption of currency in place of payment in kind. So, the existence of a market does not automatically entail profits. Nevertheless, this sort of trade without profit enriched people's life greatly.

Profit did not appear until people began to engage in long distance trade. Communication being slow in the past, traders could take advantage of the buyer's ignorance and commanded a price much higher than the actual cost of the merchandise, with the difference, less the cover for any transportation cost and risk, ending up as a net profit. But the undeniable fact is, with a growing profit generated from the "buy low, sell high" strategy, 'grain merchants getting richer than farmers' became, after 'starving to death because there's no money,' yet another counterintuitive social reality of modern civilisation. (The other being the famous paradox in economics: 'why is diamond more expensive than water?' given that we will die of thirst but not from lack of diamonds.)

Profit appeared for the second time in interest-bearing lending. Here, as in the above, profit may be regarded as necessary to offset risks. But the fact is, money lenders of all persuasions have become stinkingly rich through the ages. However, until the rise of capitalism, interest bearing lending, particularly usury, was regarded as immoral and detested by many cultures, and money lenders - aka loan sharks - viewed as parasites on the community. There was a time when the Roman Catholic Church prohibited interest bearing lending, and to this day, Sharia-compliant finance in Islamic countries and Muslim communities around the world prohibits the charging of interest on money loans.

The third manifestation of profit is the 'appropriation of the surplus value created by other people' through 'market means.' Note that here the operative word is 'market means,' because, as in the case of slavery, this appropriation is achieved by direct force and hence would not be characterised as profit.

This last source of profit brings us to the very nature of 'industrial capitalism.' Even today there are many people who think that 'capitalism' is just another name for 'free market economy,' which is way off the mark. Let us see what French historian Fernard Braudel (1902-1985) has to say about it: "There are two main types of market exchanges. The first is ordinary, open, competitive, and virtually transparent. The other is elitist, exclusive, sophisticated, manipulative, and monopolistic. These two activities follow different mechanisms and are governed by different rules. The world of capitalism is mainly about this second type of activities, and not the first." Simply put, capitalism is what the capitalists do, and not what the small-business owners do.

Further analysis has revealed that capitalism, as the dominating economic institution for the past two to three hundred years, comprises the following four parts:

1. The bulk of the social means of production, such as land, machinery, factories, capital, know-how (in the form of patents) etc, is in the hands of a few people, whom we call 'capitalists';

2. 99.9% of society are people who do not possess any means of production, whom we call the 'proletariat;'

3. All daily necessities and luxuries are obtained from a currency-mediated market exchange;

4. Of all the markets of exchange, the most important and unique market is the "labour market" in which the 'proletariat' offers their labour to 'capitalists,' in exchange for a living wage. Only by being employed (either as a white or blue collar) and thus receiving income can people get the money necessary to obtain their basic needs from the market.

Upon these four foundations, the vibrancy of an economy is dependent on the 'investment level' by capitalists, which in turn is determined by the 'return on investment,' or the 'profit rate.' The simple logic is: if the profit rate is lower than a bank's interest rate (strictly speaking it is the difference between deposit and lending rates) then capitalists are better off putting their money in a bank.

Clearly high level of investment means high level of employment means high level of consumption means vibrant business means high profit level leading to high investment level which is a virtuous circle. Conversely low level of investment means low employment means low consumption level means poor business means low profit leading to a drop in investment level which is a vicious circle. Needless to say, no government would want the economy to fall into a vicious circle. Instead, it would do everything in its power to 'maintain, promote, and create a haven for businesses,' so that the virtuous circle would go on and on. Simply put, the health of an economy now depends on the willingness of the capitalists to invest, and the governments are held ransom to their demands, including a low tax rate and lax business regulations.

But then, we might ask: how did we end up like this? German political philosopher Karl Marx (1818-1883) is the first to pose this question seriously. After lengthy research and deep thinking, Marx believed the answer includes, at least, the following:

1. Westerners became the first world-leading capitalists as a result of 'primitive capital accumulation,' made possible by the post-Columbian colonial land grab and exploitation of resources across the globe.

2. Domestically (such as England from 16th to 19th century), the 'Enclosure Movement' which expropriated farmers from their own land created immense wealth for capitalists (because land is wealth), as well as large number of 'proletariats'. Meanwhile, traditional artisans and craftsmen, driven out of business by the relentless pressure from big business, also joined the ranks of the proletariat.

3. Having been ruthlessly 'proletarianized', large number of proletariat was left with no option but to sell their labour in exchange for a wage to maintain a livelihood. 'Commodification/marketisation of labour' became the foundation stone of the capitalist institution.

Marx described the historical accumulation of primitive capital in these words, "If money comes into the world with a congenital blood-stain on one cheek, capital comes dripping from head to foot, from every pore, with blood and dirt." (To those who would like to learn more about the inherent logic of capitalism, please read my 2014 book *The Urge of Capital* which is available from Amazon.com)

Marx argued that the wage paid by capitalists to workers is invariably less than the value created by the labour of these workers. In other words, 'profit' is nothing but the surplus value appropriated without compensation from the workers. Apart from long-distance trade and loan with interest, this was the third time profit appeared in the history of humankind.

Marx also pointed out that keen competition among capitalists will invariably lead to wages being reduced to the lowest possible level, which he called the 'subsistence level.' As such, the antagonism between the 'working class' and the 'bourgeois' is inevitable.

You may ask we're interested in the future of humankind. How come we've gone at such length (actually this is just a brief summary) into the 'origin of profit' and how capitalism operates? The answer lies in the nexus between the pursuit of profit, capital accumulation, competition for resources and markets, and the relentless devastation of the environment... all of which will have important bearings on the future of humankind. More details in the next chapter.

Let's now turn to another of Marx's profound insights: when the majority of workers have become closely monitored and controlled 'paid labour,' they will be alienated from the 'product of labour,' thereby reducing drastically their passion to work, as well as their self-esteem and sense of value. Marx believed that work, at its best, is what makes us human, as it allows us to live, to cooperate, to be creative, to flourish. German philosopher Hannah Arendt (1906-1975) observed pointedly the Human Condition is fulfilled through Labour for our survival, Work for community-building, and Action for creative betterment of the world. Indeed, whether it is for the needs of daily living, or some other higher needs (for example, making a baby cot, planting flowers around the house for appreciation, or a spacecraft for going to the Moon), the feeling of satisfaction, of achievement, and the pride, are all the more felt when the person has a direct connection with the product of his labour or task. Conversely, when someone works for a living on a meagre wage and in the process becomes a 'cogwheel' repeating the same motions over and over again (vividly portrayed by Charlie Chaplin in his 1936 classic *Modern Times*), and under constant monitoring and control, he will in no time develop feelings of boredom, loneliness, numbness, emptiness, anxiety, rejection, angst, and anger, etc. Marx called this 'alienation.'

While Marx's theories of political economy met with staunch resistance from mainstream economists in the West, his theory of 'alienation' was greeted with acclaim by sociologists and psychologists. German sociologist Max Weber (1864-1920) extrapolated Marx's theory and applied it on bureaucracy (or today's culture of managerialism) which had permeated every level of society. He pointed out that, driven by a myopic 'instrumental rationality,' everything is reduced to 'targets' and 'efficiency.' The result is the loss of the individual's subjective agency, passion for life, and spirit of adventure. Locked up in the 'Iron Cage' of modern civilisation, there is

no escape. 'Existentialism,' a new wave of thought in the 20th century, was a cry for freedom and "authenticity" from a humanity in masks and shackles.

Of course, this is one big paradox. Modern society is the outcome of the Scientific Revolution and the Enlightenment, liberating humanity from the shackles of traditional way of life. These shackles include feudalistic hierarchy, "human bondage" through clanship, superstition, bigotry, rigid conservativism, parochialism, absolute monarchy, male supremacy, and female subjugation etc. Ba Jin (1904-2005), the early Republican Chinese writer, wrote his famous trilogy of novels *The Family* (1933), *Spring* (1938) and *Autumn* (1940) in praise of the on-going liberation from these shackles at his time. In Marx's view, the rise of industrial capitalism and bourgeoise values was also a major driving force behind such liberation, and he had high praise for it. But that was during the ascending stage of capitalism. In the mature stage of capitalism since the 19th century, the inherent logic of the system led inevitably to 'alienation' and the 'Iron Cage'. Humankind seemed to have 'stopped the tiger at the front door, but let in a wolf through the back.' We took three steps forward but fell four steps back.

In the past several decades, there arose an ideological debate on 'modernity' and 'post modernity.' To be more precise, it was a 'post-modern critique of modernity.' German philosopher Jurgen Habermas believes 'modernity is sick,' yet French philosopher Jacques Derrida (1930-2004) believed 'modernity is a sham from the start'. Issues such as 'science wars' and 'culture wars' also popped up in this big debate. Although it involved debates on fundamental areas in philosophy such as 'epistemology,' 'ontology' and 'existentialism,' but as I see it, in the final analysis 'instrumental rationality' and 'alienation' under capitalism remain the crux of the problem.

Finally, we've come to the end of an extremely brief review of human history, from the ascent of civilisation to the beginning of the last century. In the next chapter, we will review global developments in the last century or so, and how such developments might impact the future of humankind...if there's one.

3

**Contemporary Scene (1):
the Unique Century**

3.1 A Pivotal Point
in History

Abraham Lincoln once said "If we could first know where we are, and wither we are tending, we could then better judge what to do, and how to do it."

It is understandable that people always feel they are living at a unique moment in history, just as everyone feels they are invaluably unique. Provided we have the power of self-reflection, we would recognise the latter for what it is, namely, naïve egocentrism. As to the former prejudice on the uniqueness of the current historical juncture, we could also dismiss it it as "the fallacy of contempo-centrism".

I certainly understand the naivety of this point of view, but, against all odds, I'm still going to try to convince you, with powerful arguments and credible evidence, that our time is a most unique juncture in human history. I would leave it to you, my Dear Reader, to decide if my claims are valid or fallacious.

First, let me list some of the most influential changes which had taken place in the hundred years between 1900 and the present:

1. World population increased from 1.6 billion to 6 billion, a 3.7 fold increase, between 1900 and 2000. As of the time December 2022, world population stood at 8 billion;

2. A dramatic increase in human life expectancy from 40 years in 1900 to 70.6/75.1 at present, and a corresponding reduction in infant mortality, defined as death of young children under the age of 1, from more than 200 per thousand infants to 27.4 per thousand [2020], an unprecedented achievement from the point of view of lessening human suffering (imagine the pain endured by parents who lost their newborns).

3. The cycle of life and death, and the associated pain and suffering, is much lamented in the Buddhist faith. The main cause of non-natural death, infectious diseases, such

as cholera, smallpox, malaria, tuberculosis, typhoid, dysentery, leprosy, diphtheria, yellow fever, syphilis, gonorrhoea, was finally brought under control with the advent of antibiotic medicine in [1908/1928] and later drugs against infections caused by virus. Needless to say, these advances in medicine contributed to the increase in life expectancy. Mention must also be made of the use of anaesthetics in surgical operations, which, apart from pain reduction and control for the patient, also allows for complex and complicated surgeries to be conducted.

4. Urban population now makes up 57% [2021] of the world total. Rising from a mere 16% in 1900, people living in cities became more than those living in rural areas in 2007. On the other hand, household size has become significantly smaller, with nuclear families of 3 or 4 making up the bulk of urban population. Extended families living under one roof have become a rarity the world over.

5. Invention of the oral contraceptive pill for women and the widespread use of condoms by men allow for the first time in human evolution voluntary birth control. Increased life expectancy and reduced infant mortality rate led to a demographic transition, especially in developed countries, in which both the birth and death rate declined. Increase in global population has been offset by a steadily declining birth rate in developed countries, with some even showing a negative population growth;

6. Literacy rate of the world now stands at an average of 86.3%, more than a eightfold increase from 1900, when only about 1 in 10 persons could read and write.

7. The energy revolution of the 20th century quickened its pace, with energy consumption increasing 21 times in a hundred years. Explosive growth in the consumption of crude oil, first extracted in 1859 by drilling in the U.S., means that by now we have exhausted about half of the global reserve. Clearly, modern civilisation has been built upon the continuous supply of relatively cheap energy, in the form of fossil fuels which are unsustainable.

8. Forested areas around the world was reduced by 20% within the space of a mere 100 years.

9. Species extinction, in the 20th century alone, included the disappearance of more than 500 types of medium to large-size animals. Some researchers believe that

close to 10,000 species have gone extinct if as yet undiscovered plant species and microbial life are taken into account.

10. The amount of wildlife over the globe was reduced by nearly 80%.

11. At the same time, domesticated animals of all kinds increased drastically to 70 billion, almost 9 times as many as humans. Majority of these animals are kept and bred under very inhumane conditions.

12. Air pollution from industrial activities and transportation led to widespread premature death, from breathing and related cardiovascular illness, of a significant proportion of the world population; air pollution also contributed to Global Dimming, in which, for the first time in history, the atmosphere became more opaque to incoming sunlight, a probable cause of the slight drop in global average temperature between the 1940s to 1970s. Increased air pollution coupled with the spread of night time illumination also mean that people nowadays are less likely to appreciate the splendour of the night sky than at any other time in humankind's existence.

13. Synthetic chemistry has given us numerous new materials hitherto unknown in the natural world, with plastics being the best-known and most commonly used. Plastic pollution has since become a world problem, as these materials do not decompose easily over time, or at all. Via air, water and food channels, various synthetic chemicals, microplastics, and heavy metals have found their way into the human body.

14. Global food production increased dramatically. World total farmland area almost tripled between 1860 and 1960. Artificial fertilisers, improved crops, irrigation schemes and mechanisation of agriculture (epitomised by the Green Revolution in the mid 20th century), meant that even though world population has increased drastically, global famines as predicted by the English economist Thomas Malthus (1766-1834) in his 1798 *An Essay on the Principle of Population*, has yet to eventuate.

15. World War II, the deadliest military conflict, broke out, causing some 80 million deaths. At the end of the war, the United Nations was founded, which has been coordinating international efforts of all kinds for well over 70 years.

16. Countries in the world increased in number, from less than 100 in 1900 to more than 200 in 2000, an unprecedented event in human history. Most of these new countries are former colonies of Western powers, which led historians to describe the latter half of the 20th century as the Great Age of Nationalism.

17. In the short span of a hundred years, humankind has gone from electricity to electronics to computer to the internet. The use of electricity marked a watershed in humankind's control over nature. None of our modern day necessities and convenience would exist without electricity and electronics, and we have electronics thanks to the invention of the transistor in 1947.

18. The tremendous amount of energy locked inside the atom was unleashed, paving the way to the building of nuclear weapons and the self-destruction of the species.

19. Cars became the predominant form of person transport, rewriting the rules of human interaction and settlement, and gave rise to urban sprawl.

20. Powered flight literally gave us wings, but at the same time, the overcoming of vast terrestrial distances by flying through the air also rewrote the rules of warfare, including the extension of mass killings into non-combatant zones.

21. Humans ventured into space, and set foot on the nearest celestial body, the Moon. Unmanned space probes from Earth have since ventured into the hitherto uncharted territory of, first interplanetary space, and then interstellar space.

22. Tourism developed into a leisure activity for mass consumption, albeit still limited to those in developed countries who can afford it. Tourists can now reach the most remote places on Earth, such as the Amazon forest, Antarctica and Mount Everest, unthinkable feats to their parents and grandparents.

23. Discovery of an expanding Universe, itself an amazing achievement, and for the first time providing a solid foundation, in place of folklore and myth, to unravelling the origin of the Universe. A more profound discovery is that of the origin of ourselves, founded on the Darwinian theory of evolution and advances in both paleoanthropology and molecular biology. Humankind came to understand (instead of just speculate) its place in the Universe, and of the origin of civilisation and morality.

24. Medicine was revolutionised with the introduction of new technologies such as X-ray radiography, antibiotics, and microsurgery. Artificial insemination, organ transplant, cloning, stem cell research, genetic engineering, neuropharmacology, etc, surpassed even the wildest imagination in fictional works such as *Brave New World* (1932).

25. Discovery of the gene, followed in the early 20th century by the new discipline of genetics, culminating in the deciphering of the genetic code - the DNA - revealed the age-old secret of heredity. Subsequent advances in the field enabled scientists to map and study first the human genome then those of lesser animals and plants. Attempts at altering the natural genetic makeup of plants and animals for various purposes have caused widespread controversy, concern, and even condemnation.

26. The oral contraceptive pill and the condom not only allow people to practise voluntary birth control, they also brought about the Sex Revolution, overthrowing the traditional procreation-oriented view of inter-gender sex. For one thing, pre-marital sex has become commonplace, at least in some cultures and countries. On the other hand though, notwithstanding the increase in divorce the traditional institution of marriage has remained intact, contrary to pundits who prophesized its demise.

27. Women's liberation and the Feminist Movement have raised the social status of women worldwide, with women's right to vote alongside their male counterparts being the most important. Universal suffrage, a crucial component in realising equality in political rights, was achieved in Britain in 1918, the U.S. in 1920, France in 1944, China and India in 1947, Iran in 1963, Saudi Arabia in 2015.

28. In terms of religious belief, prediction by some scholars such as the British philosopher Bertrand Russell of a drastic reduction of followers has not come true. As of 2020, out of a world population of about 7.9 billion, 85% claimed to be practising one religion or another: 2.38 billion Christians, 1.91 Muslims, 1.16 Hindus, 507 million Buddhists, plus followers of other recognised religious faiths. On the other hand, secularisation has become the dominant tune in human societies around the world, with religion less and less influential in our everyday lives. (In a way, Jesus' exhortation "Give back to Caesar what is Caesar's and to God what is God's." has been taken to heart.)

29. The electronic computer has become an indispensable part of life, augmenting and greatly enhancing human brain power, and robots - computer controlled automatons - removing drudgery from work. Advances in electronics and computing also allowed for highly efficient storage of knowledge and data, example being the entire 32 volumes of the Encyclopaedia Brittanica condensed to the size of a pin head.

30. While the first newspapers appeared in early 17th century Europe, it was not until the late 19th century that Public Opinion became a part of social fabric via newspapers and magazines. Mass media, a conglomerate of radio, television, film, etc, is now regarded as a counterpoint to the establishment, a Fourth Estate acting as check and balance on the administrative, legislative and judicial functions of the government, and generally a keystone of modern civilisation. On the other hand, an increasingly prevalent and penetrating, and oftentimes highly commercialised, mass or Pop Culture has meant that slow-evolving traditional or Folk Cultures has been greatly overshadowed.

31. The Internet has vastly improved the spread and flow of information, aided by search engines such as Google, and knowledge sharing websites in the public domain such as Wikipedia. Social networking platforms such as Facebook and Instagram help to connect people, and yet also lead to obsessive behaviour and facilitate the collection of Big Data.

32. A global economy means almost all countries are now dependent on each other, but at the same time, globalised capitalism drives them into mutual competition, for cheap labour, natural resources, and markets. This has become the prime logic behind international conflicts.

33. English has become the lingua franca of the world, thanks to the British Empire and its offshoot the U.S., dominating the world as never before. Likewise, the American hegemony has meant that its dollar has a similar status of domination in global finance. The extents of such dominance are unprecedented in history.

34. Financialisation of the economy has meant that gross global currency far exceeds the physical wealth created by us. At the same time, gross global debt grew to an unprecedented size of US$ 300 trillion while global GDP stood at $104 trillion [2022 data];

35. Advances in audio-visual technology have enabled people to capture in vivid detail and in real time life events of themselves and others near and far. Every one of us has become a reporter - though not necessarily a journalist, and history making is no longer restricted to text. On the other hand, it has also become possible to fabricate lifelike sound and images (deep fakes) so that the old saying 'seeing is believing' may no longer be valid. In the Post-Truth era filled with fake news, the historians' task has become even more onerous and honourable.

The list above is admittedly a very personal selection and thus cannot be claimed to be comprehensive, but it is enough to show how extraordinary the 20th century has been. Likewise for those of us living in the 21st century. I was trained in science, so if I'm only allowed to choose three out of my list of thirty five, I'll go for 18 (unleashing nuclear energy), 21 (space exploration) and 25 (genetic engineering). My guess is: for those trained in sociology, their preference would be for 26 (sexual liberation), 27 (feminism) and 30 (mass media); for those trained in anthropology, 5 (population growth); for those trained in international politics, 15 (the United Nations), 16 (nationalism) and 32 (globalisation). Regardless of preference, the past 120 years is without a doubt a fast changing time with profound and long lasting influence on posterity.

My point is: choose any century in the past, and any historian could have listed dozens of epoch-making changes occurring in that century, such as the Fall of Constantinople, the Black Plague, the Renaissance, the Scientific Revolution, the Enlightenment, the Glorious Revolution, the Napoleonic Wars, the Industrial Revolution, the rise of capitalism, the French Revolution, etc. But in comparison, when it comes to the pace of change, and the impact of these changes on posterity, my choice of the three, namely the unleashing of nuclear energy which equipped humankind for the first time ever to destroy itself and the world, space exploration which expanded the stage of history from its earthly bounds to infinite space, and genetic engineering which allows us to remake ourselves, all these have ramifications that are truly mind-boggling. And all took place just in the half century between 1930 and 1980!

It is therefore not surprising that historians called this period of rapid change lasting a hundred to two hundred years the Age of Great Acceleration.

For the most part in history, social changes occurred, in times of peace, at a glacial pace. People generally expected to, and they did, live the same lifestyle as their parents and grandparents, and prepared their offspring to do the same. Such expectations and assumptions were blown to smithereens in the past century or so. Not only do we need to change our ways quickly and adapt ourselves to new situations - brand new roles and tasks in the workplace is one example - we also need to realise our children, and their children, will find themselves in a totally strange new world. Needless to say, preparing our children for unexpected and unimaginable challenges is cause enough for parental anxiety.

3.2 Compound Growth and the Ecological Crisis

Historical facts alone may not be enough to convince you of my argument that we're at a unique turning point in history. Mathematics, however, in the form of 'compound growth', presents evidence that are indisputable. The easiest way to illustrate this is to make use of a chess board, on which there are 64 squares. Put a single grain of rice in the first square, then twice as many grains in the next, and so forth. How many grains of rice would you say would fill the last square?

Answer: 9,223,372,036,854,775,808.

In fact, well before we've reached our halfway mark, one square would already be filled with more than 1 billion grains of rice! By the time we got to the last square, the weight of all the rice on the chess board would be 12 trillion tonne. This is more than 1,000 times the current rice production in the world.

Compound growth (also known as exponential growth) can be deceptively small and slow at the start, but the outcome can be astounding. Of course, the outcome need not always be disastrous, but it all depends on how small is the beginning and where the boundaries of the system lie (physicists call these the 'boundary conditions'). We're at a turning point in history because many developments in human society (including energy consumption, water use, mining, lumbering, use of chemical fertilisers, pesticides and herbicides, plastics, meat consumption…) grow exponentially, and has reached levels that is close to, or has exceeded, the limits of our planet's environment.

The increasingly devastating impact of human activities on the environment is not news anymore, so much so that people have come to accept it as staple diet in our daily news . Needless to say, such complacency is very dangerous. Many people would actually point to such news and say: we've been hearing this (and the clamouring from environmentalists) for decades. Yet society has continued to move on, and we've been

World Population from 1 A.D. onwards, with projection to 2050

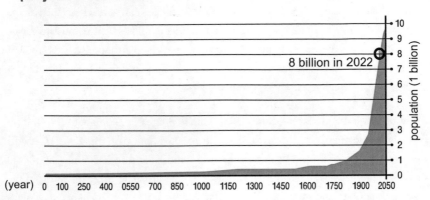

CO₂ levels over the last 10,000 years

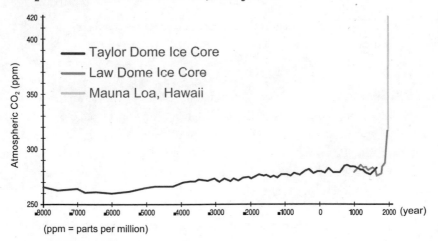

(ppm = parts per million)

living better and better. The world hasn't come to an end, as those scaremongers would have us believe! But these people missed the following points:

1. Only those surviving get to tell the story. Or: dead people don't whinge. In other words, we never hear from people who died from severe air pollution, or from those who perished in natural disasters caused by climate change (such as the more than 70,000 people who died in the European heat wave of 2003, the 10,000 people who lost their lives under Typhoon Haiyan in 2013, or those killed by the severe flooding in Paskistan in 2022, which inundated more than one-third of the country).

2. 'Time-lag effect' and 'tipping points' are part of any natural process. Environmental catastrophes may start out as trivial changes which easily escapes notice (such as a hairline crack in a high dam), but once the 'tipping point' is reached (such as the crack enlarging and multiplying resulting in a dam collapse), it is too late for us to do anything. One is reminded of the parable of the man falling off the roof of a skyscraper. Whenever he passed a floor, the people in horror heard him telling himself reassuringly: "So far so good!"

Many of you have probably heard of the famous French parable about the Boiling Frog. It is said that if you throw a living frog into a pot of boiling water, it will immediate jump out to save itself. However, if you put the frog into a big pot of cold water on top of a stove, and then slowly turn on the heat, the frog will relish in the warming, stay put, and eventually boiled to death. In essence, humankind are now 8 billion frogs in the same predicament.

I commented above that human activities 'have exceeded the limits of our planet's environment'. Was I scaremongering? Let me illustrate my argument with these two examples.

The first example came from the fishing industry. Studies have shown that in the five decades since the end of World War II, global catch increased more than 4 times. This growth has however levelled out, and in some regions actually dropped, since the 1990s. This is notwithstanding increase in the number and size of fishing fleets ploughing the ocean, and the adoption of advance technology such as weather satellites, global positioning, sonar, etc.

Collapse of the fishing industry caused by sustained overfishing has happened around the world over the years, the most famous example being the rapid decline of the North Atlantic cod industry in the early 1990s. But today, what we are facing is a rapid decline of the fishing industry worldwide. Some scientists predicted that this decline will reach its peak sometime in the middle of this century. By then, no matter what we do, the seas will yield only fish fries and seaweed. Needless to say, this will kill off countless coastal fishing communities, as well as dealing a detrimental blow to the already tight food supply globally. (It has been suggested that piracy off Somalia was the result of years of political turmoil compounded by multi-national industrial-scale fishing in its territorial waters, driving coastal Somalis off their only means of subsistence to become pirates)

One can very well say that overfishing is a stark portrayal of humankind's choice when faced with 'The Goose that Laid Golden Eggs', with 'Tragedy of the Commons' writ large on the high seas. International waters being international, one is not obligated to behave and observe fishing restrictions, especially when others are doing exactly the opposite. The result is everyone goes in for his lion share no matter what, to the ultimate detriment of all in the long term.

Now to my second example: one which has drawn worldwide concern and criticism, but not concerted action (especially in the form of shutting down coal and gas-fired power stations) - the Global Warming crisis. As we all know, this crisis is caused by our increasing use of fossil fuels such as coal, oil and gas since the Industrial Revolution, thereby releasing huge amounts of carbon dioxide which greatly exacerbated the 'greenhouse effect' in the atmosphere, causing average global temperature to rise.

Scientists know that Nature has her ways to remove excess carbon dioxide from the atmosphere. Lush green forests, a vibrant microbiology in the soil, a thriving marine plankton population, in fact the water in the seas and oceans which absorbs carbon dioxide, are all natural 'carbon scrubbers'. This can explain why, with the Industrial Revolution taking off in the 18th century and by the 19th chimneys spewing black smoke was a common sight in many western cities, atmospheric carbon dioxide level did not increase noticeably until well into the 20th century. A simple way to explain the eventual increase is that: Nature's 'carbon scrubbing' ability has reached saturation by the mid-20th century, so that any excess was left to accumulate in the atmosphere.

Which is to say: the rate at which we pump out carbon dioxide has now exceeded the limit of our planet's restorative capacity. Statistics showed that we're emitting close to 40 billion tonnes of carbon dioxide each year, half or more of which cannot be absorbed by Nature and is left accumulating in the atmosphere. Studies also showed that the atmospheric concentration of carbon dioxide is the highest in 14 million years, and keeps rising at an unprecedented rate.

This last 'excess' would have to rank the worst among the many 'excesses' of humankind, because the impact is on global temperature, and it is not as simple as 'the days' getting warmer'. It will cause more frequent killer heatwaves, more severe and prolonged wildfires, super powerful rainstorms, severe flooding and droughts, and all manifestations of abnormal and extreme weather. Moisture-laden air creates more powerful super typhoons and hurricanes (including tornadoes) killing more people. The loss of mountain ice cover and glaciers which form headwaters of major rivers worldwide will lead to them drying up downstream, while melting ice will increase average global sea level rise, inundating many coastal settlements.

Climate change is actually part of Earth's billion-year history, the onset and end of the many 'Ice Ages' through the eons being one example. But these climate change caused by natural processes (continental drift, volcanic activity, Earth's orbital change, variation in solar radiation, etc.) occurred at a glacial pace, taking tens of thousands of years to complete, allowing at least some species to adapt (such as growing a thicker fur to keep warm). In comparison, climate change induced by human activities now occurs at an unprecedented rate. The result is that large number of species cannot cope with this rapid change (compounded by habitat destruction caused by humans) and are doomed to extinction. Scientists have estimated that the current rate of species extinction varies from the most optimistic of several thousand per year to a pessimistic 50 thousand or more per year. This is more than a thousand times the basic rate of species extinction in Nature! Scientists have come to call this ecological catastrophe as the 'Sixth Extinction', following the five mass extinction events in Earth's history. (As a matter of fact we don't know exactly how many species currently exist on Earth, but the estimate is somewhere between several million to several tens of million)

Please do not think for one moment that this is only something of interest to nature or wildlife lovers. We are part of Nature, and in Nature, everything affects everything else. When Nature collapses, so do we. An ecology out of kilter could very well unleash deadly pathogens hitherto unknown to humankind. It could also lead to a drastic decline in the number of bees, which is beginning to attract worldwide attention. Bees pollinate plants, enabling many cash crops to grow. Less bees, less growth; no bees, no crops. No crops, no food. Famine and war could well be the outcome.

In the study of ecology, species which matters a lot to systemic stability and robustness are called 'keystone species'. We have no way to tell if there are other 'keystone species', apart from bees, being driven to extinction because of our actions. We are now as short-sighted and ignorant as a lumberjack sitting on a tree-top branch, enthusiastically cutting it away from the trunk for the wood, not knowing when the branch snaps, he's going to crash, branch in hand, all the way to the ground.

Viewed from another perspective, creatures big and small have all evolved over the untold eons, each one unique and precious, and has the same right as we to call Earth home. Something that's gone extinct is gone forever, and for all our wit and might, there's no way we're going to bring them back. Looking at it this way, the 'Sixth Extinction' is humankind's cardinal sin.

All the numbers and analyses point to this: that the current trends of development are largely unsustainable. The 21st century definitely is a 'bottleneck' in human history, and civilisation will experience, within this century, a big turning point. However, it makes a world of difference, and of life and death, between taking this turning point in a deliberate, purposeful, and knowledgeable way, or being forced to endure it when all options ran out. Renowned science writer Isaac Asimov made a shrewd observation on this particular foible of human nature: "What is really amazing and frustrating, is mankind's habit of refusing to see the obvious and inevitable until it is there, and then muttering about unforeseen consequences."

Due to the obvious impact of human activities on the lithosphere, atmosphere and biosphere, it has been suggested that the period of time from 12,000 BCE (the beginning of the Agricultural Revolution) to the present be called 'Anthropocene' instead of 'Holocene', as has been designated in conventional geological age reckoning. Some scientists believed the period should only cover the time from the Industrial Revolution to the present, while others argued for an even later starting point, the first atomic weapon in 1945. No matter how long the 'Anthropocene' has been, it is now in everyone's interest to know how much longer it will be.

3.3 Urge of Capital: the Hard Logic of Economic Growth

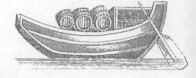

It was said that humans are the sole animal species that keeps on wrecking its own habitat. We have to ask: why is *homo sapiens* - the wise human - so irredeemably foolish?

It is the belief of many that greed is the driver behind humankind's destruction of the environment, which sounds reasonable but hollow. Imagine a shipwreck survivor stranded on a remote island with a lifeboat. He then stumbled upon a cave full of gold ingots (probably stashed there by pirates). So, before he tried his luck and put to sea in that rickety lifeboat, greed moved him to put more and more gold ingots into the boat, until it sank to the bottom of the sea, dashing all hope of leaving the island. Those who put all the blame to simple greed is saying humankind is exactly like this man. Do you find this convincing?

While some individuals may be as reckless as this hypothetical example, it begs belief that an entire human race of several billion can be just as foolish and reckless collectively. The truth is that for over half a century, dire warnings about environmental destruction and the resulting ecological collapse - supported by massive data and rigorous analyses - have repeatedly been issued by the scientists, starting from Rachel Carson's *Silent Spring* of 1962 and the *The Limits to Growth* report issued by the think tank Club of Rome in 1972. Ad yet rampant destruction continued unabated, and even worsened. How could we be so stupid?

To understand why this is the case, we must first understand what 'rules of the game' are governing the progress of modern civilisation. In short, my argument is this: it is exactly these 'rules of the game' that has landed us in the present quagmire. And what are these 'rules of the game'? In a nutshell: the logic of capitalist production.

Before outlining the logic of my argument, let's clear up one conceptual obfuscation. It has been argued that an ever-increasing trend of 'consumerism' is the culprit behind resource depletion and environmental degradation. Curbing consumption is therefore the key to reversing these dire trends. This suggestion does sound more solid than that of 'greed', but it still does not go far enough to show that, instead of some vague 'endless desire' or 'vanity', "consumerism" is actually the lifeblood of capitalism. Put simply: without consumerism, the throbbing heart of capitalism will go into immediate arrest, and the global economy will collapse.

I'm not being sensational. Remember our brief foray into capitalism in the previous chapters? Now let's turn to an inherent contradiction in this scheme of things. We say capitalists acquire profit through "institutionalised appropriation of the surplus fruit of labour of the working class", but the premise is that profit could only be realised if and when the products and services, as produced by his workers, are bought and paid for. If this does not happen, there is no profit. In fact it's all for nothing. On the other hand, consumers are highly price-sensitive, and hence capitalists are always trying to out-compete each other by offering the cheapest price for a similar product.

The only way to keep the price low while keeping the profit high is to depress the cost of production. However, the costs of various inputs such as raw materials, rent, depreciation of machinery, utilities charges, interest on loans, etc. are largely fixed by the market and cannot be easily reduced. Any capitalist worth his salt understands that among the various "factors of production", the one that is most amenable to sequestration is the cost of labour, namely the wage level. Another method while maintaining the same wage level (as too low a level might result in workers leaving for greener pastures, especially during times of low unemployment) is to increase the labour intensity, either by speeding up the assembly line, more stringent monitoring and control of the workplace, or longer worker hours. We can now come to see that why capitalists are antithetical to substantially increasing the well-being of the working class, no matter how rich they already are, and how much richer societies have grown in general. It is not because they are heartless, but because in order to survive and excel, they have to play the game by its rules.

Workers, though, have only their wages to get by. If the level is too low (or even decreasing at a time of inflation), workers will spend less. As a result, society as a whole went into under-consumption, and there would be over-production. Merchandise and service would be left unsold or unutilised, and profit would dwindle. In response, capitalists would cut back on their investment, and businesses would contract and companies foreclosed. (Don't worry they'll be fine as the wealth they possess could tie them over for a lifetime and many times more.) A slump in the business world would result in massive unemployment. With livelihood lost or threatened, people would cut back further on their spending, leading to a downward spiral. The economy goes into crisis.

Thus we see the inherent contradiction that is capitalism: between depressing as much as possible wages to achieve 'maximisation of profit' (or else face being eliminated in a cut-throat market competition), and 'maintaining worker's (which means 99% of society) consumption level', boom and bust cycles are just part of the deal. Here we see a prime example of "individual rationality resulting in collective irrationality." Suppressing wage level is entirely rational to an individual capitalist, yet when carried out by all capitalists concerned, it undermines overall social consumption, and brought harm to the capitalist class, as well as society as a whole.

Let's introduce the crucial factor of 'mechanisation', which paradoxically further exacerbates the problem. Since the early days of the Industrial Revolution, machines and production lines have helped capitalists to achieve immense cost reduction. It is admittedly a massive upfront investment but offset in the long run by lowering, or even removing altogether, labour cost. The result is that the process of mechanisation (automation. computerisation, robotisation…) has never ceased over the past two hundred years. But here, we run into same paradox of 'individual rationality leading to collective irrationality'. To any capitalist, cost reduction by mechanisation is a rational must-do, but to the collective, it would be an economic disaster when massive number of workers are laid off when their capitalist employer chooses machines over human labour. Social unrest aside, capitalists are having to face up to the risk of under-consumption, over-production and heavy business loss.

As the incessant process of mechanisation to boost productivity and competitiveness at lower cost is a road that must be taken, but which may also lead to massive unemployment and depressed consumption, should capitalism have long since undone itself and be around no more? But, time and again, crisis after crisis (the most recent being the '2008 Global Financial Crisis'), capitalism is still on its feet, going strong, and getting stronger. What is the secret behind this?

The secret is the 'sacred cow' of modern civilization: 'economic growth'. As long as the size of the economy keeps growing, labour made redundant by mechanisation and automation will be taken up. Not only that, people must also be constantly bombarded with ideas such as 'more consumption means a better life', 'shopping is not just for daily needs, it is a great pleasure in itself' . This is of course the mission of the multibillion dollar advertising industry, which employed the top pyschologists of the day adept in manipulating minds both young and old. The upshot is that people keep going after new products and new services, such as fashion apparel which keeps changing, cars, smart phones, computers, television sets, cosmetic products, gourmet food, theme parks, self-improvement courses, parenting classes.... One noticeable characteristic of modern civilisation is the majority of all consumption is driven not by basic needs but by 'manufactured wants'.

You may have heard of the business parlance of 'Blue Ocean Strategy', meaning instead of participating in the cut-throat competition within well-established markets (the Red Ocean), one should strike out and open "entirely new markets". Innovation which creates new and unique "values" (read: manufactured wants) would open up "infinite business opportunities", and is seen as the lifeline of business success.

'Spend, spend, spend!' is the *modus operandi* of capitalist production. To tell people to boycott consumerism to save the Earth is to kill capitalism and bring about a complete collapse of society.

Now is the time to introduce one more central figure in this macabre drama: debt, and her handmaiden, interest. As explained earlier, modern civilization is built on debt. Consider two capitalists in competition and starting with the same amount of capital. If one of them is able to land a big loan from a bank, he could employ the much increased capital to out-compete the other. Sure he has to provide collateral and pay the loan-interest, but if he plays it right, he could come out the winner, or even come to dominate the market. This is of course nothing but the concept of "leveraging" in Business 101. But note that the bank interest he has to pay is a compound one, so in order to re-pay the loan and still generate profit for his business, the business must grow at a compound rate *not less than* the difference between the lending rate and the deposits rate (assuming that any capital not actively employed at any time is deposited in banks). If the increase in profit (as reported in the company's quarterly reports) could not match this minimum figure, there would be no point in the investment, and the capitalist would be better off doing nothing and just enjoy the interests accrued by his wealth in the bank's deposits account. But for one capitalist who chooses to retire from the "rat race", dozens are waiting in the wing, for the game will go on.

The upshot is, any CEO, caught between 'survival of humanity' and 'business growth', will always go for the latter. Those going for the former will be fired long time ago. Likewise, capitalists caught between 'survival of humanity' and 'business growth' will go for the latter, because going for the former means he will be eliminated. They are not evil people. It's just the name of the game.

To society, or indeed the world at large, 'economic growth' (i.e. expansion of consumption) is the only way to prevent the economy from flopping. Pressing on in full knowledge of an imminent environmental collapse is the best depiction of the Chinese proverb "Hard to dismount from a running tiger." The result is that all capitalists take it upon themselves to open up new business opportunities and promote consumption. Any talk of "corporate social responsibility", "sustainable development" , "3-P triple bottom line" (People, Planet, Profit) end up as window dressing PR, incapable of bringing about any fundamental change to the course of the train heading towards the abyss.

Whether it is to absorb the surplus labour force made redundant by mechanisation, or just to re-pay the bank loan during leveraging business strategies, we can now see clearly that under the modern capitalist system, economic growth is not something in the "nice-to-have" category but the "life-and-death" category. This "urge of capital" is the driving force behind the incessant destruction of the environment, or the piling of gold ingots onto the lifeboat as mentioned as the beginning of this chapter.

At the beginning of this book, I introduced the idea of the 'selfish' gene put forward by British biologist Richard Dawkins in his 1976 book of the same name. How can the gene, a non-thinking entity, be selfish? In a similar vein, my 2014 book bears the English title of *Urge of Capital*. Again, how can capital, not even a physical entity, spawn an urge? It's really this: this is simply to highlight the fact that something which does not possess any inherent 'intentionality' produces an objective effect akin to 'intentionality' when operating in the real world. In the words of Karl Marx, "A capitalist is just capital personified." What a vivid description!

It should be patently clear by now why each and every government in the world makes economic growth their top priority. Several years ago, a high-ranking official in the PRC said that if economic growth dropped by one percentage point, unemployment would increase by five to six million. This would be absolutely ludicrous if it was to happen in ancient Persia, or the prosperous times of the T'ang dynasty. But today, in 'Red Capitalist China', it is stark reality.

Have you ever contemplated the conundrum of "What if an irresistable force meets an immovable object?" Well, if the logic of incessant growth under capitalism is the irresistible force in modern civilization, then the physical limits of Mother Nature exposed by the onslaught of compound growth is the immovable object. Einstein once said "The most powerful force in Nature is that of compound growth." Let us look at how this works out in real world situations. After the 2008 Global Financial Meltdown, Wen Jiabao, premier of the PRC from 2003 to 2013, promoted the slogan of Bao Ba, meaning to ensure at least an 8% annual rate of growth of the Chinese economy (based on GDP). Sad to say, very few people watching the news would have a true idea of what this kind of growth implies.

Mathematically, the 'doubling period' of a growing quantity can easily be calculated by dividing 72 by the rate of growth. Hence, an annual growth rate of 8% has a 'doubling period' of 9 years. Now, with 2008 as the baseline, an annual growth of the economy at 8% will double by 2017 (2008+9), quadruple by 2026 (2017+9), eight times by 2035 (2026+9)…(Remember the analogy of the chess board at the beginning of the last chapter?) One cannot even begin to imagine the catastrophic scale of things in terms of resource and energy consumption, waste generation and environmental pollution caused by a Chinese economy having grown 30 times bigger by mid-century.

Bowing to reality, the Chinese government had later revised its target from 8% to 6 % , and further to 5%. Let's be more conservative and consider the 5% scenario. At this rate of growth the doubling period becomes 14.4 years (72/5). There are five doubling periods in the 79 years from 2020 to 2099. How many is 5 doublings? Of course it is 2x2x2x2x2=32 times. Timewise it is a mere four decades and a bit later than in the previous example. And don't forget: at the next doubling it will be 64 times, and then 128 times, and then again 256 times…

How about a growth rate of 3%? Any decent economist will tell you 'only a sluggish economy grows at 3% annually'. But let's have a look: still, at a doubling period of 24 years, in 96 (24x4) years, such an economy will have grown by 16 times.

A pertinent question to ask is that the world is not ruled by the capitalists, but by policy-makers high up in the governments who are all highly educated and intelligent people. If compound growth is unsustainable, and it's so obvious to anyone, how come governments are sitting back, doing nothing, and just let the economy and the world rip? But this is exactly what's happening. Not only do governments fail to rein in unfettered growth and curb environmental destruction, they are actually doing the opposite: 'creating the most business-friendly environment', including reducing and removing tax and unwinding regulation on all fronts, in order to lure investors at home and from abroad.

Karl Marx had this figured out more than 150 years ago. He pointed out that "capital flight" (or just the threat of it) is the most powerful weapon of the capitalists to bend governments to their will. No governments will risk dealing with massive unemployment and the ensuing social instability, so they have no choice but to give in. Simply put, 'politics' is being held hostage by 'the economy', with the majority of economists worldwide being accessories to the crime. As an exception to the rule, American economist Kenneth E. Boulding (1910-1993) astutely pointed out that "To believe one can have infinite growth in a finite world, one must either be a mad man or an economist."

In recent years a cartoon has circulated widely on the internet. Under the night sky, talking to a group of children gathered around a camp fire, an adult proudly proclaimed, "Yes, the planet got destroyed, but for a beautiful moment in time, we created immense value for our shareholders." It is a vivid depiction of an absurd situation.

Let us re-capitulate. Under the inherent logic of capitalism, 'the relentless pursuit of profit' and the 'incessant expansion of capital' (or what Marx called 'capital accumulation') are the 'irresistible forces' of the system. If in the end humankind fails to control 'the urge of capitalism', and when the 'irresistible forces' meet head on with the 'immovable object' in the form of 'limits imposed by Nature', catastrophe is inevitable.

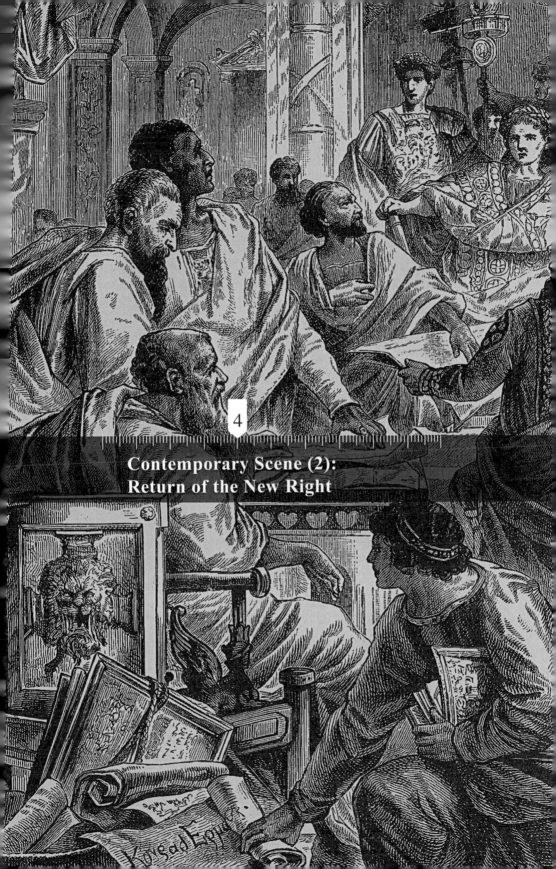

4

Contemporary Scene (2):
Return of the New Right

4.1 The Onslaught of Neoliberalism

Many historians have described the two 'World Wars' in the 20th century as essentially one war, a war in which European powers fought against each other for world supremacy against the background of 'global division of colonies'. The outcome, so it turned out, is a perfect contemporary example of the Chinese parable about the stalemate between the sandpiper and the clam on the beach, with the former's beak clammed tight by the latter to stave off being eaten. Eventually a fisherman came along and brought both of them back home for dinner. Here European powers are the sandpiper and clam, and US of A is the fisherman. As the greatest winner of WW II, Uncle Sam has been enjoying global dominance as the world has never seen. Henceforth, Europe (even after the formation of the 'European Union' in the 1990s) was relegated to that of a second or even third-rate power.

The Communism 'experiment' and its subsequent failure formed another of 20th century's main theme. The formation of the U.S.S.R. in 1917, until its dissolution in 1991, and the establishment of the People's Republic of China under the Chinese Communist Party in 1949, until its "Open Door and Reform Policy" (effectively turning capitalist) in 1979, were the most important events. Although these regimes managed to achieve big (as in nuclear armament and space exploration), but at what cost! (Countless lives were lost, not to mention laying waste to culture and morality) Apart from a rule of terror at the beginning of these new regimes, which we could regard as birth-pangs, there was also Stalin's 'Great Purge' and the Siberian Gulag, Mao Tse-tung's 'Great Famine' and 'Cultural Revolution,' and the genocide committed by the Pol Pot regime in Cambodia. Henceforth, 'communism' became synonymous with 'totalitarianism,' 'brainwashing,' and 'police state.' The 1949 novel *1984* by English novelist George Orwell (1903-1950) became an eternal warning to humankind.

On the other hand, five years before the publication of *1984*, Austro-Hungarian historian Karl Polyani (1886-1964) wrote *The Great Transformation - the Political and Economic Origins of Our Time*, in which he analysed in detail the social impacts of an increasing 'marketisation'. Polyani pointed out that the negative impacts to the individual and society were just as profound as the material gain produced by the Industrial Revolution and capitalism. Community spirit, personal relations, family ethics, moral concepts, even individual dignity were severely eroded. To counteract this, individuals collectively and society as a whole rose in self-protection, forming organisations, charities, unions, co-operatives, mutual aid societies, and political parties vowing to defend worker's rights. Polyani further contended that history in the past hundred years was a record of the ceaseless contest of power between the two forces of 'market logic' and 'community spirit.' That society had not yet fallen apart, Polyani argued, was because of the ability of the latter force to hold the former at bay.

Polyani formulated his ideas and published *The Great Transformation* in his adopted country, the U.S.A. There, he saw for himself how, in the first two decades of the 20th century, America became more and more unequal under the rapid rise of capitalism, resulting in the Great Depression triggered by the collapse of Wall Street in 1929. In response, U.S. president Franklin D. Roosevelt rolled out the New Deal, aimed at rescuing the economy, and decried by his opponents and critics as 'socialist' policies (in education, healthcare, working class welfare etc.), in a bid to reverse the adverse consequences of a '*laissez faire* market.'

Yet historians pointed out that, more than the 'New Deal,' it was World War II that saved America. Not only that, the massive consumption and rise in production spurred on by war efforts have pushed the U.S. to a level of economic might never seen before. But then, it is undeniable that the U.S. kept to Roosevelt's policies (which is also policies advocated by the English economist John Maynard Keynes) in the three decades following the end of the war. The result was a more 'egalitarian' society in which both 'public' and 'private' sectors played equal roles.

A similar situation also occurred in Great Britain and Europe. Nordic countries went even further, boasting themselves as 'social democracies' where 'high tax rate, universal welfare' is practised in a constitutional monarchy or republic.

However, the U.S. was drained of its fiscal reserve fighting the war in Vietnam. It abruptly unpegged its dollar from the gold standard in 1979. Europe, on the other hand, was plagued by wave after wave of industrial action, hurting its economy badly. Meanwhile in the Middle East, the OPEC group of oil-producing countries implemented an embargo in the earlier 1970s to give their bargaining power a push. The oil embargo dealt a severe blow to the already ailing western economy, and resulted in a 'stagflation' (a simultaneous occurrence of 'economic stagnation' and 'inflation') crisis.

This was seized upon by those in the school of thought known as 'economic liberalism' to launch a counter offensive on 'Keynesian economics,' which they have always regarded as their archenemy. They blamed all problems big and small on 'Big Government,' and 'welfarism' was criticised vehemently. Austrian economist Friedrich Hayek (1899-1992) and his American counterpart Milton Friedman (1912-2006), the two most outspoken 'liberal economists' lauding the good of a 'big market, small government' philosophy, were awarded the Nobel Prize in Economics in 1974 and 1976 respectively, which was widely regarded as the crowning glory of 'economic liberalism'. It was only a few years later that politics followed suit, with Margaret Thatcher (1925-2013) becoming the Prime Minister of the U.K. in 1979, and Ronald Reagan (1911-2004) elected in 1980 to the presidency of the U.S. Meanwhile in China, and at around the same time, the ruling Communist Party also embarked on a program of economic reform essentially embracing the capitalist ways. (Milton

96

Friedman was invited to consult the Chinese government twice, in 1980 and 1988.) Historians came to call this period in contemporary history the 'Return of the New Right,' a turning point which brought on stage the world as we know it.

To encapsulate all the characteristics of the contemporary world in one word, some would say 'market fundamentalism,' others would prefer 'extreme capitalism.' For me, among others like-minded, there's a better term with a broader scope: 'neoliberalism.'

What is 'neoliberalism'? And what has it done to our world in the past four decades? More importantly, how is it going to shape our future?

First and foremost: 'neoliberalism,' notwithstanding what the name might suggest, is NOT an extension of 'liberalism' which has a long history and featured prominently in western political philosophy. Sure, 'neoliberalism' also upholds individual values, but at heart it is first and foremost about economics and not politics. Its closest (i.e., with some differences) counterpart in political philosophy is 'libertarianism,' which says that as long as the rights of others are not jeopardised, one can do whatever one wants. Which - at least according to 'libertarians' - would disallow any government to tax its citizens, for everyone has the unalienable right to his or her income, making taxation by the government a form of theft!

What's paradoxical about 'libertarianism' is this: it lies on the far right in the ideological spectrum, but in many respects, it echoes the ideals of 'anarchism' which is a far left ideology. Of course, neither of these ideologies have made much headway in mainstream politics. The logic is simply this: 'anarchist/libertarian' societies, given they do not want someone to lead (including having the authority to tax), are doomed to be overwhelmed by other societies with a strong leadership (and levying tax).

Returning to the ideals of neoliberalism, what does it advocate in policy terms? First, domestically:

1. Wholesale privatisation of all public services and utilities, such as power, water, healthcare, education, social and retirement security, postal and communication services, public transportation, etc., on the ground that private enterprises operating on a 'profit motive' are more efficient than the government. It also offers consumers more choice. (Milton Friedman's most popular work is his 1980 book *Free To Choose*)

2. De-regulation, especially of the finance industry, but also other businesses, by removing as much as possible governmental oversight, on the ground that over-regulation stifles creativity and innovation, thereby impeding economic growth. (the most important act of de-regulation was the U.S. Congress repealing the 'Glass-Steagall Act' of 1933, thereby removing the legal separation of low-risk 'merchant banking' from high-risk 'investment banking', which was widely accepted as one of the main causes of the 2008 Global Financial Crisis.)

Next, internationally:

3. 'Free trade,' with all countries opening up their borders to import and export, and taking part in international trade, with the requirement that all trade barriers such as import duties and tariffs be removed;

4. 'Liberalisation of capital,' which means removal of regulation on foreign currency movement, allowing for the free flow of capital (and "hot money") around the world;

5. 'Opening domestic markets,' allowing investment and business operation of foreign enterprises and capital in all domains.

To ensure the economic policies mentioned above are not opposed or challenged, the following measures are often concurrently undertaken:

1. Union activities are suppressed, and unions disbanded, to remove collective bargaining and industrial action as the means by workers to enforce their entitlement, such being regarded by 'neoliberal economists' as detrimental to a 'free economic system.' However, measures such as establishing pro-establishment unions may be adopted as a 'divide and rule' tactic.

2. Increasing 'labour market flexibility,' allowing Big Corp to lay off staff even in good times, to preserve - according to 'neoliberal economists' again - the 'economic competitive edge' of business and society as a whole.

3. Big cuts to social welfare, or making it harder and harder to become eligible, or for those eligible, simply too much of a hassle - tons of form filling and countless interviews etc. - to get it, because - so say 'neoliberal economists,' again - welfare make people lazy.

4. Rolling out 'low progressivity' tax (progressive here means higher income has a higher tax rate), or implement 'regressive' 'sales tax' (since the same amount of tax will be a greater burden on the poorer people than to the rich), or outright tax cuts or offsets for the rich and Big Corp, as, according to 'neoliberal economists,' so doing will boost investment and spending and help economic growth (under the aegis of Supply-side Economics). Tax on inheritance/estate duty is also often reduced or removed altogether.

5. Removing rent control, on the ground that this leads to a more efficient housing market. At the same time, rolling out middle income 'home ownership schemes' to entice more people to be tied up in repaying home loans, generating more profit for the banking sector, as well as reining in possible future increase in resentment against the establishment - it is well known that home owners tend to be more conservative and pro-government.

6. 'Outsourcing,' and for multi-national enterprises, such as Nike and Adidas, 'off-shoring.' (For a long time, neither Nike nor Adidas have any production lines of their own)

7. Contract employment replacing pension benefits, and turning retirement security into yet another item on the investment portfolio ('Retirement funds' managed by private entities)

Further, investment and financial consultants (like Credit Swisse), credit rating organizations (such as Moody and Standard & Poor) or think tanks (such as the Heritage Foundation) post annual listings of countries according to their 'economic freedom' and 'competitiveness,' spurring them on to do even better by pitting against each other, in a bid to come up with the 'most attractive business environment' to foreign capital.

For poor Third World countries, if they are to receive the much-needed loans from the West to tie them over hard times, they have to strictly observe "fiscal disciplines" and undertake "structural adjustment programs," more commonly known as "austerity programs." More than a few commentators have described such programs as "punishing the poor for the mistakes of the rich."

Note that the change outlined above has long since gone beyond the U.K., U.S., or other developed western countries. From the Four Dragons of Asia (S. Korea, Singapore, Taiwan, Hong Kong) in the late 20th century to the BRICS (China, India, Russia, South Africa, and Brazil) in the 21st, they have all used the same 'formula' and copied the policies and measures outlined above, almost to the letter. Economic liberalism has the world in its grip.

Viewed as a challenge to the 'egalitarian society' crafted from Roosevelt's 'New Deal' and the 'Keynesian Revolution,' this is a counter-revolutionary act of 'restoration' staged by the rich and powerful, aided by their hand-picked academics. Using a '*Star Wars*' analogy, it is a real-world case of "The Empire Strikes Back."

Note also that while neoliberalism pays lip service to the 'free market' - that the market is the final arbiter of the success or otherwise of a business - in reality it works entirely differently. The fact that the U.S. government paid, out of public coffers, $700 billion to 'bail out' failed banks and businesses (such as AIG and General Motors which had gone under) in the 2008 Financial Crisis led critics to describe the disingenuous nature of neoliberalism as 'socialism for Wall Street, capitalism for Main Street'. The standard operative mantra of economic liberalism is, therefore, 'profits are privatised, costs are socialised.'

However, be as harshly critical of neoliberalism as we want, 'free trade' and 'capital liberalisation' have moulded the global economy into a highly inter-dependent system. While 'globalization' has once been heralded as the panacea for the world's problems (Thomas Friedman's *The World Is Flat* published in 2005 being a prime example), in reality, it is nothing but 'globalization of capitalism', in which businesses and countries try to beat others to the game, seeking out the cheapest means of production (energy, raw materials, logistics, etc.), the cheapest labour (both unskilled and expertise), and the biggest market. They also locate their production lines in places with next to no worker's rights protection and the slackest environmental regulation, so as to minimise overheads and maximise profit. To get to the top of the pack in business, one must first 'race to the bottom.'

This 'set of rules' has another name: the 'Washington Consensus.' The key players in this game are all deeply influenced by what goes on in Washington D.C.: the U.S. Federal Reserve, the International Monetary Fund, the World Bank, the World Trade Organisation, and those credit rating agencies such as Standard and Poor, Moody, etc. With less than 5% of the world's population, the U.S. boasted a GDP of almost half of the world total in the years after the war, and although this share of global GDP has declined relative to other economies on the uptick, it still stands at 24% [2019] "When the U.S. economy sneezes, global economy catches flu.", so the saying goes. In this highly tilted economic environment, dominated by the American dollar, countries seeking economic development have no option but to play the game the American way. This 'global economic dominance' is much more far-reaching than the Roman Empire's military dominance over its people and territory. Simply put, the 'Washington Consensus' is the upgraded version of post-War 'neocolonialism.' Not a few commentator has described it as "American imperialism."

In the past forty years, the neoliberal wave under the 'Washington Consensus' has caused a large number of public services to become private. Government regulation and oversight of private enterprises has been severely undermined. Multi-national corporations have expanded their scale and scope to unprecedented levels through repeated mergers and acquisitions, becoming more powerful than some small nations. The sustained 'financialisation' of the economy means that the total amount of 'hot money' circulating around the globe has reached an astounding ten to twenty times that of the global GDP, with an astronomically huge gross global debt looming in the background. There are scholars who pointed out that modern civilization has entered a 'super-debt era' under 'globalised monopolistic financial capitalism.'

4.2 Trickle-Up Economics and the Precariat

It must be pointed out that, while becoming part of this "modern-day Roman Empire economy," many developing countries did get rich (prime example being the group of countries known as BRICS), but more often than not at the expense of

1. Massive selling off of their natural resources (minerals, timber, oil…);

2. Widespread environmental degradation (pollution, deforestation, and biodiversity loss);

3. Damage to the health, dignity, sometimes even the lives of their people (witness the spread of 'sweat shop factories' worldwide; and disasters such as the garment factories fires in Bangladesh, the spate of suicides in Foxconn, Shenzhen, China, the detrimental effects of cobalt and sulfur mining…., just to name a few).

While the economy booms and GDP rises, not everyone is benefited to the same degree, and some are even worse off than before. Enclosure of traditional living space, expropriation of the people living in it, and the subsequent proletarianization which leads to cheap labour crowded into urban slums are processes that have been repeated many times over numerous Third World countries. Even for the white-collar workers, the sad irony is that with increasing social affluence, people work longer and longer hours, and under more and more stress.

Even in developed countries, it used to be the man of the house as the sole bread earner. Now it is husband and wife on a double income and yet still barely making ends meet. Working multiple jobs is now a norm. So is spending on credit (witness the pervasive advertisement enticing people to borrow). Upward social mobility has grinded to a snail-pace. Inter-generation poverty has become prevalent, and "Rich Dad, Poor Dad" has now become the dominant factor in determining one's success in life.

One doesn't need to be a university professor to realise that, starting from fundamental logic, a 'free economy' free from any constraints will necessarily end up an 'unfree economy.' This is because in any competition, there's going to be a winner and a loser. He who wins goes on to win more, and so on and so forth. Or 'success breeds success.' This feedback loop works in such a way that the strong gets stronger while the weak gets weaker. The final outcome of course is 'winner takes all.' Monopolies and oligopolies take hold, and the 'free economy' becomes an empty word. Sociologists call this simple logic the Matthew Effect, for in the Gospel there is a saying that "For to everyone who has more be given, and he will have abundance; but from him who has not, even what he has will be taken away." (Matthew 25:29, RSV)

Actually, many scholars have pointed out long ago that 'neoliberal' economic policies would lead to a widening gap between the rich and poor. They therefore urge governments to implement tax reforms and welfare measures in a bid to 'redistribute wealth' and reinstate social equity.

"Absolutely not!" is the response from supporters of the 'neoliberal' agenda. They claimed that such 'Robin Hood' policies would destroy people's incentive to work and to create wealth, dooming the economy and ending prosperity, in which case the poor would only end up worse ("the path to hell is pathed with well intentions," so they will exhort). What we should be doing instead, argued these supporters, is to make sure the economy keeps growing, (to grow a bigger pie) and when that happens, even though the poor will not get a bigger share, the absolute value of their share will still be bigger than before, meaning their livelihood will improve. In other words, a bigger pie feeds everybody better. This school of thought, based on 'a rising tide lifts all boats,' is the basis of the famous 'trickle-down economics' narrative.

Facts have shown, however, that to the majority of the working population, the outcome promised by 'trickle-down economics' has not materialised, the fundamental cause being the logic of 'the race to the bottom,' or wage level always depressed to the 'subsistence level' as explained in previous chapters. The anticipated 'trickle down' sharing of prosperity became a 'trickle-up' transfer of wealth instead, meaning more and more wealth goes to the top, and the rich-poor gap gets even wider. A comprehensive study of this development is presented in the book *Capital in the Twenty-First Century* (2013) written by the French economist Thomas Picketty. According to Oxfam's study, since 1995, the top 1% have captured nearly twenty times more of global wealth than the bottom 50%. The pandemic since 2019 is making matters even worse. A Credit Swisse report finds that the world richest 1% now owns nearly 46% of global wealth. Another study undertaken by *Forbes* reveals that the combined wealth of the 10 richest persons on Earth is greater than the GDP of many countries.

Warren Buffett, commenting shortly after the 2008 global financial crisis on the 'Return of the New Right', said, "There's class warfare, all right, but it's my class, the rich class, that's making war, and we're winning." Buffett had the guts to say this because while a billionaire, he is dead set against such a trend of development, and went so far as to suggest making the rich pay a 'Robin Hood tax.' No wonder his comment was met with dismay and scorn from the rich and powerful. Some even queried if it was his failing mental faculty which caused this outburst.

'Neoliberalism' is absolutely successful, and the hallmark of its success is the majority hasn't even heard of 'neoliberalism' (just like fishes don't know they're living in water). It succeeded immensely by planting this idea in people's head: 'Politics is about choice, while economics is about laws,' and what we're doing now is 'playing it by the rules of economics,' namely, it is something non-ideological. Nothing is of course further from the truth. And yet, so successful is this ideology-in-disguise that 'politics' has been hi-jacked by 'economics.' Margaret Thatcher has a famous and often-quoted saying, "There is no alternative!" (acronym TINA). For decades, from university professors to government bureaucrats and down to the man in the street, all have become victims of this 'cognitive capture.'

'Neoliberalism' has a profound impact. An important outcome of Roosevelt's 'New Deal' was the making of a robust 'middle class.' It's true the middle class tends to be conservative politically, but politics aside, the improvement of livelihood of an increasing majority in society is something to be celebrated. However, the relentless drive from 'the race to the bottom' and 'trickle-up economy' have been gnawing away the middle class. First put forward by William Ouchi and then popularised by Japanese management consultant Kenichi Ohmae, people are alerted to the rise an 'M-shaped society', in which diminishing upward social mobility, financialization of the economy and the stagnation of wage level etc has led to the erosion of the middle class, with income distribution in our society changing from a 'bell curve' of a 'normal distribution' to an 'M-shaped curve', with a widening and deepening dip in the middle.

To a certain extent, this fits in with what Marx has predicted, namely that capitalism will invariably lead to social polarisation. (For many years, the rise of a middle class has been seen as a powerful rebuttal to Marxist theory)

By 'polarisation,' Marx was referring to the 'bourgeois' and 'proletariat.' In recent year, scholars have pointed out that, bombarded by waves of outsourcing, contract employment, and layoff, the current situation is no longer the same as a century (or just several decades) ago, when people worked for the same or maybe two employers for their life. A name was given to this new class of unstable employees (whether 'white' or 'blue' collar): Precariat, a combination of *preca*-rious and proleta-*riat*. I call this new class 'drifters.'

This new class of *precariats* is characterised by inherent employment instability, need to supplement income with part-time work, lack of vocational identity, fluctuation in real wage (oftentimes an overall decline), lack of employee benefits and retirement security, sometimes even chronically indebted. *karoshi* か ろ う し for Japan, and 'Working Poor' for the rest of the world.

More and more people took up freelancing, often not entirely voluntarily, or temporary or short-term employment (i.e., from 'employed' to 'self-employed'), giving rise to the present-day 'Gig Economy'. Yet many of the so-called 'self-employment schemes' are really scams which deepened the exploitation of the workers, as poignantly highlighted in the 2019 movie *Sorry We Missed You*. This development is the practice of the 'neoliberal' philosophy carried to the extreme.

Today, university graduates make up the bulk of the drifter class. A much lower upward social mobility, compounded by an ever-increasing property price tag which practically shut out these newcomers to society to home ownership, many turned to pursuing LOHAS (Lifestyles of Health and Sustainability) or 'down-shifting' in a bid to 'de-materialise' their lives, while others went all out to devote themselves to realising cherished ideals, becoming boutique bookshop owners, running experimental drama troupe, or going to live and work in a farming village. In short, they are refusing to join the "rat race" which have consumed the lives of their parents and grandparents. The 2006 Hollywood movie "The Devil Wears Pravda" gave us a glimpse of such awakening among the younger generation. In China, there is in recent years a movement among the young people with the slogan *Tang Ping*, meaning "lying flat /low" as a philosophy of life: no houses, no cars, no marriage, no kids, and a minimum level of desire and consumption. The reason behind all this is to "refuse being a machine or even slave exploited by the capitalists for their profits." This extremist response is a sad logical conclusion to the evils of capitalism.

Needless to say, this fall in marriage and birth rates is fuelling the demographic implosion crisis already experienced by many countries. Parents can help financially to some extent (lending money to their kids for mortgage down payment and even their wedding expenses), but the uninvitingly cramped living environment in high rise shoebox apartments in most major cities only work to discourage family formation.

Apart from this nihilistic response, people also try hard to push back the tide. Increasing wealth disparity and social injustice have driven many to the streets in protest, a most convincing and powerful rebuttals to 'neoliberalism' and 'globalisation's feigned promise of opportunity and prosperity. An 'Occupy' movement broke out bang in the middle of the throbbing heart of capitalism - Wall Street in New York, and thereafter, similar 'Occupy' movements spread to major cities around the world. The *Mouvement des gilets jaunes*, Yellow Vest Movement which first broke out on the streets in Paris in November 2018, is still very much alive, as are many other popular movements around the world championing a similar cause.

In October 2019, massive protests broke out in Chile, a country on the 'global periphery'. (according to Wallerstein's classification). You may still remember that following the overthrow of Allende in the 1973 coup (as related earlier), Chile became "the world's first test-bed of neoliberal economics". Professors from the School of

Economics of the Chicago University - nicknamed the "Chicago Boys" - became consultants to Pinochet for his economic and social reforms. What followed was a reign of terror not forgotten by the Chilean people until today. So, during the 2019-20 protests, you could well imagine my elation when I saw a photo of a Chilean woman on the street holding up a placard which reads "Neoliberalism was born in Chile, and will die in Chile". Of course, I would love to see this come true, but viewed objectively, this will be a prolonged and agonising struggle.

To anyone who wants to understand the impact of 'neoliberalism' in the past decades, I heartily recommend Canadian author and social activist's 2007 book *The Shock Doctrine: the Rise of Disaster Capitalism*, and another book *Blessed Unrest* published by social activist Paul Hawken in the same year. As to how we could possibly counteract this trend of development, my recommendation is two books by Nobel Laureate American economist Joseph Stiglitz: *People, Power, and Profits* (2019) deals with national reforms, and *Globalisation and its Discontents Revisited* (2017) deals with reforms to international organisations such as the World Bank and the International Monetary Fund. I do hope that a ray of hope will be glimpsed by you the Dear Reader after reading them.

The Trap of
Managerialism

'Neoliberalism' causes damage not only to the economy by worsening social inequality and creating a class of precariats. It has also done immense harm to society through the engendering of 'managerialism'.

The first to let in this curse was the British Prime Minister Mrs Margaret Thatcher, when she rolled out 'public sector reform' in the 1980s, under the guiding principle that backward and conservative thinking public service operating at below par efficiency must learn from private enterprises dictated by efficiency and cost effectiveness. To this end, objectively measurable targets and outcomes must be established beforehand for practically everything, augmented by unceasing supervision, monitoring, and assessments.

In the same period of time, a revolution arose in business management. To counter the impact of the rather successful 'Japanese style' management, 'innovative theories' blossomed in the field of management in the U.S., and CEOs of major enterprises compete to wow investors with more and more exotic ways of boosting business revenue (boosting their own pay check at the same time). The most famous example has to be General Electric's Jack Welch, who 'raised competitiveness' by wielding the axe on the workforce under him, with massive lay-off of staff euphemised as "streamlining" and "re-engineering". This was copied by other CEOs in almost no time, who also copied Welch's another cost-cutting measure: 'performance-related pay'. Welch made his subordinate middle managers implement annual assessment on worker's performance to replace the traditional fixed pay scale as the basis of any pay rise. More drastically, he demanded department managers to lay off the lowest performing 10% of workforce every year (disregarding the actual performance), ostensibly to 'eliminate the weak and keep the strong' and to keep the entire workforce at peak performance, by keeping everybody on their toes.

Here, we run yet again into the tragedy of 'individual rationality equates collective irrationality'. For a business, making it 'lean and mean' may help raise competitiveness. But if all businesses go the same way, society eventually will be left with troubled people, people without security, without community spirit, without a sense of belonging. And they will be filled with anxiety, angst, anger, and indifference. Society ends up paying a hefty price (including alcoholism, drug use, obesity, domestic violence, rise in crime rate, decline in mental wellbeing, even random killing). When Jack Welch was nick-named "Neutron Jack" for his destructive ruthlessness, few people would have imagined how apt it is in a wider sociological context.

More lamentable is while the business is pushed to the brink of losing the last gram of compassion, its management is lauding 'Vision, Mission, Values' as their lofty goals, and dressing it up in euphemisms such as 'Caring Organisation'. What a stark contrast between the cruel reality on the one hand and the thin veneer of civilised modernity on the other! Among this veneer is the "exit interviews" (also invented by Jack Welch) for staff suddenly laid off with no justifiable reason. For the horrible impacts of this "humanistic" innovation, I recommend the 2009 Hollywood movie *Up in the Air*.

Unfortunately, the ill wind that is 'managerialism' has not only blown over the business world, it has reached public services worldwide. Government departments, public organisations, education, academia, culture, sports, even religious bodies, and charities. No aspect of human life can escape its onslaught.

Managerialism's mantra is, 'everything can be managed' and 'whatever can be managed *should* be managed'. The result is that not only do we now have a university degree for 'business management', we have proliferating courses and diplomas in customer relationship management, event management, wealth management, culture management, sports management, creative arts management, education management, spouse relationship management, parent-kids relationship management, time management, health management, anxiety and anger management, conflict management, self-image management, pet management... etc.

Viewed from a wider perspective, this is the logical outcome of the philosophy of neoliberalism, in which business thinking and the market hold sway over everything. We are asked to "leave everything to the market", "turn everything into a business", "manage society just like a business" because "the market knows best" and "efficiency and tangible results" trumps everything.

But then, what exactly is 'management'? Under the banner of 'scientific management' (which I could call "managerialism"), everything has to be 'objectified', 'quantified', 'target-based', "out-come based" and 'operationalised', 'proceduralized' and 'standardised'. That which cannot be reduced to any of the above is deemed anachronistic and unscientific. The upshot is that nowadays, whether it is the teacher-student relationship, physician-patient relationship, or social worker-welfare recipient relationship etc, conformity to the above requirements is mandated without questions.

To show that we're up-to-date, everything we do these days must be characterised by 'target-based objectives', 'benchmarking', 'demonstrable deliverables', 'key performance indicators', 'value-added-ness', 'impact assessment' etc, with 'assessment/ evaluation' being the most crucial. These days even stage performances (concert/ play/opera etc.) will come with an 'evaluation questionnaire' to be filled in by the audience; teacher performance is determined by 'student evaluation'; academic papers are assessed on their 'citation index' and 'impact factor'; a curriculum-design to be assessed by 'outcome based objectives'. Furthermore, everything needs to go through a detailed 'SWOT' analysis (strengths. weaknesses, opportunities, and threats), meet onerous 'Quality Assurance' standards, as well as providing '3- (or 5-) yearly plan/ budget' and constant progress review etc.

I do not deny the value of management, but what transpires under the name of 'managerialism' in the previous half-century has obviously gone too far. Workers in all fields of employment are having to deal with a constant and heavy load of extra paper work (in the form of endless stream of assessment reports). It also weighs heavily on their mental wellbeing. School teachers seldom commit suicide due to a heavy teaching workload, but such tragic incidents have become part of the modern scene because of ever-increasing *administrative* workload. How can this not be a sad state of affairs of the modern civilisation?

The fact is, 'questionnaires' and 'evaluations' have become our new religion. But oftentimes it is just an expensive trick to delude oneself and trick the public. Just think back to the 2008 global financial crisis: credit rating agencies such as S&P and Moody were still awarding AAA rating to Lehman Brothers and AIG on the eve of the bust. If this is not deception, what is?

From a historical perspective, managerialism is just the extension of the monitoring and control of physical labour (blue collar) to the realm of mental labour (white collar). The "optimization of work process" by breaking it down into minute segments, pioneered through Taylorism (temporally) and Fordism (spatially) more than a century ago, is now elevated to a high religion. As sociologist Max Weber so presciently pointed out, our "instrumental rationality" has led to an "Iron Cage" of our own making, with dehumanising results. Against the background of worsening social inequality and long working hours, ongoing development in this direction will only lead to more resentment, apathy, and perfunctory formalism, further depressing the individual's initiative, enthusiasm, and creativity, and turning people into stressed, angry, indifferent, and hypocritical beings.

In recent years, an 'obituary' has circulated widely on the internet. It was not for a person. It was something we call 'commonsense'. Reading it makes you wonder if humankind has already lost its collective sanity.

Today we mourn the passing of a beloved old friend, Common Sense, who has been with us for many years. No one knows for sure how old he was, since his birth records were long ago lost in bureaucratic red tape. He will be remembered as having cultivated such valuable lessons as:

• Knowing when to come in out of the rain;

• Why the early bird gets the worm;

• Life isn't always fair; and

• Maybe it was my fault.

Common Sense lived by simple, sound financial policies (don't spend more than you can earn) and reliable strategies (adults, not children, are in charge).

His health began to deteriorate rapidly when well-intentioned but overbearing regulations were set in place.

Reports of a 6-year-old boy charged with sexual harassment for kissing a classmate; teens suspended from school for using mouthwash after lunch; and a teacher fired for reprimanding an unruly student, only worsened his condition.

Common Sense lost ground when parents attacked teachers for doing the job that they themselves had failed to do in disciplining their unruly children.

It declined even further when schools were required to get parental consent to administer sun lotion or an aspirin to a student; but could not inform parents when a student became pregnant and wanted to have an abortion.

Common Sense lost the will to live as the churches became businesses; and criminals received better treatment than their victims.

Common Sense took a beating when you couldn't defend yourself from a burglar in your own home and the burglar could sue you for assault.

Common Sense finally gave up the will to live, after a woman failed to realise that a steaming cup of coffee was hot. She spilled a little in her lap, and was promptly awarded a huge settlement.

Common Sense was preceded in death, by his parents, Truth and Trust, by his wife, Discretion, by his daughter, Responsibility, and by his son, Reason.

He is survived by his 4 stepbrothers;

• I Know My Rights

• I Want It Now

• Someone Else Is To Blame

• I'm A Victim

Not many attended his funeral because so few realized he was gone. If you still remember him, pass this on. If not, join the majority and do nothing.

To go into the details of this obituary would require a separate booklet at least. Without knowing the background of the author, I would venture to say that he (or she) is most likely from a conservative background - the Conservatives in the UK, and the Republican in the US. Many of the scathing criticisms are levelled at the Liberals or the Progressives - the Liberals in UK and Democrats in the US.

It is true that many of the absurdities pointed out in the obituary are the results of "political correctness" carried to the extreme. First championed by the Liberals/Progressives in the 1970s and rising to prominence in the 1990s, the "political correctness movement" is an attempt to fight racism, sexism, and elitism based on wealth and class. However, the underlying egalitarianism, solidarity, compassion, and sense of brotherhood run counter to the beliefs of the Right, who subscribe to the view that whatever is produced by the free market is the best. Any attempt to over-ride market-driven outcomes (such as comprehensive social welfare programs) would only make matters worse. "Life isn't always fair." and "Maybe it's my fault." propounded at the beginning of the obituary encapsulate the underlying philosophy.

Paradoxically, the ills lamented by the obituary are in essence the results of Right-wing managerialism more than the results of Left-wing political correctness. It all boils down to this: when 'social norms' are replaced by 'market norms', and formalised 'standards', 'procedures' and 'targets' replace 'intuition', 'compassion' and 'common-sense', personal autonomy and the sense of duty will be eroded, and the absurdity in the obituary will become reality.

Over the years, many entrepreneurs with heart (mostly from the younger generation) have strived to come up with a more 'humane' philosophy of business management. Regrettably, notwithstanding occasional positive outcomes achieved, management has remained in the main subservient to the 'urge of capitalism' and 'urge of managerialism', which are really two sides of the same coin.

All in all, the 'managerialism' invented by the West (and fervently copied by the rest of the world) is akin to a super-efficient way of digging graves, from which the world cannot now escape. Looking into the future, are we able to reverse its trend? The 'Managerialism Trap' is a problem we must face, together with the traps of agriculture and capitalism, in our quest to map out our future path.

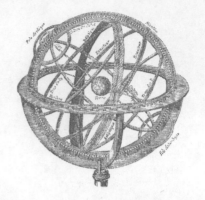

4.4 The Expanding Circle

In our examination of the contemporary 'Human Condition,' from the 'Ecological Crisis' to 'Neoliberalism Rules the World,' it would appear that human society has somehow 'took the wrong turn' and gone astray. However, looking back at the chapter on 'The Second Enlightenment,' and the 35 points in 'History's Turning Point', it is clear that civilisation has truly ascended through progress made in many areas, a fact which is very encouraging.

Here, we are more concerned with the ascent in the non-material aspects of civilisation. Aside from advances such as in life expectancy, literacy and quality of life, there are also the following key points, some of which have been covered before. These include:

1. Liberation of the other half of humanity - women. Generally speaking, women around the world are enjoying a much higher social and economic status and have more freedom and greater political rights than 100 years ago, let alone 500 or 1000 years ago. But this is 'generally speaking,' as there can be a significant disparity between women of different countries and in different socio-economic strata. Even in developed countries, 'equal rights between men and women' are still very much works-in-progress, as could be seen in the 2017 #MeToo social movement, first initiated on social media, against sexual abuse and harassment of women. There is still a lot that needs to be done.

2. End of slavery and racism, the former being a historic achievement of the 19th century, the latter, from the 1960s 'civil rights movement' in the U.S. On the other hand, the recent 'Black Lives Matter' movement illustrate all too well the difficulty in achieving true and complete racial equality. True, the South African Apartheid ended in 1994, yet even now the black population fares far worse than the white.

However, notwithstanding the detours and set-backs, statements like "women is the weaker sex," "women's place belongs to the kitchen" or "coloured people are mentally inferior" and is therefore the "White man's burden" are no longer acceptable in any civilised conversation. This of course is one big step for civilisation.

3. Secularisation and harmony between religions. Firstly, with 'secularisation,' which means 'what's religion is religion, what's secular (politics, society, culture...) is secular,' one is not worse off or persecuted for being an 'atheist;' secondly, freedom to believe, which means for people, they have a choice of religious faith - or none - free from fear of discrimination or persecution, and for religions, they are not to attack one another. (Note that 'harmony between religions' is actually nothing new: the Chinese culture is inclusive to different faiths; the Ottoman Empire (1299-1922), though Muslim, allowed religious freedom).

'Secularisation' and 'harmony between religions,' like the fight against 'sexism' and 'racism,' are still very much works-in-progress. For the past seven decades or more, the Middle East has been in a state of constant conflict, caused not in the least by the establishment, supported by the West, of Israel, a Jewish state in the midst of Palestinian land. This triumph of Zionism was spurred on by the horrors of the Holocaust, while bigger reasons are a scramble for valuable oil and gas (not in Israel itself, but in neighbouring regions), US military dominance, and the bigger picture of geopolitical contest of power. As a result, countless lives have been lost, cities even entire regions reduced to rubble. From the ashes of destruction has risen not hope or salvation, but Islamic extremist terrorism, championing the vanquishing of the infidel West through what they called *Jihad*, by attacking mainly civilian targets and blowing themselves up in self-sacrifice and redemption (the 9/11 attacks on U.S. soil is a prime example). On the other hand, Islamophobia led to hate crimes targeting Muslims, a most notable incident being the mass shooting of Muslims outside a mosque in March 2019 Christchurch, killing a total of 51 people. Such horrific events have made people think that a 'clash of civilisations,' brought about by rifts in different religious faiths, is both unavoidable and worsening.

In my view, this is all a misunderstanding. 'Peaceful co-existence' among religions is entirely achievable, both in the past and in the future. The extremism and bloodshed we have witnessed so far is actually more an outcome of Western colonialism compounded by extremist Zionism. It is true that some Islamic countries tend to secularise slower than others, but if we look at Malaysia, we can see that a secularised Islamic country is entirely possible.

As we move further into the 21st century, there are worrying trends that once secularised Islamic countries are moving backwards, a notable example of which is Turkey. And there are countries like Iran which still aspires to replace the modern legal system by "Sharia" the sacred law of Islamism. The Taliban regime in Afghanistan is another example. What is urgently needed is that the West/Israel adopt geopolitical policies that would defuse such fervour, instead of fuelling it. (The re-election of the far-right Netanyahu government in Israel at the time of writing is sadly not encouraging)

4. Regulating wars and banning torture, of which 'progress,' as in the above domains, is full of setbacks. From the moment humankind's first aircraft took to the air, the distinction between combat and non-combat zones vanished, subjecting countless people to the threat and fear of airstrikes. The *Geneva Protocol* of 1925, banning all forms of chemical and biological weaponry, did not stop Nazi Germany from committing genocide with poisonous gas, or the Japanese Imperial Army from conducting bacterial weapon test on live human beings, or the U.S. releasing enormous amounts of 'Agent Orange' during the Vietnam war, or the use of white phosphorus munitions in Syria. The 'Geneva Protocol' also requires for the humane treatment of prisoners-of-war, but this has not stopped the U.S. government from obtaining information through torture (such as waterboarding), under the excuse of 'War on Terror.'

Be that as it may, whether it is 'waterboarding' or 'video-ed confession' practised in the PRC (widely believed to be confessions obtained under severe duress), it has been roundly criticised and widely condemned by the civilised world.

In summary, whether it is a prisoner-of-war or a prisoner in time of peace, they are being treated much better than 500 or 1000 years ago.

Domestically, prisoners in many countries can now vote in elections, and more and more societies are now offering them re-integration support.

5. Sexual liberation that challenges established and accepted codes of behaviour related to sexuality and relationship allowed people to dress more sexily, people in love displaying intimacy in public, pornography (including sex scenes in movies) to be more daring, sex shops to open without restriction, premarital sex becoming commonplace, and red light districted regulated - and protected - by law, it also enabled the most important progress - a more inclusive attitude to people with diverse sexual orientations (grouped collectively as LGBTQ), as well as recognising the legitimacy and lawfulness of same-sex marriage. (U.S. president Barack Obama's 2015 legalisation of same-sex marriage is a big step in this respect). As well, it also included the introduction of equal rights and protection of law to sex workers.

6. Embracing disability, including the physically and mentally disabled, removing all forms of discrimination against them, and supporting them to be part of society. A notable progress was the beginning of the 'Paralympic Games' in 1960.

7. Animal protection. It was Charles Darwin the great English naturalist who said, "The love of all creatures is the most noble attribute of Man." Over the past hundred more years, humanity have done good and harm equally in this respect. The good is that, regardless of the pace and magnitude of change, the majority of countries have legislated against cruelty to animals. Furthermore, following the start of the 'anti-vivisection movement' in the 19th century, most countries have banned the use of live animals for the purpose of testing and experiments unless absolutely necessary. And when these are done (such as in the development of new drugs), strict regulations have to be observed, with pain and suffering of the animals kept to a minimum.

As the idea of 'animal rights' grew in public awareness, there is increasing criticism of and opposition to 'recreational hunting,' and toward animal suffering brought about by their being kept in zoos or trained to perform in circus. The result is that killer whales have largely disappeared in the Seaworlds of the world, and circus with performance of lions, tigers, bears, and elephants etc. have become a relic of history. Zoos have also improved animal habitat design under the constant pressure from animal rights activists.

During the writing of this book, an international movement to extend the concept of personhood and its associated status and rights to include the great apes (chimpanzees, bonobos, gorillas, and orangutans) was in full swing, a legal personhood being the ultimate goal, by which time tests and experimentation involving great apes would face a total ban, and they capture and detention made unlawful, thereby requiring all zoo-kept animals to be set free.

Given this measurable progress in advancing animal rights, what is the 'harm' referred to at the beginning of this section? This has everything to do with the rapid expansion of livestock farming and its industrialisation over the past century or so. As the world gets richer on the average, people are eating more meat (China being one-fifth of the world is the best example, but of course is still no match to the Americans on a per capita basis). The result is that traditional free-range herding of meat animals (think free-range chickens) has given way to 'feedlots' of increasing size: enormous number of animals (chicken, pig, cattle…) packed and kept in an extremely crowded, and therefore very unhygienic, environment, kept growing by pumping them with growth hormones, and kept disease-free with lots of antibiotics. These animals never see the light of day - or their parents. Overgrown animals become so heavy they cannot even stand on their own feet…

The harm which humanity has done is this: worldwide, wildlife has been on a rapid decline, when at the same time animals kept in cruelty simply for our culinary delight have drastically increased in number, the newest estimate being 80 billion animals slaughtered for food each year (fish not included), this number being more than 10 times the world population. And the number is still on the rise.

On the other hand, 'veganism' has also been on the rise, at least in developed countries. In the past, religious faith was the main motive to become a vegan. Modern day vegans do so also for the sake of the environment, their conscience or for their own health. Sadly, this trend remains largely a fad of developed countries, a drop in the ocean compared to the two-thirds of the world's population living in developing countries.

To reduce doing further harm, as well as to halt livestock farming encroaching on the environment leading to its eventual collapse, it has been suggested that a 'meat tax' be levied, and 'man made meat' be developed. 'Man made meat' includes plant-based products with textures rivalling animal meat, as well as laboratory grown meat using stem cell technology. We shall await with anticipation the meat of the future.

Now, let's return to the spiritual aspect of the 'ascent of civilisation.' Summing up the 7 points listed above - and setting aside the setbacks and regressions for the time being - we can see a common theme: humankind's 'Expanding Circle of Inclusiveness'.

The Circle of Inclusiveness has always existed. Simply put, it is the circle of 'us': parents, siblings, partners, in other words, people with ties of kinship. Next, the extended family. In the primitive society of 'hunter-gatherers,' this circle would have included a dozen to several dozen persons.

After the appearance of garden farming, this circle expanded to a size of several tens to hundreds of people, about the size of a hamlet. When large-scale farming began, this circle further expanded to several hundred to several thousand people, making up a village or town.

A clarification is necessary here. "Inclusive" here does not mean there is perfect harmony without any conflict or war. We all know that there can be bitter rivalry even within a household, let alone between offspring of a common ancestor but from different lineages. But generally speaking, such conflict would be regulated by the moral codes to which all these members subscribed, and unresolved disputes referred to the highest authority (heads of family, tribal elders, chieftains, etc.) who would have the final say.

Diametrically opposite to this in-circle are those 'not of my kind.' So, within the circle are 'Us,' and without, 'Them.' As the Chinese saying goes, "Those not of our tribe would always harbour alien thoughts." We must therefore be constantly alert to 'Them,' for ultimately they bear us ill and want us dead.

In this confrontation between Us and Them, a tendency is to denigrate such 'alien races' as 'sub-human,' so that moral rules that apply to 'us' don't apply to 'them.' Needless to say, 'sub-humanising' or even 'de-humanising' 'them' has been the source of much atrocity in human history. A typical example is the Holocaust: Nazi Germany labelled Jews 'rats' and 'vermin;' another example is during the 1994 Rwanda genocide, when the Tutu perpetrators called their Tutsi victims 'cockroaches'.

The demarcation of 'us' from 'them' forms a main theme of human history, with such demarcation based on 'totem' (tribes), creeds, religion, culture, language, race (skin colour), gender ('women are inferior to men'), sexual orientation ('gay people are bad people'), or species ('animals don't feel'), etc.

Historically, the overcoming of bigotry in its various forms is a major theme in the ascent of civilization. However, it has been a prolong and arduous journey, and invariably, the progress has never been a result of the magnanimity of the oppressors, and rather a result of the heroic struggle and sacrifice undertaken by the oppressed. But still, whether it is overthrowing the institution of slavery, the liberation of women, de-colonization and the rise of nation states, the fight for equality in sexual orientation, or the rights of animals, the "Circle of Inclusiveness" has been covering more and more creatures under the sky.

The last item outlined above - that of animal rights - is of course not fought for by the persecuted animals themselves, but by human beings with a heart. Australian philosopher Peter Singer, with his 1975 book *Animal Liberation*, is a forerunner in this respect. His 1981 book *The Expanding Circle* pointed out clearly that expanding humankind's circle of inclusiveness to include other animals is an important landmark in the ascent of civilisation.

In fact, as early as 1957, English science fiction writer Arthur C. Clarke (1917-2008) wrote the following passage at the end of his novel *The Deep Range*, "Sooner or later we will meet types of intelligent life much higher than our own, yet in forms completely alien. And when that time comes, the treatment man receives from his superiors may well depend upon the way he has behaved toward the other creatures of his own world."

No one knows when we will encounter aliens, but facing up to ourselves with increasingly powerful weapons of destruction will pose an equally great - if not greater - challenge. The crucial question is: Will the Circle continue to expand, and universal brotherhood brings everlasting peace, or will the tribal mentality of Us and Them persists, and bring upon the downfall of the human race? This leads us into realm of the power contest between nations, a theme to which we now turn.

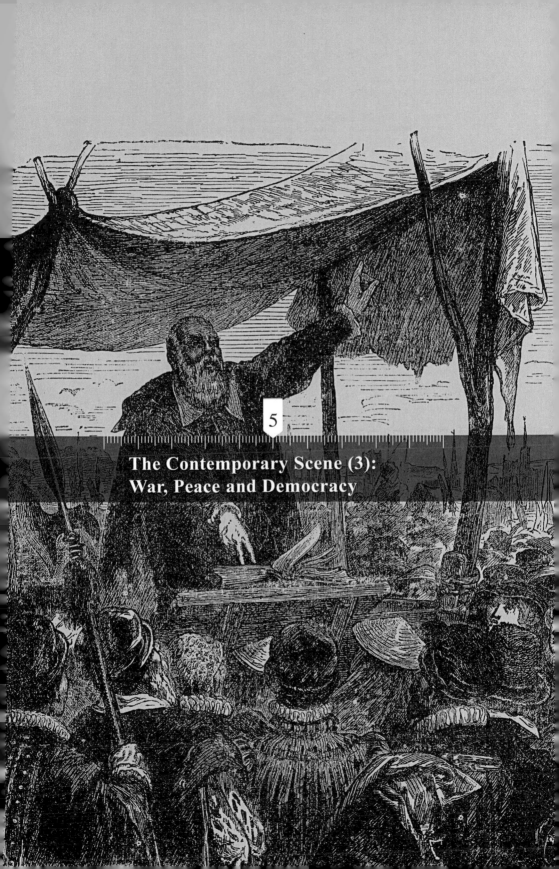

5

The Contemporary Scene (3):
War, Peace and Democracy

5.1 Geopolitics and the Prospects of War

The Peace of Westphalia, encapsulated in two treaties signed in 1648, was widely regarded as the foundation of modern international politics. Although the Westphalian treaties did not prevent further wars (such as Napoleon's conquests), the concepts of 'sovereign state' and 'international law' became enshrined in what is known collectively as 'Westphalian sovereignty.'

By the end of the 19th century, just as people - at least those in Britain, Europe, and America - thought they were entering a bright new age of peace and prosperity, the dawn of the twentieth century was soon followed by the unprecedentedly bloody World War I (which is the Eurocentric name given to a regional conflict, albeit it is a region ruling large parts of the world).

The League of Nations, one of the most significant outcomes of the Paris Peace Conference, was the first international body in history to be charged with the duty to maintain world peace. However, excessive demands by the victors on the vanquished led to the rise of Nazism in Germany, and subsequently to the outbreak of World War II (now this is truly a World War). The League of Nations and the ideals behind its conception was left in tatters, and the body finally dissolved in 1946.

The United Nations, established after World War II in 1947, is humankind's second attempt at pursuing, and maintaining, a world in peace. The UN has been successful in its prime mission so far, as there is yet to be a World War III, but countless armed confrontations and conflict of varying severity - including genocides - happening on both a regional and local scale - is more than enough to raise serious doubt about the effectiveness of the UN as a peace-keeping international organisation. In the eyes of pacifists - especially in view of Russia's blatant invasion of Ukraine - the UN is a complete failure.

Quite a few scholars have also pointed out that it is "nuclear deterrence" rather than the UN that has managed to prevent conflicts and confrontations, in particular the Cold War between post-war U.S. and Soviet Russia, from becoming an all-out world war. If not for this deterrent effect, the 1962 'Cuban missile crisis' would have pushed the world over the brink.

Soviet Russia was the world's first communist regime, but it broke up in 1991-2. This also ended its four decade long contest for global domination with the U.S., and for a time, people thought this was the beginning of true world peace. Japanese American political scientist Francis Fukuyama, best known for his 1992 work *The End of History and the Last Man*, argued, with a generous dose of optimism, that after a bitter contest in the 20th century between communism and capitalism, capitalism has emerged as the undisputed winner. He went on to suggest that, as capitalism encapsulated liberal democracy which represents humankind's highest ideal, the victory of capitalism marks the end-point of history, with what lies in the future merely variations on the same theme.

However, an almost diametrically opposite viewpoint was put forward at around the same time. Samuel P. Huntington (1927-2008), an American political scientist at the Harvard University, wrote an essay titled *The Clash of Civilisations?* published in the *Foreign Affairs* magazine in 1993, the arguments of which was later expanded in a book *The Clash of Civilisation and the Remaking of World Order* (1996).

I described Fukuyama as an optimist. If so, Huntington would be the pessimist. Huntington put forward his view that the end of the communist-capitalist confrontation, which he considered to be a form of 'ideological struggle' - and was an 'exception' rather than the 'norm' in history - marked not an 'end of history' as Fukuyama had suggested, but a return to the conventional/historical mode of 'clash of civilisations.'

Huntington divided the world into three major 'civilisation groups': the predominantly western 'Christian civilisation,' the 'Islamic civilisation' of the Arab world, and the 'Sinic civilisation' dominated by China and its neighbouring countries. These civilisation groups subscribe to vastly different core values, and geopolitical interests clashed every now and then. In Huntington's view, the future will still be full of conflicts and confrontations.

At first, these two contesting theories attracted equal attention. Those in favour of Fukuyama's theory even went so far as to envisage a future in which the world, with the U.S. as the 'sole superpower,' would evolved into a 'Pax Americana,' a state of affairs not unlike that under the 'Pax Romana.' The 9/11 terror attacks shattered this wishful thinking, and people were rudely awakened to the prospect of a 21st century just as tumultuous as the 20th. The 'Clash of Civilisations' overcame 'End of History' as the mainstream narrative.

Between Fukuyama and Huntington, who got it right? With something as complicated as war and peace, any simple explanation would be like the blind groping an elephant - no one would get it all right. But I wouldn't mind playing the role of that blind person and summarise the causes of war in five main headings, which are interrelated and influence each other.

The first one is the conventional 'geopolitical struggle,' which has always been the major cause of war. Biologists have long pointed out that most species are equipped with an innate 'territorial imperative' to protect its habitat and the extended territory the resources of which are essential to their survival - grazing ground for herbivores and hunting ground for carnivores. Humans, of course, is no exception.

Since the Agricultural Revolution, this imperative was elevated and glorified in the desire of empire-building by mighty rulers, resulting in the urge of incessant territorial expansion and the conquest and subjugation of other races. Notable examples are the unification of Persia by Cyrus, Qin Shi Huang's unification of China, and Ashoka's unification of India, all accompanied by huge amounts of bloodshed. The Greco-Persian Wars, the conquests of Alexander the Great, the Punic Wars between Rome and Carthage, the Mongolian Empire, the Crusades, the Napoleonic Wars, the Arabian Empire, the Ottoman Empire, the British Empire etc. are all testaments to the human urge vying for geopolitical dominance.

On a practical level, conflict over land is first and foremost a conflict over resources since the land is the source of all types of resources. One main historical theme is the conflict between sedentary agricultural communities and nomadic tribes, especially when the livelihood of the latter was threatened by adverse weather conditions. In particular, conflicts could focus on a specific resource, such as petroleum in modern times, bird droppings in the Guano Wars, or female population in ancient times.

Apart from megalomaniac empire-building and the actual scramble for resources, yet another source of confrontations and conflicts are ethnic, cultural, and religious differences, i.e., the theory of the 'Clash of Civilisations' as propounded by Huntington. Notable examples are the Islamic *jihad*, the Crusades in the 12th and 13th centuries, and the 'Thirty Years' War' in Europe. Note that for the sake of simplicity, I have grouped the factors of ethnicity, culture, and religion together. In principle, people from diversely different ethnic and cultural background can co-exist in peace and harmony, and history abounds with such examples. However, and for various reasons, when ethnic tension escalated to war, the wedge of 'difference' would drive the antagonists to see each other as 'less than human,' leading to horrendous bloodshed. Throw in the difference in religious belief, and it would inflame the conflict further ('Kill the infidels!'). Conversely, even if both sides have a basically identical ethnic and cultural makeup, with the only difference being religion, this could still lead to massive killings, one notable example being the 'Thirty Years' War' mentioned above, which tore through 17th century Europe (with a high degree of cultural homogeneity). We can classify these conflicts as "cultural," although it should be remembered that purely cultural struggles are rare, as there are always geopolitical (territorial/resource) undertones.

The third kind of war is one fought between the ruler and the ruled, with the warring parties either from the same ethnic background, or different. Peasant uprisings in Chinese dynastic times, the American War of Independence, the French and Russian

Revolutions are all examples of the former, while the slave uprisings in the Roman Empire, the Taiping Rebellion, the Chinese Republican Revolution of 1911, and the many Post-WWII nationalist wars of liberation, such as the Algerian War from 1954 to 1962, and the First Indochina War from 1946 to 1954, both fought against France resulting in its defeat.

The fourth is about ideological struggle, something new in history the origin of which could be traced to the 1848 *Communist Manifesto* by Marx and Engels. In simple terms, supporters of communism believed that capitalism was evil and must be overthrown by force, in the form of a revolutionary coup to take power from and unseat the capitalists, in order for any meaningful social reforms to take place. Conversely, capitalist supporters believed communism was evil, and they must do everything in their power to 'nip it in the bud' so as to stop it from infesting others. The result is that this contest of ideologies led to civil war in China between the Nationalists and Communists, the 'Cold War' between the U.S. and the U.S.S.R. which lasted for decades, and spawning many regional 'proxy wars' such as the Korean War and the Vietnam War. Needless to say, these wars also contained the elements of traditional power struggle, as testified by the Civil War between the Nationalist Party (KMT) and the Chinese Communist Party after the Japanese occupation.

However, as Fukuyama argued in his 'End of History' thesis, since the collapse of the Soviet Union, ideological struggles between nations have by and large become a historical relic. (But on the other hand, 'ideological struggles' between 'leftist' and 'rightist' political parties within a single country - or a confederation of countries such as the European Union - have yet to cease. This will be a very important issue in the examination of humankind's future)

The fifth reason - which is seldom mentioned outside the "leftist" circle - is the 'urge of capitalism' described earlier. Simply put, pursuit of profit and capital expansion is the hard logic of market competition. Just as 'small fish get eaten by big fish,' so to avoid being eaten all capitalists in the race (the highest form of manifestation being the super multinationals and conglomerates) must play by the law of the jungle, and to achieve maximum 'capital accumulation,' capitalists must scramble for (1) the cheapest source of raw materials, (2) the cheapest labour, and (3) the biggest market. As this world-wide competition is essentially a 'zero-sum game,' it constitutes a fundamental reason why nations can never co-exist in peace. Conversely, this will remain the powder-keg for future wars. This insight is nothing new. While it may be hard to believe, it was first propounded by Lenin is his 1916 book *Imperialism, the Highest Form of Capitalism.*

Taken in all, it can be seen that out of the five reasons examined above, Fukuyama's emphasis was only on the fourth, Huntington only on the first and second. Both neglected the crucial effect of the fifth.

In my view, the recent invasion of Ukraine by Russia notwithstanding, no country will seriously consider 'frontier expansion' by annexing another country as a *modus operandum* in the modern international system. However, this does not mean that the first reason of 'geopolitical contest' has disappeared altogether. Today, the contest between nations is one of regional or global influence and domination rather than that of territory. This is why future historians would characterise the transition from the British Empire not to an 'American Empire' but to 'American Hegemony.' Indeed, the U.S. did not take over former British colonies after World War II. The reasons are twofold. The first is that this would impose too great a cost to the Americans, and the lesson of "imperial over-reach" was still fresh in their mind, especially at a time when Post-War nationalism was on the rise in the Western colonies world-wide. The second and more salient reason is that America had found a much more effective way to stay on top, which is to roll out a global financial and economic monopoly by means of an 'American dollar hegemony.' The Federal Reserve, Wall Street, International Monetary Fund, World Bank, these are all U.S. weapons to enforce such a monopoly.

Of course, it is also backed up by the overwhelming military might of the U.S. With a mere 5% of the world's population, the U.S. defence budget is the total of the 20 countries behind it, and makes up almost half of the world total. The U.S. has some 800 military bases in more than 150 countries around the world, is the world's largest arms manufacturer, and is in possession of some of the world's most advanced weaponry (cruise missiles, stealth fighter jets, drones, etc.), plus the largest collection of ICBMs carrying nuclear warheads. The seven carrier battle groups (actual number of aircraft carriers is 19) of the U.S. are in constant patrol wherever accessible, and each carries supersonic fighter jets capable of reaching target airspace anywhere in the world within an hour.

You may wonder why the U.S. would bother to maintain such a powerful military capability given that it has shown no intention to attack or annex any territory. The answer, of course, lies in its intention to maintain global hegemony, in particular an economic hegemony. Oil from the Middle East is of course of important concern to the U.S. So is the American dollar as a world currency. Some scholars pointed out that the ultimate demise of Iraq's Saddam Hussein and Libya's Muammar Gaddafi were both caused by their actions in trying to go against the 'American dollar hegemony,' and their execution served as a warning to those who might be tempted to follow suit. (The most telling episode was the death of Gaddafi, as years before his death, he had openly declared an end to his support to terrorism and a wish to reconcile with the West. As such, there was no compelling reason to have him eliminated)

Summing up, and looking into the future, the gravest threat to world peace would come not from any 'ideological struggle' or unavoidable 'cultural or religious conflict' but from geopolitical contests caused by the 'urge of capital.' As pointed out earlier, Lenin had clearly pointed out that the logical outcome of the 'globalisation of capitalism' is the expansion of imperialism.

What Lenin failed to foresee is the rapid rise in nationalism causing the number of national states to double in the century after 1917, a phenomenon unprecedented in human history. Some scholars believe, therefore, that as old-style colonial rule has been superseded by 'neo-colonial' domination, the 'American hegemony' is no long a form of conventional imperialism. It is 'neo-imperialism.' Labelling aside, the risk of warfare remains the same.

It must be noted that, under the 'hard logic of capitalist expansion,' 'geopolitical contests' are often dressed up as 'nationalism' and 'patriotism.' The reason behind this is simple: to spur hotheaded young men to take up arms and go to war, killing complete strangers or getting themselves killed in the process, 'defending national pride and interests' would obviously sell much easier than 'defending the interests of the capitalists.' The result is that 'Make China Great Again!" 'Make America great again' (Or 'Make Mother Russia/India/Türkiye/France…great again') becomes a rallying cry, and 'stability and unity above all' in order to 'fight against foreign force' have become the dictatorship's best excuse in suppressing dissent.

Progressive thinkers - such as British philosopher Bertrand Russell - have long since pointed out that 'nationalism' is outdated and no longer serves in humankind's best interest. As such it should have been consigned to the rubbish bin of history. Russell's outspoken view against World War I cost him jail time. Be that as it may, nationalism remained a strong rallying cry. Polish-German socialist revolutionary Rosa Luxemburg (1871-1919) pleaded to workers soldiers on both sides of the war to refuse being party to the massive killing for the sake of capitalists struggle. Her efforts were in vain.

Simply put, 'national identity' is an extension of 'tribal identity,' an attribute which has a significant effect in 'inter-group competition' in the evolutionary process. 'Class consciousness,' with its short history of less than a hundred years (up to the time of Luxemburg), is no match to evolutionary instinct.

Honest be told, I do not categorically write off nationalism or patriotism. In a different time, these qualities had proven indispensable in national unity and had led to grand achievements in civilisation. Yet, I insist that these sentiments must be founded on a 'complete respect and inclusion of other peoples and their cultures and history.' 'Nationalism' of an ethnocentric, exclusive and jingoist kind must be resolutely rejected. As to patriotism, a love of the land of one's hometown and mother country, of one's fellow countrymen, and of one's history, language and culture…all these come naturally and are commendable. However, love of one's country is not the same as loving the ruling regime. If the regime does wrong, everyone is duty bound to criticise and castigate it.

The birth of the 'European Union' in 1992 marked a big step forward in humankind's effort to overcome, albeit to a limited degree, the myopia of nationalism and patriotism. European countries, having experienced the horror of two World Wars, not to mention the many wars fought between different states and peoples over the past centuries, have come to the realisation that cooperation is to be preferred to competition. The 27 member states (28 before Brexit) making up the EU each retains its own political, legal and defence institutions, but are otherwise highly integrated. All members have removed cross-border duties and tariffs to form a common market. Furthermore, 19 out of the 27 member states form the eurozone in which the euro becomes their primary currency and sole legal tender. Removal of border control means that people from member states has unrestricted freedom of movement, and can study and work in any country. In terms of foreign relations, the EU poses as a single political entity, thereby creating an enhanced diplomatic profile and influence than before. It could be said that the EU is a proud achievement of humankind's Expanding Circle.

Does this mean therefore, given the EU is a great example of different peoples coming together and living in peace, that if humankind continues to strive and make progress in a similar way, the two hundred countries on Earth might just form themselves into an 'Earth Union'?

In the early days of the EU, many people were hopeful. After three decades, the optimism has weakened considerably. In recent years, the EU has been plagued by the 'Eurodebt crisis' (bankruptcy of the PIIGS countries) triggered by the '2008 global financial disaster', the influx of immigrants and refugees, 'Brexit', keen competition from Chinese products, and over-reliance on energy supply from Russia. It remains to be seen if the Russia invasion of Ukraine would be a blessing in disguise in strengthening the solidarity of member countries.

Externally, the U.S. wants the EU - through NATO - to curb the rise of a powerful Russia. This seemed to have backfired as the "Eastern expansion of NATO" is seen as the trigger for the 2022 Russian invasion of Ukraine. There are however conspiracists who believe that this is all part of a grander plan masterminded by the strategists in the Pentagon. One is of course hard put to prove one way or the other.

On the other hand, the US is always wary that the EU may become too strong and independent, and decides to move out of her orbit. In particular, any chance that the euro would challenge the 'American dollar hegemony' would have to be nib at the bud. Another development that irked the Americans is EU moving too close to China, which is considered the up-and-coming superpower capable of challenging the American Empire in the 21st century.

Domestically, people in member states are not happy with the EU leadership in Brussels (where the EU headquarters is). On the one hand these bureaucrats are not popularly elected (hailed as 'EU's' 'democracy deficit' problem) and therefore cannot represent the people. On the other hand, it is felt that these bureaucrats (as well as the European Central Bank) ultimately serve only the interest of the rich and powerful and Big Corp, not that of the common folks.

There is a more important reason why the 'EU' may not be the best example for humankind's future development. EU member states and their people share a common ethnic, cultural, and religious heritage. No many how many wars they have fought among themselves, they are tied by deep cultural roots under the names of Zeus, Apollo, Dionysius, the Homeric epics, Socrates, Plato, Aristotle, Greek tragedies, Hippocrates, Roman laws, the Bible, Christ and the Gospels, Santa Claus, Camelot, Dante, Michelangelo, Da Vinci, Shakespeare, Dickens, Bach, Mozart, Beethoven, Galileo, Newton, Darwin, Kant, Hegel… This great homogeneity among the European people is not available to other peoples and cultures of the Earth, making the formation of an Earth Union highly inconceivable in the foreseeable future.

Let's return to the theme of nationalist struggles. Even though the 'EU' may not, in the short term, become the best example of humankind's future development, its achievement in peace keeping are really good revelations. Let me stress once again that the possibility of 'frontier expansion' and 'nationalist annexation' as a *modus operandum* no longer exist in the modern world, as such there is no compelling reason why different peoples have to go to war. Any nationalist struggle under the banners of 'nationalism' or 'national honour' is simply the 'urge of capital' in disguise.

Italian economist and sociologist Giovanni Arrighi (1937-2009) took a rather pessimistic view of this 'urge of capital'. In his 1994 work *The Long Twentieth Century: Money, Power, and the Origins of Our Times*, Arrighi examined the relationship between capital accumulation and the outbreak of war over the past seven hundred years, and came to the profoundly insightful conclusion that 'systemic cycles of accumulation' would culminate in large scale wars. Arrighi counted at least four such cycles since the rise of capitalism:

1. End of 14th to mid 17th century, with the centre of accumulation in the city states in northern Italy (Venice, Florence, Genoa; briefly shifted north to Antwerp, Belgium);

2. 17th to end of 18th century, with the centre at Amsterdam, the Netherlands;

3. End of 18th to early 20th century, with the centre in London;

4. World War I to present, with the centre in New York (the Great Depression in the 1930s was just birth pang).

In Arrighi's analysis, each cycle ended as a result of 'over concentration' and 'over accumulation' of capital leading to over-investment, over-production and fall in profit.

With capital searching for other source of profits, this invariably led to the rapid financialization of the economy, with speculation running amok and booms and busts becoming more and more destructive. And the ultimate solution to this? An all-out war to nullify surplus capital (including population, factories, machinery, credit), so that the process of capital accumulation can start all over again. Ordinary historical narrative describes wars as a struggle for hegemony between rival powers. Arrighi's analysis points at a much more fundamental, and structural, cause.

Looking back at those four cycles proposed by Arrighi, the end of the first cycle coincided with the 'Thirty Years' War,' resulting in the rise of the Dutch hegemony. The second cycle ended with the Napoleonic Wars (1792-1815), resulting in the rise of the British Empire. As to the third cycle, it ended with the two World Wars (1914-1945), resulting in the emergence of the American hegemony.

It must be pointed out that the above are macro-scale historical changes. Within these big cycles of the economy there are lesser cycles, such as the 'Kondratiev cycle' caused by the appearance of new technologies and new industries, and the 'Minsky cycle' caused by periodic fluctuation in investor confidence.

Arrighi made one more interesting observation about these big cycles which always ended in war: they are becoming shorter and shorter. It took more than two hundred years for the first cycle to end, a hundred and fifty for the second, slightly longer than a hundred for the third. We are now in cycle four (with the centre of accumulation in New York), and a hundred years have passed. Does it mean the end of the cycle is imminent?

After the 2008 global financial crisis, the U.S. government has been rolling out 'quantitative easing', which actually is an act of global exploitation. While paying lip-service to the lessons of the crisis (in the form of hypocritic "compliance" during transactions), the pace of 'financialization' of the economy hasn't slowed down. What followed was the rise of populism and the extreme right (fascism), Trump becoming the U.S. president, 'Brexit', waves of refugees, the return of trade protectionism, the escalation of U.S.-China confrontation, hate crimes and terrorism, the return of strong-men politics in many countries, worsening climate crisis, violent civil unrest and protests around the world…It'd hard not to relate all this to an imminent end of the fourth cycle.

What differentiates the current cycle from the previous ones is that we now have a frightening nuclear arsenal at our disposal which could destroy the world many times over. This is both good and bad news. Good news because the prospect of mutually assured annihilation might just hold the warmonger at bay (the so-called nuclear deterrence). Bad news because it might be equally possible for some madman, or something (an AI algorithm perhaps), to trigger World War III, dooming the entire human race.

The prolific Hong Kong writer and senior newspaper publisher Lam Hang-chi wrote in February 2020, "The Americans have been spending 'future money that isn't there'. It will take a nuclear war to turn this debt to ashes." Let us hope his insightful observation will not materialise.

After the end of World War II, the great physicist Albert Einstein said, "I know not with what weapons World War III will be fought, but World War IV will be fought with sticks and stones." Eighty years later, this poignant comment has become more relevant than ever.

Democracy Vs
Despotism

The 20th century marked the time when 'hereditary monarchies' with absolute power retired from the stage of human history. It all began with the 1911 Revolution in China, in which the last imperial dynasty, the Qing of the Manchus (an ethnic minority from northeastern China) was overthrown. This was followed in 1917 by the October Revolution in Czarist Russia. Soon, Turkey and Iran followed suit.

Most of the monarchies which had gone through the throes of nationalist movement had gone down the road to constitutional democracy. Others, such as Japan after the Meiji Restoration and Thailand in the 1930s, chose to go the way of Britain in 'keeping a titular monarch' and setting up a 'constitutional monarchy'. If the Empress Dowager, or Cixi as she's known in China, hadn't stood in the way during the Wuxu Reform of 1898, Imperial China might have gone this way too.

We saw in Chapter 2 'The Second Enlightenment' that the first country to implement a 'constitutional monarchy' was Britain, and the first country to overthrow the hereditary monarch was France in 1789. Although after the French Revolution (a *coup d'tat* in which 'capitalists' usurped the power of the 'aristocracy') there was a 'Reign of Terror' and the brief restoration of Napoleon Bonaparte, France as a nation finally got on the road to a constitutional democracy.

In comparison, Russia, having gone through a so-called 'proletariat revolution' in 1917, became the U.S.S.R. The same happened when China became the People's Republic of China (PRC) in 1949. The sad irony is that in the name of "liberating the people," both became autocratic regimes. Revolutionary leaders and their cadres became the new ruling class (Yugoslav politician Milovan Djilas (1911-1995) wrote *The New Class: An Analysis of the Communist System* in 1957, in which he described the party-state officialdom as 'using, enjoying and disposing of nationalised property.') The result is that what was meant to overthrow oppression became the new form of oppression, the removal of privilege created new privilege, and the pursuit of justice got gross injustice in return - the biggest farce and worst tragedy in human history.

Stalin's 'Great Purge' and his Siberian Gulags, Mao Tse-tung's 'Great Famine' and 'Cultural Revolution,' the Pol Pot regime in Cambodia with his 'Killing Fields'... these atrocities betrayed the ideals of Marx and Engels. But the man in the street is not so much concerned with 'betrayal' but the actual impacts. And the effects are that "Communism" is seen as repugnant and evil ever since.

The success of the U.S. strategy of 'blockade' on Soviet Russia and 'Red China' - aided by many Third World countries conducting bloody Communist purge campaigns (which were in turn aided by the US government) - meant that the spread of communism world-wide (under the slogan "Workers of the world unite. You have nothing to lose but your chains!") was largely curtailed, with North Korea, Cuba, and Vietnam as the rare exceptions. And with the revulsion and disgust felt by people worldwide toward crimes perpetrated by Communist regimes, it was curtains down on Communism when the Soviet Union collapsed in 1992. The "communist experiment" of the 20th century has failed.

In the last two to three decades of the 20th century, half of the countries around the world were having their leaders elected through universal suffrage, at least in principle. This led to an optimism in the continued and unimpeded progress in 'democratisation' worldwide, until in the end 'democracy and freedom' is there for all. Needless to say, Francis Fukuyama, whom we've met before, is one such optimists.

In fact, democratisation has been beset with difficulties. Not only is the spectre of 'despotism' looming in the background, it has resurrected itself and made a big comeback, in worse shape and degree than before. Hereafter we will briefly examine what happened.

The biggest disillusionment has to be from China. For a country comprising one-fifth of the world's population, 'Reform and Opening' would only lead to 'economic liberalisation' then on to 'political liberalisation.' Or so some people believed, and wished. They were sorely disappointed. Not only that, people were shocked to find that in China, 'economic freedom' and 'political un-freedom' is now a package deal.

And then, there are those countries which are 'democratic' in nothing but name. North Korea (aka the Democratic People's Republic of Korea), Laos (Laos People's

Democratic Republic), and Congo (Democratic Republic of the Congo) are just the best-known examples. But then the consolation is that even to these despotic regimes, the 'democratic' label is both desirable and smacks of being 'civilised.' Democracy has triumphed, at least in name if not in practice.

The role of the U.S. is a paradox though. A simple question to ask is whether America is a friend or foe to democracy. Here the answer is nothing but simple. For those who view Uncle Sam as the Great Satan, it was the global American push to 'export democracy and Western values' that caused such a strong 'anti-America' reaction world-wide. The facts, however, are more complicated.

On the one hand, the U.S. as the major victor of World War II did play a crucial role in the rebuilding and rehabilitation of democratic Germany and Japan, but on the other hand, the U.S. had also propped up, mainly in the Third World, 'pro-American' autocratic regimes, such as the Park Chung-hee regime in South Korea, the Chiang Kai-shek regime in Taiwan, the the Ngô Đình Diệm and Nguyễn Văn Thiệu regime in South Vietnam, the Ferdinand Marcos regime in the Philippines, the Suharto regime in Indonesia, and the Pinochet regime in Chile etc. Many of these regimes had been accused of committing heinous crimes against humanity while suppressing dissent.

Worse, if a democratically elected government is somehow shown to be insufficiently 'pro-American,' the U.S. will, without hesitation, bring about its demise. Notable examples are Syria in 1949, Iran in 1953 (because a popularly elected government planned to re-nationalise oil rights), Indonesia in 1965, Chile in 1973 (the popularly elected government wanted to re-nationalise copper mining rights), and Egypt in 2013.

For some countries who are able to defy the will of Uncle Sam (China and Russia being the most prominent, followed by North Korea and Iran), "American imperialism" give the perfect excuse to maintain the iron fist of despotism. I say 'excuse' because in those countries, 'despotism' has had a long tradition. Absolute rule did not arise as a 'novel' response to any 'foreign threat.' More specifically, reigns of terror such as the 'Ivan the Terrible-esque' Stalin, and the cruel autocratism of Zhu Yuanzhang (founder of the Ming dynasty in China), cannot be excused simply by blaming it on 'foreign threats.'

It must also be noted that, although the despotism practised in Soviet Russia and China, both in imperial and republican times, might have a root in their respective histories and cultures, they both surpassed traditional forms of despotism and developed a much more terrifying 'totalitarianism.' What's 'novel' about the 20th century is that, under the principles of 'pan-politicised' and 'ideology above all', a government exercising near-universal and highly penetrating brainwashing, thought control and silencing, through government-sanctioned education programs, media (the press, books, radio, television, and these days the internet) pumping out propaganda and setting up surveillance. What's more, making citizens keep watch on and dobbing in one another, in an act of 'guilt by association.' This sort of reign of terror 'from womb to tomb' far exceeds the most horrendous cruelty ever practised in Czarist Russia, or in the several thousands of years of imperial Chinese history. Its devastation of human nature (most notable during the 'Cultural Revolution,' when even marriages required the permission of the party cadre) has set a historical precedent.

It would be a serious mistake to think that, just because I quoted the notorious examples of Soviet Russia and Mao's China, 'totalitarianism' is reserved for communist regimes. In fact, the first powerful totalitarian state in the 20th century was Nazi Germany, followed by Fascist Italy. These were 'rightist' (capitalist) not 'leftist' (communist) regimes. Other similar examples would include Spain under Francisco Franco, Pahlavi Iran, Saudi Arabia, Indonesia under Suharto, South Korea under Park Chung-hee, Chile under Pinochet, the military dictatorship in Brazil from 1964 to 1985, etc. Isn't it obvious that evil doesn't have any political inclinations?

A movie depicting the horror under a rightist regime is the 1968 *Z*, in which any movie fan can tell (although not spelt out in the movie) it's about Greece in the 1960s. For Chile under Pinochet, the movies *Missing* (1982), *Death and the Maiden* (1994) and *No* (2012) are highly recommended. For Korean, *When the Day Comes* (2017) and *A Taxi Driver* (2017) are not to be missed.

True, there are countries which, after a long and tortuous struggle, finally assume the form of a liberal democracy. Examples are South Korea, Taiwan/ROC, the Philippines, Indonesia, Chile, and Brazil. However, the 21st century opened with disturbing trends. 'Political strongman' appeared on stage and countries suffered a setback in democratising. Syria's Bashar al-Assad and his father before him, Turkey's Recep Erdogan, Rodrigo Duterte in the Philippines, and India's (the world's largest democratic state) Narendra Modi are all political strongmen. The monarchy of Thailand, having gone through a prolonged confrontation between the opposite camps of the 'Red Shirts' and 'Yellow Shirts,' has been ruled by a military junta since 2014, and at the time of writing, it is still not sure if the 2023 election will be able to bring back – at least partially - constitutional democracy.

The Chinese Communist Party's insistence on the 'One Party Dictatorship' would look to many to be last word in autocratism. History, however, has shown otherwise. With the ascendency of Xi Jinping, the concentration of power - party, government, and military - in a single individual has become unprecedented, far exceeding that wielded by his predecessors Hu Jintao or Jiang Zemin, and marking a clean and irrevocable break with Deng Xiaoping's 'collective leadership' which was a move to rein in any over concentration of authority and leadership cult. In early 2018, Xi had the two-year term limit on state presidency removed, paving the way to lifelong rule for himself, and earning the moniker of 'Emperor Xi' in the process. In December 2022, amidst a total lockdown of the country because of the COVID-19 global pandemic and defying any speculation to the contrary, Xi entered into his third term.

On the other side of the Eurasia landmass, the collapse of Soviet Russia in 1991 brought hope to its people and the prospect of democratisation. However, it was not long before Vladimir Putin appeared as the political strongman and assumed the Russian presidency. Putin played democracy like his own pet, and dissent was silenced.

As a matter of fact, poll rigging, and outright election fraud are not uncommon among "democratic" Third World countries. According to a review undertaken by *The Economist* in 2021, countries in the whole world which can be classified as "full democracies" amount to only 12.6% of the total, against 35.3% classified as "authoritarian regimes". A full 31.7% are classified as "flawed democracies" and 20.4% as "hybrid regimes." If we add the last two categories together, more than half of the countries on Earth - even though not outright authoritarian/despotic regimes - still fall short in their strive towards full democracy.

While we may not fully agree with this classification of *The Economist*, it is obvious that humankind still has a long way to go. It is interesting to note that while many people consider America as the leading democratic country in the world - in terms of influence rather than population, as India would have the claim to the latter - it is classified as a "flawed democracy." In terms of scores, she is lower than Austria, Iceland, Uruguay, Mauritius, Costa Rica. In the past, many would query this surprising ranking result. However, the election of the racist, misogynistic and megalomaniac Donald Trump as the American president, and the violence at the Capitol Hill when he failed to secure a second term, are giving people second thoughts. "What has happened to our democracy?" is a question on many people's mind. Needless to say, leaders of authoritarian regimes are quick to seize this debacle and point out to its people that if this is what democracy would produce, is this the system you want for our country? For sure such regimes are never tired of pointing out that Adolf Hitler came to power through democratic elections.

On the other side of the Atlantic, and just as shocking to those who hold democracy dear, is the 'Brexit' referendum and the rupturing of social cohesion that resulted, together with the resurgence of 'populism' (with 'xenophobia' the main characteristic) and the extreme right in the political arena.

Broadly speaking, the resurgence of populism and the extreme right in Europe both came from the same root cause: 'influx of migrants' and 'influx of refugees' impacting many Europeans. Let's look at these in more detail.

These 'influxes' have commonalities and differences. First, the migrants. Western countries have been experiencing problems caused by a consistently low birth rate which resulted in the gradual aging of the population. Plagued by a shrinking workforce and the ever increasing age-related public expenditure, Western countries turned to mainly Third World countries for labour, enticing more and more people with attractive immigration schemes. In France, for example, a substantial number of immigrants are from its former colony Algeria.

It must be pointed out that undersupply of labour is always a crisis for capitalism. This is because it puts an upward pressure on wages, hence leading to a 'profit squeeze.' If the profit rate falls below the bank rate for loans (or the difference between loan rate and deposit rates, to be exact), there would be no incentive for capitalists to make any investment, and the whole economy will grind to a halt. To enhance labour supply and drive down wage levels, employers will band together and pressure the government to let in 'foreign labour.' Some even resorted to illicit schemes of importing labour (Mexican workers in the U.S. is a notable example).

Large numbers of migrants are bound to impact local people in various ways. First and foremost is of course 'they snatched our jobs' while driving down the wage level at the same time. Then there are the social, ethnic, cultural, and religious conflicts that ensue. The upshot is that 'anti-immigration' sentiment will accumulate, sometimes to a breaking point. Vowing to take back the jobs from China and building a wall to stop Mexican migrants, Donald Trump rode this wave and won the presidential election.

While "China bashing" is good for winning votes, what was left unspoken is that U.S. manufacturing was offshored *en masse* to China exactly because U.S. employers wanted to keep the wage down. In other words, 'letting in large number of migrants (foreign labour)' and 'offshore manufacturing' resulting in massive unemployment in the U.S. was a result of the 'urge of capital.' It is the logic of capitalism running its course.

As for the influx of refugees into Europe, a main reason is that since the 'Jasmine Revolution/Arab Spring' of 2010/11, the West had not done much by way of facilitating democratisation in the many countries involved. Instead, geopolitical considerations such as oil-related interests, support and defence of the hawkish Israeli regime, suppression of Iran, and curbing the expansion of Russian influence, were prioritised over the interests and welfare of people in the Middle East (and Libya in North Africa). Endless war raged (the worst being Syria). Countless lives were lost. Those who survived did so by fleeing, seeking refuge in distant lands, and many perished on the way (on land or at sea).

Owing to the separation by the Atlantic Ocean, mainland U.S.A. did not bear the brunt of the European refugee crisis. Europe in the form of the European Union, however, has to share this immense economic and humanitarian burden among its member states. The U.K., long since seeing itself as special (its currency never converted to the Euro), was not happy with this arrangement. Hence the 'Brexit,' with its resounding cry of 'taking back control.'

From 'anti-immigration' to 'anti-refugee' to 'racial discrimination' to 'white (Aryan) supremacy' to random killings caused by 'racial hatred'…the spectre of Nazism is haunting the West once again. This is one background to the resurgence of extreme right ideology. On the other hand, this resurgence also has a background of class struggle to it. 'Neoliberalism' led to the '2008 global financial crisis', and awakened a lot of people (young people in particular) to the gross injustice of capitalism. As a result, the 'Occupy Wall Street' broke out in 2011 in New York, the heartland of the capitalist empire. Its slogan of 'We're the 99%' touched the raw nerve of the '1%' (or even less), the class of super rich and powerful people. No wonder they saw this 'left-leaning' ideology as dangerous and must be suppressed at all costs.

In 2015, the Coalition of Radical Left-Progressive Alliance, a Greek political party more popularly known by its acronym SYRIZA, won the seat of government to the roaring applaud of the European and global left. But it did not last long. Greece, having gone bankrupt, was desperate to get financial assistance from the EU, and in the end the new government was unable to make good its promise to voters (which was to create a more just and equal society), and succumbed to the demands of Troika (European Commission, European Central Bank, International Monetary Fund). In the 2019 parliamentary election, the Coalition lost to 'New Democracy', a centrist-right political party, thereby ending the brief 'leftist experiment'.

On the other hand, Brazil, with its population of 210 million (20 times that of Greece), also experienced a 'leftist recession and rightist advance'. Rightist politician Jair Bolsonaro became president in 2019, and moderate left-wing policies since 2002 was abandoned. And just as the ascendency of Trump and his withdrawing from the 'Paris Accord' dealt a severe blow to humankind's effort against climate change, the 'return of the right' brought nightmare not only to the environmental movement in Brazil but to the whole world.

Under the pretext of economic development, Bolsonaro gave the green light for a massive onslaught by Big Corp on the Amazon rainforest, either for cattling, plantation of soya bean or exploitation of other resources. The rate of forest clearing in 2022 was the highest for the past 14 years, even though large-scale forest fires over the past few years had already led to the worry of many scientists for the forest's long-term fate. On the one hand, valuable native ecologies were devastated, displacing, or even killing many indigenous tribes, many of whom have minimal contact with the outside world. On the other hand, the Amazon rainforest, being the largest on the planet, acts as the 'lungs of the Earth' and plays a crucial role in maintaining an optimum level of atmospheric carbon dioxide. The wanton destruction of rainforest by the Bolsonaro government, committed for short term economic gain, is an act of madness akin to digging one's own grave. Although Bolsonaro was ousted in an election at the end of 2022 (with his supporters storming the Supreme Court and Congress in January 2023, akin to the storming of Capitol Hill by Trump supporters two years earlier), it awaits to be seen if the come-back of the Lula Da Silva government could turn the tide and save the Amazon forest from further harm.

In general, since the beginning of this century, whether it is international or domestic, developments have been disheartening. The 'financial debt' and 'ecological debt' created by 'neoliberalism' have pushed humankind to the brink, but the brief period of sobriety post 'global financial crisis' failed to turn the tide. Instead of embracing a 'democratic socialism' like northern European countries, in which 'equality of wealth' and 'sustainable development' feature prominently, the world has been hijacked by strategists employed by the rich and powerful, and steered wrongly onto the road to rightist 'populist nationalism.'

In the traditional political narrative of the U.S., the Democratic Party has always been seen as 'left-of-centre,' while the Republican is 'right-of-centre.' However, for the past several decades both camps displayed no noticeable difference in rolling out 'neoliberal' policies. A similar situation prevailed in the U.K. Margaret Thatcher came from the 'rightist' Conservative Party, but when Tony Blair from the Labour Party (traditionally of course leftist) became Prime Minister in 1997, there was no departure from his predecessors whatsoever in terms of 'neoliberal' policies (some scholars even thought it is in many aspects worse than before). Hillary Clinton was of course a staunch 'neoliberalist,' and her loss to Republican's Trump in the 2016 presidential election was simply a black farce in which 'neoliberalism' was supplanted by an even more radical right-wing aristocracy (but cunningly dressed up as 'fighting for the people' and "draining the swamp" ...).

It has been pointed out that Bernie Sanders, the leftist senator who was widely supported by younger voters, might well have won over Trump, if only he was 10 years younger, cut his ties with the Democrats, and run as an independent. Sadly, history has no buts. At the time of writing, Joe Biden has been in the White House for over a year. It awaits to be seen if he could achieve more - in the face of strong Republican obstruction - in terms of social justice and fighting climate change than Barrack Obama, the president he had served.

Today, people around the world march on the street in protest either of the autocracy of the 'left,' or the plutocracy of the rich and powerful. During the period 2019-2023 when this book was researched and written, footages of such protests were common sights in the daily news on television. In the developed countries, while the post-2008 Occupy Movement seemed to have died down, in was succeeded in spirit by the Yellow Vest Movement in France. Starting by the end of 2018, it has been compared to the French Revolution of 1789. While modern capitalism is much more tenacious than the French aristocracy of the 18th century, social protests experienced its ebb and flow but has never gone away.

The police crackdown of such protests had been widely condemned, but this was nothing compared with the cold-blooded crackdown by the police and even the military in despotic regimes such as Myanmar, where nearly 2,700 people had been killed - some in execution style - during the anti-government protests of 2021/22. In Iran, more than 500 people were killed during the protests of 2022. The fact is that in this unprecedented super-affluent era of human civilization, many people are not enjoying the fruits of progress either in terms of freedom, dignity, democracy, basic livelihood, equality, social justice, and life opportunities. Whether it is in Chile, Peru, Bolivia, Venezuela, Colombia, Algeria, Lebanon, Iraq, Hong Kong or even Mainland China (the so-called "White Paper Revolution" of late 2022 protesting against the draconian pandemic lockdown regulations), people are standing out and trying to get their voice heard. If we add to these the marches for pay rise organised by trade unions, and the marches protesting the incapacity of governments in fighting global warming, then there is not one single country on Earth that can be exempted from this unrest.

To those unfamiliar with the thoughts of Karl Marx, it may be a surprise to learn that Marx had categorically stated that "Democracy is the road to socialism". ("The dictatorship of the proletariat" is a doctrine invented by Lenin.) On the other hand, Marx did ridicule "bourgoise democracy" as practised in the 19th century as a system whereby "the oppressed are allowed once every few years to decide which particular representatives of the oppressing class are to represent and repress them."

Marx wasn't wrong in terms of economics and politics on the macro-scale, but looking at all the many rights people enjoy across the world these days - basic human rights, protection under the law, freedom of expression, independent media, universal suffrage, political participation and a civil society - one can only say that humankind's 'Second Enlightenment' which gave us 'democracy' among other things, has also given us something, however fake it is, that is far better than a 'real dictatorship'. It has been shown time and again that, given the choice, people will always go for - with their feet if not their hands - 'fake democracy' rather than 'real dictatorship.'

Churchill famously said that "democracy is the worst form of government - except for all the others that have been tried," which he uttered after being voted out as Britain's prime minister just months after World War II ended. At a deeper level, and before we free ourselves from capitalism's bondage, our mission must be to make 'fake democracy' real. We must try our very best to resist the spread of 'real dictatorship,' whether it be a dictatorship from the Left or from the Right.

The 21st century regression in democracy can be disheartening, but that doesn't give us even the right to give up in despair. Not only must we persevere, we must also do everything within our power to make democracy better (including bring democracy to the people through the internet). Irish orator and politician John Philpot Curran (1750-1817) said, "Eternal vigilance is the price of liberty." Eternal vigilance is also the price of democracy.

There is no such thing as a perfect democracy. And just as nothing is perfect, there may never be one. In this light, democracy can only be a never-ending experiment and never a "finished product." In our pursuit for greater democracy, we should look at our efforts as an 'asymptotic curve' in mathematics: we will get closer and closer, but never really getting there. But as they say, the journey is often more important than the destination.

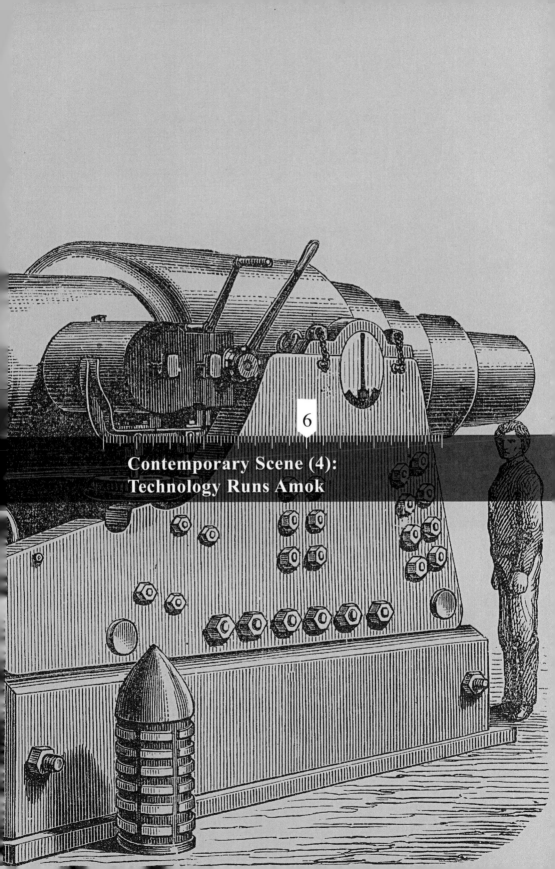

6

Contemporary Scene (4):
Technology Runs Amok

Knowledge Explosion and the Technological Threat

To examine the current human condition and how it will evolve, a theme of paramount importance is the explosive growth of human knowledge in the last several centuries, and in particular over the last several decades. This is because the technological innovations so engendered have had profound impacts on the human conditions, which will only deepen in the foreseeable future.

Let's first take a look at knowledge. Just pick any discipline at random: anthropology, history, archaeology, sociology, economics, politics, mathematics, physics, chemistry, biology, medicine, psychology, linguistics, geology, meteorology, oceanography, astronomy, cosmology, architecture, engineering…The growth of human knowledge in the 20th century alone has far exceeded the sum total of the past several millennia.

Using a simple yardstick: there were less than 100 academic journals worldwide in 1900. By 2000 the number has increased to more than thirty thousand, and is still increasing. An estimate in 2018 put the number of research papers published in these journals each year at over five million. If we say arbitrarily that the sum total of human knowledge comprises one thousand disciplines (I named only twenty in the previous paragraph), then each discipline will have five thousand papers published each year, far more than anyone can possibly read.

Today, over-specialisation in research has reached a worrying level. An 'expert,' said someone, is one who 'knows more and more about less and less.' To offset this 'missing the forest for the sake of one tree' kind of trend, 'trans-disciplinary research and integration' has been promoted, with some positive results. And, impacted by 'information overload,' more and more tertiary education institutions have been putting increasing emphasis on 'liberal education' to equip students with the ability to integrate and relate large amount of knowledge. As I see it, this is one direction in which we must continue to forge ahead, and where there is still a lot of room for improvement.

Knowledge explosion has its own inherent logic. Acquisition of knowledge is cumulative, and existing knowledge is the key to knowledge yet unknown. Further, knowledge begets more knowledge, otherwise known as synergy. The simplest way to look at it is this: between two points there is only one connecting line, and between three points three lines. But there can be 6 lines connecting four points, 20 connecting 5...45 connecting 10...190 connecting 20. Obviously, 'non-linear increase' is a major characteristic of knowledge growth. The result is that our knowledge of the world around us grows exponentially, with the 19th and 20th centuries at the point where this exponential curve shoots upward.

Hot on the heel of knowledge explosion is the rapid advance in technology. As we've seen in Chapter/Part III, technological advance in the past century or so has raised our living standard immensely, and progress in printing, publishing, audio-visual technology, broadcasting, and the internet has brought the arts into everyone's home, greatly enriching our life. Nevertheless, technological advance has always been a double-edged sword. We have already encountered the concept of 'Civilisation Backfiring' under the 'Agricultural Trap' and 'Industrial Trap'. More specifically, each advance in civilisation was accompanied by significant negative impacts:

• Fire, improper use or when uncontrolled can cause untold damage to life and property;

• Metals, the use of which greatly increased the lethalness of wars;

• Printing, which can be used to spread false information and incite hatred;

• The compass, which pointed the way for global colonial exploits;

• Gunpowder (and later the rocket and missile), vastly increasing war casualties;

• Machinery (used in factories) turned humankind into robot-like slaves;

• Fossil fuels, which brought about widespread and severe air pollution, endangering people's health;

• Aircrafts, which spread the fear and suffering of war far and wide;

The last of which brought us into the 20th century. In the past hundred years or so we also found:

• The automobile has greatly increased the mobility and convenience for humankind, but at the same time, gross road toll by now has exceeded epidemic fatalities in the 20th century (latest estimate is about 1.3 million each year);

• Unleashing the energy locked in the atom was thought to be the answer to humankind's ever increasing energy need. Instead, humankind is presented with the nightmare of a nuclear holocaust. Latest statistics showed there are still more than 13,000 nuclear warheads worldwide, with each one three or four times more powerful than the one dropped on Hiroshima. In other words, we now possess the power to destroy ourselves several times over;

• Radio, television, and the internet allow us to 'know the world from afar' without leaving our ken. On the other hand though, many people become addicted to it - especially through social media platforms and video games - leading to worsening alienation, and giving rise to the '*hikikomori*' (a Japanese term meaning social recluse; also called '*otaku*');

• The mass media contributed to better representation of public opinion and social sentiment, leading in principle to better governance, but on the other hand, it has also been exploited by those in authority and Big Corp to perform political and commercial brainwashing;

• The 'Information Revolution', brought on by the internet, has allowed us to obtain huge amount of information with relative ease (including virtually unlimited data from sources such as Wikipedia); yet at the same time autocratic regimes can still lock out such sources of information with powerful 'firewalls'; on the other hand, even in societies branding themselves as free and open, artificial intelligence enabled 'search engines' track our browsing history and posts, filtering out information we don't want to know about, making us even more short-sighted and narrow-minded than before;

- The almost universal adoption of social networking service on the internet has enabled us to connect and re-connect with friends and strangers far and wide, but on the other hand people holding the same view tend to fall into an in-group to the exclusion of others and their different opinions. The outcome is that people can become less and less open and liberal in their thinking. Radical contents which could incite racist, misogynist, religious and political hatred tend to spread quickly, sometimes resulting in tragic consequences (such as hate crimes and mass shootings);

- Just as machines of the past alleviated the burden on menial labour, 'Artificial intelligence' (or AI in short) alleviates the burden on mental labour. The flip side is that this could lead to massive unemployment in many white-collar sectors - including highly esteemed professions - impacting the livelihood of many and rocking the foundation of the economy and society (we will come back to this point in more detail later);

- Recent advances in medicine and biotechnology have increased our ability to repair injuries and cure disease immensely, but it also raises serious questions of 'bioethics;' the development of 'cloning,' 'stem cell repair' and 'gene editing' which would enable us to modify ourselves, have for the first time brought us face to face with a 'Frankenstein' (the protagonist in the 1818 novel *Frankenstein*) nightmare;

Any one of the above 'traps' poses a challenge to our wisdom. We shall explore some of these in latter chapters on 'The Next Fifty Years' and 'The Next Five Hundred Years.' For now, let's focus on those which have raised grave concern in recent years.

Of all the "backfirings," environmental disasters brought on by global warming has to be the overarching and most urgent. We have seen in Chapter 3.2/Part III, this blowback has already manifested itself over the decades, and at an accelerating pace: more frequent and more lethal heatwaves, more severe and longer lasting wildfires, super hurricanes, super rainstorms, and prolonged droughts are all abnormal and extreme weather events severely impacting almost every economic activity in the human world. Food production is impacted by pest and disease, brought on by prolonged heat and ecological imbalance. The flow rate of major rivers is reduced when mountain glaciers and ice cover disappear, leading to water scarcity and drought downstream. The mean sea level will rise, drowning coastal settlements around the world, when ice now covering Greenland, Antarctica, and mountain tops melt.

The conclusion is inescapble: if we don't cut carbon dioxide emission drastically by banning the use of all fossil fuels (coal, oil, and gas) as soon as possible, the collapse of our weather system and ecology will nullify all that we cherish: social harmony and stability, economic growth, prosperity, social justice, national revival, democracy, international justice, and world peace, etc.

Regrettably, today's world is still one in which nationalist pride and predominance is the main theme, such that 'fighting global warming' has become a typical problem of the 'Tragedy of the Commons' and 'Prisoner's Dilemma' in game theory. The logic behind it is this: if it's only me (one country) doing it and not the others (or just pretending to do something), then not only is it not helping at the end of the day, it's going to hurt my development and international competitiveness, casting me to the back of the pack. Conversely, as the world is so concerned about this, why don't I just sit back and let others do it and I enjoy the result of their hard work? I can keep my lead in economic standing as well. This is also known as the 'free-rider problem' in game theory.

Exactly because of this, although the United Nations has convened a global climate change conference in Kyoto Japan way back in 1997, with the *Kyoto Protocol* as the outcome, and pleaded for serious global efforts to curb carbon emission, followed by conferences such as the one in Copenhagen Denmark in 2009, and agreements such as the 2015 *Paris Agreement*, global carbon emission has continued to rise instead of dropping. The amount of carbon dioxide in the atmosphere today far exceeds that of the past three million years. We have managed to push the Earth, an incredibly complex system, into *terra incognita*.

Viewed as a 'technology trap,' the culprit behind the global warming crisis is not any new technology. On the contrary it is the unwillingness to let go of old technology: energy generation via fossil fuels. The reason behind this unwillingness is the huge investment necessary (and hence giving rise to the 'Tragedy of the Commons' problem described above) to transition from fossil fuel to zero emission 'renewable energy,' and the massive redistribution of social interest. In more concrete terms, huge, vested interests (multi-national oil companies in particular), in the protection of their own interests have tried their best to obstruct any solution at every step. A huge disinformation campaign employing the best PR experts that money could buy has spread confusion and doubts in the mind of the public. Hints were even made that all this is just a fraud perpetrated by funding-starved scientists. And any indication of introducing a "Carbon Tax" by any government to discourage usage of fossil fuels and re-directing resources to develop renewable energy sources have been vehemently opposed by heavy political lobbying and social propaganda.

Scientists are most concerned at this moment about the grave crisis called the 'permafrost time bomb.' It turns out that Siberia, Alaska, northern Canada, and the Tibetan Plateau (comprising 17% of land) are covered in a thick layer of permafrost. Permafrost contains a vast amount of methane from decomposed biomass. In a frigid environment, methane bonds with water to form a stable ice-like crystal (methane hydrate). As temperature rises, this crystal melts and methane is released as a gas.

What's so frightening about all this? It turns out that methane is a 'super greenhouse gas,' one which is 20 times more powerful than carbon dioxide (calculated based on a "standardised" 100 years of mean atmospheric residence time; actually nearly 100 times if we focus on the actual residence time). Once released, methane will accelerate the warming of the atmosphere, causing more melting of the permafrost, releasing more methane in the process. This cycle repeats itself in a positive feedback loop, like a small avalanche begetting larger and larger collapses. Research has shown that, if this vicious circle comes true, human effort to 'de-carbonise' will be rendered fruitless, and average global temperature rise (up to the end of this century at least) will no longer be the 4 or 5°C as predicted by United Nations experts, but 8 or 9 °C, or more.

What are the impacts then? Let's focus on one impact which no human effort can possibly avert: mean sea level rise. The 2014 report from the United Nations expert panel estimated a mean sea level rise, by the end of this century, of about 90cm, in the worst scenario where the rise in atmospheric carbon dioxide level goes unabated. A report from NASA pointed out in June 2019 that this could be as much as 2.5m, after revising with up-to-date data. This would mean increasing devastating flooding of coastal cities. And where are these hundreds of millions of people going to go? (In the longer term, complete melting of Greenland's ice would mean a rise of 7 m, and of the very unstable West Antarctic ice shelf, a rise of 23m)

How far are we from this 'point of no return'? According to a release in October 2018 from the United Nations expert panel, unless we can achieve massive and urgent 'emission reduction', the deadline before the 'permafrost time bomb' is triggered would be reached in 2030. The fact can't be clearer: humankind is on the brink of a planet-wide catastrophe.

6.2 The Nightmare of *1984*

Lately, one 'technological trap' created by the rapid advance of technology has led to worldwide concern. The prevalence of the internet and electronic monitoring devices has meant an ever-increasing level of mass surveillance and invasion of privacy. This has generated widespread fear for the future of human rights, freedom and basic decency and dignity. From a certain perspective this is a regrettable sideshow for when the world goes up in flames (or goes under water) in the global warming castastrophe, the protection of personal privacy would be the least of our concerns…

English novelist George Orwell (1903-1950) is famous for the slogan 'Big Brother is Watching You' from his 1949 dystopian novel *Nineteen Eighty-Four*. Orwell, who lived through the 1940s, could not dream of the day when, not only was his prophecy realised, it was far more complete and terrible than he imagine.

The fact is, with the omnipresent electronic video recording and surveillance (including with microdrones and mechanical beetles, as well as that we willingly wear on our wrist), uninterrupted real time monitoring by global positioning satellite networks, the almost universal adoption of electronic payment, online communication and commerce, internet traffic (including visiting which website and when, comments/ feedbacks posted, books borrowed from libraries), instantaneous genetic identification, AI-enabled 'facial recognition' or 'gait analysis', and the ever widening scope of Big Data etc, we have become completely naked and transparent to Big Gov, Big Corp, criminal syndicates, or even teenage 'hackers' who are just out for some mischief.

From birth to academic records, from employment, marriage, friends, health, hobbies, political persuasion to day to day movements, we are being watched more and more closely by 'Big Brother.' The massive leak in 2013 by former U.S. intelligence analyst Edward Snowden awoke and shocked the world of this sort of already commonplace practice by 'Big Gov'; the 2018 Facebook personal information leak scandal made us realise 'Big Corp' was also an 'accomplice'. Obviously, these two instances are merely the tip of the iceberg. Unless we retreat into the wilderness and become a hermit, the loss of privacy looks inevitable.

Where there is still a relatively robust democracy and legal institutions, people can still attempt - although it would look like 'Don Quixote Tilting at Windmills' - to counteract this trend (such as through media exposure, civic action, legal proceedings, and democratic supervision). But in an autocracy, any Don Quixote will be silenced as soon as it emerges.

A prime example is China. The Chinese government has set up, in stages, a 'social credit system' aimed at 'commending and exemplifying trustworthiness, and penalising the untrustworthy,' so as to 'cultivate citizen quality.' In this system, citizens will each have a 1000-point score to start with, and, depending on subsequent scoring, fall into categories such as 'trustworthy', 'relatively trustworthy', 'trustworthiness alert', and 'untrustworthy'.

Preliminary observation revealed that citizens' scoring went up with the following: 'pay card balance on time,' 'pay social insurance,' 'did not exceed the allowed number of births (since rescinded after the dropping of the One-Child Policy),' 'volunteering,' 'blood donation,' 'publicised in media reports,' 'commended at county level,' 'commended at the state level,' etc. Scoring deduction happened with the following: 'falling behind with loan repayment,' 'owing tax,' 'owing utility payments (such as water and electricity),' 'drink-driving,' 'overloading,' 'prostitution,' 'failing to care for elderly,' 'slander and false accusation,' 'spreading false information,' 'making and selling counterfeit goods,' 'involving in a cult,' 'attack on government office,' etc. (Details of this system were still changing at the time of writing) Citizens graded as 'severely untrustworthy' are not allowed to buy air- or train tickets.

In reality, the impact on the individual would be much more far-reaching than not being able to fly or travel. Once someone is graded as 'severely untrustworthy,' he or she faces immense restrictions to his or her social activities. Clearly, such a system is meant to be means of governance above and beyond current legal institutions. It works because of total electronic surveillance in this age of the internet.

Yet another worrying development is that of robotic weapons or killer robots. Although called 'robots,' these weapons can take any form or shape other than that of a 'person,' such as a four-legged animal (its size could range from a mouse to a dog, a tiger, or an elephant), a bird, or an insect. Regardless of the outward appearance, however, they have a common purpose: seek and destroy anything and anyone according to pre-programmed orders.

In the past decade or so, the U.S., in the name of 'counter-terrorism,' has launched countless extremely deadly airstrikes around the world with 'drones.' Until now, the deadly strike (pushing the firing button) remains in human hands, by a pilot flying the drone remotely, and supervised by a senior officer. But with the increasing sophistication of artificial intelligence to identify, assess, and decide, this last step can well be handed over to a computer. Then, the armed drone would become a truly 'Lethal Autonomous Weapon' (LAWs), bringing in a new era in warfare.

Imagine a robot dog with a sharp sense of smell just like a real dog but armed with a deadly assault rifle? It is programmed not to attack those emitting a coded signal, but will relentlessly - and tirelessly - hunt down those without. It is not hard to imagine the killing power of such a 'robot dog' in battle. (Such a situation was depicted in the episode "Metal Head" in the acclaimed TV series *Black Mirror*)

Or imagine robot hornets, flying silently day or night, seeking out targets with their infrared sensors and stabbing them with their deadly poisonous stinger. An even more gory imagination is a chainsaw-equipped 'robot slasher,' only this one slashes so much faster than a human one ever could…

I need not go further for you to realise that this is all a terrifying trend. 'Autonomic weaponry' in itself is terrifying enough. Imagine how much worse it could be if the computer glitched, or the instruction hacked, or someone forgot to delete something… This is before we go on about the science fictional runaway computer or 'machine revolt'…

Supporters of such development claimed that by changing warfare from fistfights between people to 'a duel between robots,' it might well reduce the casualties. (Those who always think in dollar and cents even stress that governments could save big on war-related compensation and on veteran support and welfare etc.) But on the other hand, those in opposition pointed out that 'robotisation' would eventually numb the public to the trauma of war, making it easier for governments to engage in armed conflicts, thus detrimental to the cause of promoting and maintaining world peace.

The most severe criticism is this: by delegating, to a machine which does not have any feelings, or conscience (including the most basic compassion), or idea of morality and ethics, the right to take a life, and impossible to turn back after the switch is thrown, amounts to the worst corruption of human morality, and akin to opening the 'Pandora's Box.' Humanity would have brought doom upon itself.

It is because of these arguments that people around the world launched a 'Campaign to Stop Killer Robots,' and has, since 2013, garnered support from thousands of experts working with artificial intelligence, well known scientists (such as Stephen Hawking), entrepreneurs (such as Elon Musk), as well as people in politics. Antonio Guterres, Secretary-General of the United Nations, pleaded openly in 2018 for the immediate cessation on all such weapon developments.

Unfortunately, these exhortations have mostly fallen on deaf ears. The U.S., which was in the lead in developing this type of weapon, has not slowed down its pace, with Israel, Russia and China following closely behind. Many experts have pointed out that, just as with the fight against global warming, the 'opportunity window' in which action is taken to avert disaster is narrowing. We must work hard together to raise the world's awareness and stop the 'killer robot' dead in its track.

6.3 Life 3.0 and
Technological
Singularity

'Universal electronic surveillance,' 'Big Data,' and 'robotic weapons' are all natural extensions of 'artificial intelligence,' or AI. While AI is the product of the Computer Revolution beginning in the latter part of the 20th century, what distinguishes it from previous generations of computers is its ability to learn.

It was exactly their ability to learn, rather than the brute force of high-speed computing, that enabled a computer called 'Deep Blue' to beat eleven-time world chess champion Garry Kasparov in 1997. Nine years later, with the advance in 'deep learning' enabled by sophisticated artificial neural networks, AI program AlphaGo defeated South Korean professional Go player Lee Sedol.

Today, people speak enthusiastically about 'driverless cars,' 'fully automatic medical diagnostic system' and even 'surgical operations without a surgeon.' Over the past decade, fully automated production lines, warehouses, supermarkets, and freight terminals are becoming reality. Many fear that professions such as real estate and insurance agent, bank teller, accountant and solicitor might follow in the wake of telephone operators, to be replaced by an artificial intelligence, the latest incarnation of which is the ChatGPT system released by the company OpenAI in 2022.

Key figures in the high-tech frontier, ranging from Microsoft's Bill Gates to Tesla's Elon Musk to Facebook's Mark Zuckerberg, have warned of the possible adverse outcome of rolling out AI on a big scale: massive unemployment and the subsequent social unrest.

It could be argued that computers are like any machines that replaced humans in the workplace. While unemployment was inevitable in certain sectors, those made redundant have subsequently rejoined the workforce on new roles providing new services. Therefore - at least according to optimists - new kinds of jobs will always come to the rescue of those displaced by new technology, and the talk of 'massive unemployment' is scaremongering.

But pessimists disagree unlike in the past when workers were displaced from manual labour by machines, AI is now displacing human workers from the 'cognitive domain' - jobs requiring the brain not brawn. And this time round, the "brainpower" made obsolete is not just computing power, but that which requires contextual knowledge, deep analysis and complicated decision making. As such, the impact this time round will be much broader and deeper. We need to come up with strategies and measures to deal with this change to pre-empt the consequent social dislocations.

Who is correct? By now it should be clear that neither of these viewpoints has gone deep enough. Taking a closer look, mechanization, and automation, such as what happened during the Industrial Revolution with the introduction of textile machinery, did lead to massive unemployment. This in principle would lead to reduced consumption, overproduction, and even economic recession. However, these crises were resolved in the end because of one thing: 'continued economic growth.' Viewed from this perspective, AI is just the newest wave of mechanization and automation. To say it will lead to social calamity is being ignorant of the rules of historical progression. Continued economic growth will always absorb what workforces have been made redundant by the machines.

The question is: will this 'economic panacea' still work this time round? Let's examine two arguments against the continued effectiveness of this 'panacea.' Firstly, the human economy growing at a compound rate has already reached, or exceeded, Nature's physical limits, with environmental disasters occurring around the world, and is getting worse. To count on future economic growth to absorb displaced workers will only accelerate environmental collapse and push humankind closer to the brink.

Apart from this, there is reason to believe that there is a fundamental difference between AI and the waves of mechanisation and automation in the past. Powerful 'self-learning' algorithm plus huge advances in 'robotics' mean that robots will replace humans faster and in greater numbers across all professions. Take for example a caregiver in an elderly home. To become a proficient worker conversant in the daily routines, the dietary and exercise requirements of different clients, the ways in maintaining a congenial relationship with clients and colleagues, and the skills in tackling complaints and emergencies etc, a newcomer would need considerable hands-on experience requiring a period of 3 to 6 months. With the current state of the art, we could also use the same amount of time to train a caregiving robot which in the end could perform parlour tricks, share jokes, and play poker or chess with the elderly. And don't forget that this caregiver - or any nanny for kids - would never get tired, be absent-minded or ill-tempered.

And yet, it makes no sense to say, "machines will replace humans." What we are really worried about is the loss of (1) jobs and hence the income for livelihood, and (2) human dignity in accomplishing a meaningful task.

When analysed at a deeper level, though, even these fears are misguided. Let's look at the following example. Suppose you are living in ancient times in a village, and you are the fire-keeper in the temple of worship. This is because most people have forgotten how to start a fire, and in the rare occasion when all fires in the village accidentally burnt out, the fire you are keeping is the only source to keep the fires going. Needless to you, yours is an important job, and you are highly respected by the village inhabitants. Now suppose a time-traveller from the future appeared, and left as a gift a large batch of lighters. All of a sudden, anybody could start a fire easily, and your sacred duty is longer required. In the short term, you would certainly feel a loss of worth and dignity. In the long term, however, this is a big leap forward for the whole village.

Let's reframe the issue from the economic perspective of income and livelihood. Suppose a village is situated on very fertile soil, and yet the nearest reliable source of water for irrigation is a river several kilometres away. A team of people is therefore needed to carry water from the river to the village every day, and they are paid for the effort. In addition, people are needed to turn the mill to turn grains into flour. Now suppose a master craftsman passed by this village, and taught the villagers to build water wheels and conduits upstream so that water will flow to the village automatically. And with the construction of wind mills and water wheels, he also freed the villagers from the drudgery of turning the millstones. With these technological advances, mass unemployment led to economic crises and social unrest....

By now of course you'll realise I was being sarcastic. Technology in the service of humankind, whether it is something replacing muscle power, or something else which increasing productivity, ought to have freed up people so they enjoy more leisure time and generally a more comfortable life. How come there will be 'unemployment,' 'economic crises' or 'social unrest' instead? By now you should understand that this has all to do with the "capitalistic mode of production" in recent times, namely just the past few hundred years compared with the nearly ten thousand years of civilization. I have pointed out that what we need is not a 'job.' It's an 'income.' An 'age of abundance' should be a logical outcome of mechanisation, automation, computerisation, and AI robots, by which time the remaining economic issue is one of 'distribution' not 'production.' In the latter chapters on 'The Next Fifty Years' there will be more discussions on this issue of 'distribution' and the solutions.

Having done away with the spurious "economic threat" which is particular to capitalism, I do concede that there is something unnerving about the recent development of AI. It is far more complicated than the appearance and adoption of 'smart robots' in our everyday lives. Swedish-American physicist Max Tegmark, in his 2017 book *Life 3.0*, proposed a 3-tier classification of 'life' from its origin to the present day as follows:

1. 'Life 1.0,' in which life forms possess a fixed and unchangeable body structure (hardware) and directives for a behavioural pattern (software), at least in the short term. Note that in the long term, both can change over time due to 'hereditary (genetic) variations' when breeding, as well as 'natural selection' acting externally (which is together called biological evolution). The time taken, however, stretches many generations (counted in decades or millions of years). A good example is bees, equipped with a body structure and behaviour pattern developed as a result of evolution, and therefore is not unchanging. But in a short time-span (say in one or several hundreds of generations), these are relatively stable and unchanging. Regarding behavioural patterns, we call the unchanging behavioural pattern 'biological instinct.'

2. 'Life 2.0,' in which while life forms possess a fixed and unchangeable body structure (hardware), the directives for a behavioural pattern (software) is changeable to a certain extent. On Earth, the earliest such life form was the primeval 'Homo habilis' which emerged about 2 million years ago. The breakthrough is in the nature of the 'software.' In 'Life 1.0' the 'software' is the 'coding' carried in the 'DNA,' large molecules with a double spiral structure. Although the execution of this 'behaviour

162

coding' has to be done through a 'central nervous system' which is constructed by 'structural coding,' the autonomy of the 'nervous system' in the process is very low. For example, when a beehive is under threat bees attack the invader to their death. Their nervous system gives the instruction, but the ultimate command remains within the genetic code.

'Homo habilis,' on the other hand, became the prototype of 'Life 2.0' because its 'central nervous system' - mainly the cerebral cortex - developed over time the characteristics of 'plasticity' and autonomy, thereby enabling self-learning to happen. The result is that it probingly began making various kinds of tools. Note that such knowledge and skills were not acquired inborn as in the case of bees, which were inherited from past generations. Instead, it was learned by each and every individual over generations. This mode of behaviour, which transcends 'biological instinct,' is what brought humankind on the way to wisdom.

Contemporary humans are of course the best example of 'Life 2.0,' with the 'memetic evolution' (knowledge, thoughts, ideas, values, and behaviour) constantly upgrading the 'software.'

3. Tegmark argued that the 'AI' we have today has to some extent overtaken 'Life 2.0,' and has already evolved to 'Life 3.0.' This is because 'AI' capable of self-learning can not only perform 'software upgrades,' it can also perform 'hardware upgrades.' In other words, 'computer/robot A' designs a 'computer/robot B' which is better than itself, then B designs C, which is better than itself, then C designs D which is better than itself...and so on and so forth.

To a certain extent, human beings at the apex of 'Life 2.0' are closing in on 'Life 3.0.' With rapidly advancing genetic engineering, we may soon be able to modify our bodies so we can live in the deep ocean or breathe in the thin atmosphere of Mars. Further, quite a few scholars have pointed out that while the 20th century is the 'century of physics', the 21st will be the 'century of biology' especially the 'century of the brain', and propelled by both 'genetic engineering' and 'neuro-technology', we may soon be able to elevate our intelligence so much so we come up with 'Superman 1', who will make 'Superman 2', who will make 'Superman 3'...and so on and so forth. The majority of us believe this could only happen in a science fiction not just because of the complex technology involved, but more so because of the enormous ethical and moral concerns.

On the other hand, AI 'evolving' toward 'Life 3.0' is different from that of human beings. On the face of it, this does not involve ethical concerns. But we only need to pause and think to realise that once the genie is let out of the bottle, there's no way we can put it back.

Due to AI's much faster 'evolution' compared to biological organisms (even with the aid of genetic engineering), explosive changes can occur with computer- or network-based 'Life 3.0,' overtaking and surpassing humans in leaps and bounds in no time.

Conceptually, there could be two types of AI in principle: a 'strong AI' in which a computer somehow evolves a 'self-consciousness' and thereafter 'intentionality.' Most science fiction stories and movies depicting computers going rogue and attacking their human masters (such as the movie series *Terminator and Matrix*) fall into this category.

It is a strange fact that most IT experts do not believe in "Strong AI." On the one hand, the emergence of Strong AI could never be proved (how do you prove someone is truly "self-aware"?). On the other hand, it is argued that as 'self-consciousness' has taken millions of years to evolve and is unique to higher animals. A computer, however sophisticated in its design and construction, can never become aware that it 'exists,' and therefore entirely incapable of 'going rogue' and 'harming people.' This argument keeps science fiction in its rightful place: in books or on the silver screen.

Even the best in the field of AI expertise is at a loss as to how AI would turn out, but quite a few has pointed out that it matters not a bit if Strong AI ever becomes reality. Now that our lives are so intricately tied to computers and AI, even a 'Weak AI' with no self-consciousness whatsoever is still threatening enough to bring about doomsday. The slightest mistake it makes, be it a malignant sabotage from the outside or a faulty logic or even random error from the inside, is enough for civilisation to come crashing down. These days a total blackout is bad enough for society. In an AI dominated future, a small glitch is all it takes for the whole world to grind to a screeching halt.

In fact, as early as 1909, English writer E M Forster (1879-1970) has already described a fictional future of this sort in his story *The Machine Stops*, a future in which every human was taken care of by machines, until one day these machines broke down, as witless and helpless people watched in horror and died. Judging by the way things are going, it might well be that Forster's fictional future is becoming real…

We can extend this further and say: it's more than dependence. It's indulgence. It's addiction. In mid-20th century, scientists located the pleasure centre in a rat's brain. They then experimented with rats by inserting electrodes into this pleasure centre in the rat's brain, and placing it inside a cage. There were three switches which the rat could activate: one for food, the second for water, and the third to send pulses of electric current into its brain. The rat with an electrode in its brain, it turned out, learned in a short time to keep activating the third switch, so it could get to feel a dose of electric pleasure, eventually leaving the switches for food and water altogether, until it died of exhausting from overstimulation to its brain.

This is a truly shocking result. By extension, immersed in ultra-realistic electronic experience, - the Metaverse promoted and even glorified so much by Mark Zuckerberg - might humankind one day follow the footsteps of those lab rats? And would the end of humanity come not as a result of an all-out nuclear war, or an alien invasion, but because of addiction to electronic stimulation to the brain's pleasure centre?

Let's return for a moment to the question of AI. If the assumption of 'strong AI' stands and it became so pervasive (such as the internet), what if one day it 'woke up'? To most people this would be a nightmarish prospect, but to a few enthusiasts this is a moment in human history worth celebrating. They have even come up with a name for it: 'technological singularity.' Note that the term 'singularity' was first used in relativistic physics to describe what exist at the heart of a black hole, where ordinary time and space as we understand them no longer exist. Here, the term is used for a quite different purpose, meaning the awakening of machine intelligence.

To take a step further, there are those who eagerly await the arrival of the "singularity," which is understood as the moment when humans and machines merge into an 'ultimate amalgamation,' an apotheosis giving birth to an entirely new form of existence (or even moving to a higher "spiritual plane" …). More specifically: they are waiting for the moment when we can 'upload' our minds to the internet, thereby attaining 'immortality.' The Hollywood movies *Transcendence* in 2014 and *CHAPPiE* in 2015 both depicted such a scenario.

Based on the possibility that 'life/mind' might experience a significant breakthrough and upward boost due to 'man-machine amalgamation,' it was proposed in recent decades the idea of 'trans-humanism' or 'post-humanism,' that is to say that (1) this trend is a historical inevitability and (2) this is an outcome worthy of pursuit and celebration. For us, we should enthusiastically embrace our role as a midwife in this 'breakthrough.'

I am somewhat sceptical to this 'historical inevitability', and am strongly against it being 'worthy of pursuit and celebration.' Warts and all, 'human nature' is what every one of us cherishes most, and ranks as the one of the most complex thing in the Universe. Before reaching a complete and thorough understanding of it, any talk of 'super,' 'post-' or 'trans-human' is premature and smacks of being unwise and irresponsible. The ancient Chinese sage and philosopher Confucius, when asked by one of his most critical students on the topic of 'death and dying,' admonished him saying, "If we don't understand even the living, how can we talk of understanding the dead?" I will say instead, "if we don't understand humanity, how are we able to talk about post-humanity?" As I see it, even if AI or the internet wakes up one day, it would be advisable to keep it at arm's length and treat it as a 'friend' and 'counterpart,' and not to instead pursue any sort of 'coming together.'

But history often takes surprising turns. Clearly, whether it is 'computer awakening,' 'uploading our minds' or 'man-machine amalgamation,' it will have a profound impact on our future. There is yet no way to tell which direction things will go. I shall keep these possibilities open in my discussion on the future in 50 and 500 years, but place them in the category of 'hard to tell'.

6.4 ▶ The Technological
Trap

Having gone through the discussion in the previous pages, a question that begs to be answered is "Does advances in technology invariably backfire?" Responses to this question generally fall into two categories: one that believes technology is simply a tool at our disposal, and this tool is amoral in itself. Just as a knife can be used to cut or kill, it falls on the user of the tool to decide on the purpose. Hence the problem is with the user - us, not the tool - technology. Such view is called technoneutralism.

Yet other people view this neutrality as naïve if not divorced from reality. History has shown time and again that technological advances brought unintended consequences, often resulting in profound impact on posterity, altering the course of history, and reshaping our thinking, values, and morals. Taking the examples of the Four Great Chinese Inventions - paper-making, magnetic compass, gunpowder, and printing - and their influence on the course of European history and the world at large. Language in the broadest sense is also a form of technology, and it is common wisdom that while higher-order thinking led to the development of higher-order language, higher-order language also leads to the further development of high-order thinking. So as humankind uses technology to change the world around him, he himself is also changed by the world so created.

Pessimists who hold this view also believe that our morality is bound to be outstripped by technological advances. African American church leader and human rights activist Martin Luther King Jr. (1929-1968) said, "Our scientific power has outrun our spiritual power. We have guided missiles but misguided men." The result, of course, is like a kid let loose in a science laboratory full of dangerous inflammable chemicals: it's a matter of time when he burns the whole thing to the ground, consuming himself in the process. This view became popular during the height of the Cold War, when the world was brought to the brink of nuclear self-destruction spurred on by the tension between the U.S. and U.S.S.R. bloc of countries.

A world teetering on the edge of destruction thanks to a nuclear armament deadlock was exactly the argument employed by optimists in rebuttal. By the mere fact that no nuclear war has broken out for more than seventy years, it shows, so said the optimists, that humankind possesses both the wisdom and ability to rein in any risk posed by advances in technology - if he so wishes. Other examples cited by optimists include acid rain and the ozone hole, both having been much remediated by human effort. What we need to do is to stay wise, so that technology can remain in the service of humankind, and not become a curse.

I would say that both the optimist and pessimist viewpoints make perfect sense - except neither takes into account the fact that, today, in the service of capitalism, science and technology has become a money-making tool, and no longer a means to solve humankind's problems. Examples such as Big Pharma pouring big dollars into drug R&D of age-related diseases (such as senile dementia) but not for those which affect many more people especially in poor developing countries (such as the many deadly infectious diseases).

Worse, dictated by the unyielding assault of consumerism, new knowhow and new techniques almost always end up as money making merchandise, regardless of their possible detriment to body and soul. Examples abound, from toxic pesticides and herbicides, antibiotics and growth hormones in cattle and poultry feed, genetically modified (GM) crops (in particular those with so-called 'suicide gene'), industrial fishing with sonar and floating factory ships, food additive chemicals for flavouring and appearance, silicone inserts for breast enhancement, Botox in the so-called medical cosmetics industry, disposable plastic utensils and packaging, glow sticks for pop concert audience, addictive electronic games - especially those using the newest in virtual or augmented reality technology, etc.

The hype on krill oil serves as a more recent example. Touted as a supplement with more and better omega-3 than fish oil, health food business started putting more and more krill oil supplement on the market. Krill, a tiny crustacean not unlike a shrimp (remember Will and Bill from *Happy Feet 2*?), is the main source of food for marine animals, from fish to squids to whales, penguins too, but not widely regarded as having much economic value. But the drive to dive into new business opportunities has meant that it is now under threat from overharvesting, with consequential impact on marine animals dependent on it for food. This could well be the last nail in the coffin to some species of whale already threatened by extinction.

In other words, "runaway technology" is to a large extent the runaway commercialisation of technology driven by capitalism.

Aren't governments around the world supposed to regulate the use of technology? And prohibit the use of any when it is shown to be detrimental to the interest of society at large? The fact is: government regulation and control might be tough on guns and drugs, but when it comes to fast changing technologies, they either simply can't catch up with the pace of change, or don't hang around long enough to witness the damage which sometimes can take years or decades to show - witness the case of plastics, or both. Political ideology and influence also play an important part in government's failure. In the mantra of the free market, any regulation is overregulation, and - so say free market advocates - detrimental to innovation, freedom of choice, and economic growth. Regulators can be influenced by Big Corp: an outright bribe, or an offer of a well-paid chief executive role after leaving public service - the so called "revolving door" in which the government appoints the ex-CEO of a drug company to the chair of the drug advisory board, only to return to the private sector on retirement, etc. This happens often in the U.S.

Of course, governments too can be abusers of technology, a nationwide electronic surveillance system is just one nightmarish example among many. Sadly, the fact remains that the man in the street is sandwiched between Technocratic Statism and Technocratic Corporatism. (For people in Third World countries, in the grip of neo-colonialism as well)

There are techno-optimists who believe that new advances in technology would be able to break the spell and create a better world for all. The Printing Revolution is an often-cited example. With the rise of the internet at the end of the last century, many people saw it as a powerful means not only for the diffusion of knowledge and promotion of social interactions and participation, but also as a means in the decentralisation of power and empowerment of the ordinary people. As so often happens in history, however, the Big Boys always come in, with their huge amounts of capital, and any egalitarian and romantic aspirations for the internet are now snuffed out by the profit imperative of the Big Techs.

In recent years, the advent of the Blockchain Revolution and the proliferation of cryptocurrencies, decentralised finance, non-fungible tokens and smart contracts etc. have once again fired the hopes of some people as to the chance of subverting society's dominant power hierarchy. It awaits to be seen if this promise will be fulfilled, or will go down the way of the internet.

As I see it, the only way to counteract these dire trends is to deepen public education and the democratic institution. Abraham Lincoln said of a government, 'of the people, by the people, for the people.' In the same spirit, we should also promote 'science of the people, by the people and for the people.' For this to come true, we need both a well-developed and vibrant civil society with democratic institution, as well as a comprehensive science education.

As we shall see in Chapter 9.4, the necessity for democracy extends beyond the realms of political governance. Not only do we need political democracy, but economic democracy is equally indispensable. Democracy must be allowed to fully bloom, both in spirit and in practice. Institutional changes and spiritual changes must go hand in hand. Only so could we turn the world around, and realise the goal of 'technology in the service of man' instead of "man in the service - and enslaved - by technology." There is no other choice. We must rein in the genie of technology, and to make sure that it will work for, and not against, the welfare of humankind.

Predicting the Future:
Lure and Trappings

7

Lure of
the Crystal Ball

In the previous six chapters, we've had a quick look at the ascent trajectory of human civilization, as well as various aspects of the current human condition. At long last, it's time to ask the grand question, "What lies in wait for humanity?"

The urge to predict is irresistible. To be able to predict in a timely and accurate fashion gives one a unique advantage over everybody else. Or so it seems.

Logic dictates that we cannot foretell the future, which is, by definition, something yet to happen. Of course, it also hinges on our understanding of the nature of existence and time, which in itself is a profoundly philosophical exploration. Einstein once said, "Past, present, and future are but an obstinate illusion and do not actually exist." According to Einstein's Theory of General Relativity, the flow of time is relative in different inertial frames. What is absolute is events in the space-time continuum. However, causality is still conserved in general relativity, and it is impossible for anyone to foretell an outcome before the occurrence of a cause. If a vase was still standing firmly on the table, and in the absence of any plausible cause for it to change its position, any prediction of its smashing to pieces on the floor simply would not stand.

However, there is nothing to stop us from making informed forecast about the future. With relatively simple systems, as long as we know enough of their inner workings, we should be able to foretell the chain of causes and effects, allowing us to predict the state of a system at a particular moment in the future. If our imaginary vase in the previous paragraph was given a big enough push, our prediction of its smashing to pieces on the floor would hold true.

From the rather mundane task - or so it would seem - of weather forecasting, to the movement and position of heavenly bodies, such as the spectacular celestial sights of the eclipses of the Sun and Moon, forecasting the future is very much part of daily life. Here, a word of caution is due: unlike the heavenly bodies, our Earth's atmosphere is a much more complex system, such that even with the best of mathematical models and the most powerful super-computers, Chaos Theory tells us that a fortnight is about the maximum period for which we could hope to have reliable forecasts, and even so subject to stochastic uncertainties. No wonder the saying 'Just like weather'!

Human society, however, is much more complex than weather systems. In fact, it is the most complex system we've ever known, we ourselves being part of it. Forecasting the collective behaviour of it, let alone its long-term development, poses a challenge well beyond current technological capabilities. But this has never stopped people from trying.

Ancient societies entrusted the task of prediction to shamans and priests. More than three thousand years ago in China, people attempted to foresee the future with oracle bones, pieces of tortoise shell or animal bones on which questions were carved with a sharp tool. Intense heat was then applied with a hot metal rod. Depending on the resulting cracks and fissures the shaman would pronounce the will of the spirits and deities, after which he would carve it on the piece of bone. This practice of divining the future with fire gave rise to the first known collection of East Asian ideographic writing.

Fortune tellers of all persuasion still claim to be able to foretell the future, these days with the aid of technology. Celebrity fortune tellers and psychic mediums pronounce their annual forecast on every New Year's Eve, mostly getting sceptic reception, because all these predictions would carry the caveat of 'barring unexpected circumstances' which, practically, includes everything unpredictable in life. The biggest failing of fortune-telling and the like is that none of it stands up to the bare minimum of scientific scrutiny, for unlike any scientific experiment, they are never falsifiable.

That human behaviour is complex is obvious. What makes it especially hard to predict, and with any degree of accuracy, lies in the fact that human being is a species capable of self-reflecting cognition, giving rise to self-fulfilling and self-defeating prophecies in the study of psychology.

Imagine in a time of economic turmoil, rumour spread that a bank, which was soundly managed, was going bust. The rumour eventually triggered a bank run, and the bank went under. The prophecy, which began as an unfounded rumour, realised itself.

In a self-negating prophecy on the other hand, is where the reaction to the predicted outcome turned out to be negative. Imagine a brand new theme park was opening and a big turnout was predicted. As a result, fearing traffic congestion and long queues, people stayed away during the opening week, and admission was sparse. In short, the prediction caused people to behave in exactly the opposite way.

Yet another scenario is where the same prediction results in two diametrically opposite outcomes. Let's say I warned my two friends to drive safely on a certain weekend, citing my sixth sense which suggested that a crash might happen. As a result, one of them took extra care at the wheel and there was no crash (self-negating), but the other was so unnerved that he ended up crashing his car (self-fulfilling). Here, as in previous examples, a feedback mechanism was at play, which might increase the magnitude of complexity such that no meaningful forecast of human behaviour is possible.

Human society is a vastly complex system. Apparently insignificant and local events might lead to an upheaval totally beyond expectation. A nursery rhyme 'For want of a nail' nails it thus:

> For want of a nail the shoe was lost.

For want of a shoe the horse was lost.

For want of a horse the rider was lost.

For want of a rider the message was lost.

For want of a message a battle was lost.

For want of a battle the kingdom was lost.

And all for the want of a horseshoe nail.

Minute changes that happen by chance can give rise to powerful and decisive effects, so the nursery rhyme goes. We have seen how the workings of the chaos theory impose limitations on the accuracy of weather forecasting. The most famous, and popularly quoted, of such workings would have to be the Butterfly Effect, in which a butterfly flapping its wings in Brazil ultimately set off a tornado in Texas! The technical term for this is "sensitive dependence on initial conditions."

The Chaos Theory, developed in the 1960s and 70s, have put ancient intuitive wisdom on a robust foundation of physics and mathematics. Repeated iterations of seemingly simple and deterministic equations and dynamic systems may result in random and unpredictable outcomes, due to the effect of non-linearity. The discovery of 'deterministic chaos' has been hailed as the third revolution in 20th century physics, after the Theory of Relativity and Quantum Mechanics.

It is always easy to be wise after the fact (say, after a stock market slump, or when war broke out between nations), but for any dynamic systems that harbour non-linearity - which includes most systems that are of interest to us - the crystal ball is murky most of the time. No matter how hard we try, surprises are always waiting round the corner. In recent years, such surprises go by the name of "Black Swan." Mathematically, traditional risk assessment algorithms are based on normal distribution (the Gaussian curve) analysis in statistics. Black Swans, otherwise known as "long tail" or "fat tail" in statistical jargon, are outcomes that fall well outside the 99.9% probability region of the bell-shaped curve of the Gaussian function.

Of course, as with all jargon, Black Swan is now suffering from over-use: 9/11, the 2008 global financial meltdown, Brexit referendum, the election of Donald Trump, the

COVID-19 pandemic, the Russian invasion of Ukraine…Such is the misuse and abuse of technical terminology. But it does counsel caution whenever we attempt to predict the future. However meticulous and careful we go about our business, events always take a surprising, and totally unexpected turn, even to experts. British biologist J.B.S. Haldane (1892-1964) once said, "the Universe is not only queerer than we suppose, but queerer than we can suppose." Whatever wisdom we distil from our daily life tells us, "it is more often those risks which we have not considered than those we did that will do us in."

7.2 ▶ From Dialectical Historicism
to Psychohistory

We need to know the past to see the future. Hence this question: does history follow any rules? Or is history just 'one damn thing after another' as some have suggested? An answer to this question would be immensely helpful in predicting what the future may hold for us.

Of the many schools of thought on the topic of laws governing history, the most notable has to be dialectical historicism proposed in the mid 19th century by German philosophers Karl Marx (1818-1883) and Friedrich Engels (1820-1895)

According to Marx and Engels, human history began, in the time of the primitive humans, with a communal society, a form of primitive communism. The advent of civilization, however, threw humankind into class societies characterized by oppression and exploitation. Slave society is the outcome of this oppression. The next stage is the feudal society, after which the Industrial Revolution brought about the rise of the capitalist society.

Capitalism, it is true, unleashed the productivity potential locked up in previous stages of human society. But Marx and Engels also foresaw the unsolvable contradiction inherent in a capitalist society. There is bound to be a cycle of boom and bust in a capitalist economy, driven by the inherent contradiction between (over-) production and (under-) consumption.

According to a dialectical historian, the increase in productivity would eventually elevate humankind from the present capitalist society to a communist society of unprecedented prosperity and super-abundance. When that time finally arrives, it would be a world where 'from each according to his ability, to each according to his need.' There would be no more oppression or exploitation. However, in real life, we would need to first pass through the transitional stage of socialism, which is 'from each according to his ability, to each according to his contribution.'

So, what Marx and Engels had done was firstly to sum up and re-interpret history, and secondly forecast the future, doing both as they saw it. Needless to say, it is the second part of their theory - the prediction of a world free from oppression and exploitation - which appeals more to us. And this is exactly this second part of their theory too, that has so far been humankind's greatest disappointment and worst tragedy: witness the countless disasters and tragedies all committed under the guise of communism in the 20th century.

Critics often point out that, apart from the abject failure in the real world, the fatal defect in the political theory of communism lies in its underestimate of the importance of what it calls 'societal superstructure': attributes such as gender, ethnicity, religious and philosophical beliefs, together with the many cultural outcomes driven by these attributes. They certainly carry some imprints of class structure, yet at the same time are not entirely dictated by social class differences. A simplistic 'economic determinism' cannot account for the boundless complexity and variability that is human society. Money, after all, is not the measure of all things, contrary to what communist theorists want us to believe.

And there is still one conundrum Marxists must resolve. Marx insisted that his was a scientific socialism, which would set it apart from the kind of utopian socialist theories propounded by his contemporaries and predecessors (Charles Fourier, Saint-Simon, Robert Owen etc.). It is 'scientific,' because the evolution of human society, from the ancient slavery society to feudal to capitalist and eventually on to socialist then communist, follows a set of objective and immutable laws, laws that cannot be changed by our will, however hard we try. Yet immediately a paradox arise: if the march of history follows inexorable logic, then why bother setting up communist parties to promote the political agenda? Why bother getting aggressive and violent, even staging coups and waging wars to achieve a regime change? If what's going to happen will happen anyway - because it's so inevitable, why not just sit back and wait for the communist paradise to come to us?

Turns out ther's a catch, and only the Marxists can explain it. Objective laws, so they say, fall into different kinds. Those governing the planets going round the Sun, for example, are by nature different from those governing the human world. Therefore, although inevitable and immutable, human effort is nonetheless required to bring forth and accelerate the changeover to a communist world free of exploitation and oppression. You may find this kind of argument unconvincing, but it does provide hope and encouragement to millions who are fighting against injustice around the world.

Not long after the end of World War II, a young American science fiction writer named Isaac Asimov (1929-1990) began to write a series of short stories on the decline and fall of a Galactic Empire set in a distant future. Asimov was inspired to put pen to paper after he read English historian Edward Gibbon's monumental work *The History of the Decline and Fall of the Roman Empire* (1776-1788). Asimov's stories were subsequently collected into three full-length novels, and *The Foundation Trilogy*, published between 1951 and 1953, and went on to become one of the most popular and widely read work of science fiction in history.

If Asimov had just moved the history of the decline and fall of the Roman Empire to a distant future, his trilogy would not have been so highly regarded. The love and respect it garnered was due to one brilliant science fictional idea: psychohistory. According to Asimov, while the behaviour of a single individual, acting under free will (together with various other factors as discussed before), is unpredictable, the collective behaviour of a sufficiently large number of individuals would start to follow certain rules, and mass psychology would become predictable.

In his trilogy, Asimov imagined a distant future when humankind would have settled the length and breadth of the Milky Way galaxy, and would number in the trillions if not more. Such an astronomically huge population would behave and think in ways that could be reduced to mathematical equations, and hence could be analysed, and more importantly, predicted, statistically. An analogy would be the behaviour of a gas. While the motion of one single molecule is entirely random and therefore unpredictable, a gigantic cloud of gas consisting of thousands of trillions of molecules would follow natural laws such as Boyle's Law and Charles's Law.

In Asimov's *Foundation Trilogy*, the protagonist mathematical genius Hari Seldon founded the study of psychohistory, with which he was able to predict the future development of the Galactic Empire. To his surprise, the mathematical solutions predicted that the empire, which was at the apex of its power and glory, was actually in decline and heading for a complete collapse. Humankind would be thrown into a dark age lasting thirty thousand years.

Further analysis, so the story went, revealed a sliver of hope: while human effort would not be able to arrest the irrevocable tide of history, and the eventual collapse is inevitable, fine-tuning the course of events in the next several centuries might shorten the ensuing dark age to a mere thousand years, and the turmoil and suffering to humankind thus greatly reduced.

There is no way to know if Asimov was familiar with the concepts of dialectical historicism. Yet the inevitability of historical development as propounded in his trilogy echoes perfectly the idea of dialectical historicism as propounded by Marx and Engels. One can even draw the parallel between the postulates that (1) human agency could not prevent the fall of the Galactic Empire but could shorten the ensuing Dark Age, and (2) human agency cannot prevent the coming of communism, but could hasten its arrival.

The best was yet to come in the trilogy. Asimov pointed out that if the general population were to know about how the future was unfolding, in particular the fine-tuning which psychohistorians were to perform to steer the trend of future events in their preferred direction, their forecasts and predictions would be rendered ineffective by both positive and negative feedbacks from human behaviour. Therefore, such fine-tuning must be carried out in utmost secrecy for them to work. For this, Seldon established a clandestine organization which he named the 'Foundation,' and, just as another semi-fictional protagonist, Zhuge Liang, did in the 14th century Chinese historical novel *The Romance of the Three Kingdoms*, Seldon instructed his followers to open his "time capsules" (in the form of pre-recorded holographic videos) after his death to receive his prescient instructions from time to time on what to do in times of crises

I shall leave it to you to explore the full scope of Asimov's imagination, except to reveal a twist in his plot a little bit further. Halfway through the story, the absolute authority of the galactic empire was seized by a usurper possessing superhuman capabilities, including the ability to read minds. This unexpected development caught the psychohistorians completely off guard, to the point of upsetting all of Seldon's predictions…almost! Once again, Asimov's vision as a science fiction writer leaves one in awe. In today's parlance, what he was describing is exactly what is referred to as a Black Swan event today.

Asimov penned two prequels and two sequels to the *Foundation Trilogy* in the 1980s, by which time chaos theory had established itself. Deterministic chaos posed a grave challenge to the predictability of long term development. Asimov responded to this challenge by invoking the idea of "achaotic equations" in the fictional science of psychohistory, which to be fair is the most a writer of fiction could do.

But let's get back to the question which started this discussion: does history follow any laws? If it does, can we, by discovering these laws, predict the future? We have seen two affirmative answers, one academic, one fictional. Let's turn to a forceful response in the negative.

We have come across 'falsifiability' as a concept for defining what science is. This concept was put forward by the Austrian-British philosopher Karl Popper (1902-1994), who, in 1936, wrote and presented a paper titled *The Poverty of Historicism*. It was enlarged and published as a book in 1957, and became the most cogent and powerful rebuttal to the idea that there are laws governing historical development, and that such laws could be known to us.

Popper's rebuttal was founded on a simple precept: the predominant driving force behind any historical development is progress in knowledge (which, incidentally, was also the cornerstone of the thesis of dialectical historicism). But here's the catch. By definition, it is impossible to foretell how knowledge would progress. If we are able to predict humankind's future knowledge of chemistry, then that knowledge will no longer be "future knowledge" but the knowledge of today! Similarly, suppose we could foresee the style of dress 500 years from now, people are bound to adopt that style for the sheer fun of it, and that style will no longer be a "future style" but a style in the 21st century. The upshot is that it is logically impossible to know the future course of history when that course depends on the future growth of scientific knowledge which is unknowable in advance. Just as future knowledge cannot be foretold, so is history.

Popper argued and denounced dialectical historicism as dangerous and bankrupt. Dialectical historicists, in prophesying the future development of human society as heading toward an idealistic endpoint, provokes a rejection of the status quo, posing a threat to existing social order, and therefore becomes a bane to humankind. Popper did not deny the ongoing need for social reforms, of which he counselled caution and patience. What he advocated was "piecemeal social engineering," in contrast to the violent upheavals of a Marxist revolution.

Popper's logic is unassailable, but the fact remains that the course of history hasn't changed in any fundamental manner, despite the growth of human knowledge in the last two centuries. Technology and productivity have come a long way, so has the cumulative wealth of the human society. And yet, the man in the street is still desperately trying to hang on to his paid job to put food on the family dinner table, to pay his bills, to provide education for his children and occasionally - and these days more than ever - struggling to pay off a sizable home loan. Some are even taking on multiple jobs to make ends meet. It's true most of us in the developed countries are using the newest model of smart phone, and paying our bills with a tap of the phone (previously plastic cards), racking up a big debt in the process. Other than that, nothing has changed.

The global geopolitical picture of a centre and a periphery hasn't changed materially either, with the exception of a handful of nations such as South Korea and Singapore who have managed to move themselves from the periphery to a semi-periphery status.

American writer and futurologist Alvin Toffler (1928-2016) wrote three of his best known books *The Future Shock, The Third Wave and Powershift* between 1970 and 1990. I read all three as soon as they were available. Looking back after some thirty years, Toffler's predictions of technological change have all been superseded. Power shift from top to bottom? Hardly!

No wonder people pointed out that while change is inevitable, the more the world changes, the more it stays the same, as exemplified by a simple yet popular cartoon picture circulating on social media these days: bombs falling from planes, under which are the head shots of U.S. presidents Bill Clinton, George W. Bush, Barack Obama, and Donald Trump. The description reads, "The rich stays rich, the poor stays poor, and the bombs never stop!"

My conclusion is this: as long as Western domination and the capitalist mode of production persist, nothing changes. No change is possible even with the most massive growth of knowledge and the most advanced in technology. In fact, these changes will only help to reinforce the political and economic order of the day.

Whether this trend will continue, or whether some new knowledge will come along and bring total disruption to the present social and world order is of course not a foregone conclusion. It may yet turn out that a quantum jump in scientific knowledge and technology tomorrow will turn the table and bring down those in power, and make human oppression and exploitation forever history. However, looking back at similar claims throughout history, from the printing press to the steam engine, and then onto telegraphy, the telephone, television, computers, PCs, the internet, smart phones, the blockchain-bitcoin revolution etc., one is not inclined to be optimistic.

Popper's advocates may wish to point out, that although capitalism stays the same, the labour movement over the past century or two has led to dramatic improvement in pay and working conditions, thereby confirming, if not completely proving, Popper's piecemeal social engineering correct. On the other hand, although Western domination has not been completely sidelined, nationalist movements in many parts of the world have brought about significant improvement to the dire situations in many Third World countries, vastly reducing the proportion of their population living in extreme poverty. In other words, there is change for the better.

This is a topic of such scope and complexity that I believe best to leave it at that, instead inviting readers to make their own judgment. To assist, I recommend Dutch-American sociologist Saskia Sassen's 2014 book *Expulsions - Brutality and Complexity in the Global Economy*, and American economist Joseph Stiglitz's 2019 work *Globalization and Its Discontents Revisited - Anti-Globalization in the Era of Trump*.

Lastly, I wish to address this 'law of history,' one that appeals even to those professing no interest in history: where there is oppression there is resistance, and the greater the oppression the greater the resistance.

The emergence and development of both aggressive and retaliatory behaviour is governed by the laws of biological evolution. On the other hand, history has shown time and again that overwhelming oppression could and did succeed in suppressing retaliation and rebellion. Slavery under Roman rule lasted more than a thousand years, black slavery lasted about 350 years. Oppressive regimes, such as the Manchu Qing dynasty in China, remained in place for 270 years. To say after the fact that "oppression will always be overcome given time" is at its best disingenuous, and at its worst insensitive and cruel, especially to those still suffering the oppression.

7.3 Stochastic and Dynamical Forecasts

This Chapter on forecasting the future carries a subtitle of 'temptations and pitfalls.' While we have gone through many of the pitfalls associated with predicting the future, the temptation is just too strong for me to resist, or else I wouldn't have written this book on the future of humankind. From this point on, I shall attempt to achieve the impossible by predicting the future of humankind, first and foremost to satisfy my very own curiosity, but also to map out some pointers for readers and the public at large to follow, in the hope that future catastrophes may be averted.

As an academic inquiry, predicting the future can either be in a restricted sense, as in technological forecast, or in the much broader scope of futurology, which deals with future changes in human society.

Readers may ask: can predicting the future ever become a legitimate field of academic inquiry? By now you may have concluded that predicting the future is just pie in the sky. I worked in the Hong Kong Royal Observatory, core business of which is weather forecasting. So let me use the example of a typhoon/hurricane forecast to show what we can do in predicting the future to make it less of a pie in the sky.

Let's assume a tropical cyclone has formed over the northwestern Pacific Ocean, and was intensifying and tracking north-northwest toward the east of Luzon. Where would the cyclone be, and how strong would it get, every 12 hours thereafter? There are several forecasting methods we can use to find out.

The first method is called persistence, otherwise known as linear extrapolation. If the tropical cyclone has been tracking north-northwest at 15 kilometres an hour for the past 24 hours, then we assume it would do the same in the next 24 hour period. Simple, but crude. Some might call this the dummy's guide to forecasting. Given the inertia usually associated with natural phenomena, this simple and crude method nonetheless has its worth in the short term of say, 6 to 12 hours.

As the accuracy of linear extrapolation tends to decrease with time, we need another method to forecast in the longer term of, say, 24 to 48 hours or longer. Here we may resort to the climatology method, in which past records of tropical cyclones occurring at around the same time of the years and in roughly the same location were analysed to obtain a set of mean positions, speed, and headings. Obviously, all this analysis of past record makes the climatology method at least more 'scientific' than simple "persistence," with the big assumption that tropical cyclones past and present occurring at around the same time of the year all behave in very similar ways.

In practice, the results from linear extrapolation and climatology analysis are combined and a mean value obtained, i.e., ½ (P+C), P being Persistence and C Climatology. In 24-hour weather forecasting, this value is the first approximation for reference.

Next at our disposal is the analogue method, in which multiple meteorological parameters such as air pressure variation, surface and high altitude wind fields would be taken into account. Archived data would then be searched for the closest match, which would become the reference against which a forecast is made for the development of the current cyclone, making corrections based on the disparity between the two.

Given the number crunching power of computers these days, we are able to combine the climatology and analogue methods to perform a statistical regression analysis. In the main, statistical methods are premised on inductive reasoning, which tells us that if something happened in the past, something similar will happen in future. For example, the Sun has been rising in the east so it will do the same tomorrow and thereafter. And the bigger the amount of past data, the more accurate the statistical forecast.

Of course, there are some more forecast methodology at our disposal: time series analysis, the Monte Carlo method, and so on, which I will not go into here.

For some like me with a background in physics, none of these statistical methods is satisfactory. Physical systems all follow specific dynamic equations, so the best forecast methodology is one which makes use of these dynamic equations. Once the initial and boundary conditions are determined, a set of snapshot data is entered, and the equations would calculate results for any chosen moment in time. In other words, we need deductive, not inductive, reasoning.

Dynamical methodology based on deductive reasoning, while much more ideal, is much more challenging than its statistical/inductive counterpart. Simple enough if it's predicting the motion of a billiard ball, but with a vastly more complex and dynamic system such as a tropical cyclone, with the Earth's atmosphere as the backdrop, the technical challenge increases several orders of magnitude. (Note that 'dynamic methodology' is a category of equations including the various laws of conservation in physics. A more accurate name is 'analytical methods')

Significant advances in weather forecasting have since been made over the past several decades, thanks to the advent of super computers. Now, atmospheric equations are already able to calculate weather forecasts up to a fortnight, and with much higher accuracy than before.

From the above we can see the methodology employed by Toynbee the historian in his comparative study of human civilizations and his 'challenge and response' theory was one of statistical analysis, whereas both Marx and Engels' dialectical historicism and Asimov's fictional psychohistory both belong to the category of dynamic analysis. Asimov wrote in his novel that just as Newton devised calculus to deal with the complex motion of heavenly bodies, Hari Seldon invented a whole new field of mathematical analysis to study the laws governing human behaviour *en masse*.

Methodology aside, in real life, it is whatever works that matters. Most of the time, it is a combination of inductive and deductive reasoning, with a pinch of personal intuition - being the secret ingredient - added. To a certain extent, this secret ingredient had been incorporated in the form of Bayesian statistics, which has been revived in the second half of the last century, and supplemented the purely frequency-based Fisherian statistics which had reigned supreme previously. Today, Bayesian inference is widely used in areas ranging from forecasting the performance of shares on the market, box office revenue, race outcomes, company quarterly results, GDP growth, drug and surgical efficacy, and epidemiology.

By far the most interesting forecast methodology is one in which a group of experts are asked the same question. Their respective answers and comments are then passed around anonymously for others to comment on. It is believed that after repeating this process multiple times, the disparity in the answers will decrease and the experts' views will converge towards a "correct" answer - if at all. Incidentally, this process is known as the Delphi method, so named after the Oracle of Delphi, the high priestess at the Temple of Apollo at Delphi, in Greek mythology.

Is the Delphi method then the most powerful forecast method? In the seminal book *Noise: A Flaw in Human Judgment* (2021) written by Daniel Kahneman and his associates, it is recommended as one of the best methods we have to reduce "noise", and hence make the crystal ball a bit clearer.

Suppose we rounded up a hundred experts (both Western and Russian) on Soviet Russia in late 1989, and asked them to predict the future of the U.S.S.R., or in 2006, put a hundred of the world's top financial analysts on the task of forecasting the state of the market in the next couple of years. Would these experts have forecast the downfall of the U.S.S.R. or the global financial crisis? For the second example, such a forecast actually exists. That is the report of the World Economic Forum held in February 2008 in Davos. You are invited to try your luck (and skill), but when this author tried to find it in the relevant website a couple of years afterwards, it was no longer available, probably because it is too embarrassing to all those who had attended the Forum and expressed their expert opinions.

Since even the topmost experts of the world could not foresee such a calamity as the 2008 Global Financial Meltdown just months beforehand, it gives me great encouragement to venture forth my own projections for a world 50 and 500 years in the future. These projections will in all likelihood be way off the mark, but what is there to lose?

7.4 Courage and
Imagination

Having been introduced to several different methods of forecast, let us now return to the subject of futurology, which, as the name readily suggests, is all about the future. American futurologist Alvin Toffler's 1970 ground-breaking book *Future Shock* first introduced futurology as an area of academic inquiry, at least to the general public. Two years later in 1972, *Limits to Growth*, a report compiled by the Club of Rome (an international think tank of politicians and academics drawn from a wide range of disciplines that concerned themselves with how to solve problems faced by humanity collectively...), concluded for the first time ever that

'...the exponential economic and population growth would most probably result in a sudden and uncontrollable decline in population and industrial capacity.'

Readers of science fiction will say that initial attempts to forecast the future long predates academic works such as *Future Shock* and *Limits to Growth*. While Asimov concerned himself with the distant future in his Foundation trilogy, French writer Jules Verne (1828-1905) had already made a series of spectacular predictions on future technologies such as space flight to the Moon (*From the Earth to the Moon* 1865) and undersea voyage in a submarine (*Twenty Thousand Leagues Under the Sea* 1869-70), all these in the latter 19th century. Toward the end of that century, English writer, futurist, and visionary H.G. Wells (1866-1946) elevated the imagined future to a whole new level. In his novel *The Time Machine* (1895), considered one of Wells' best, he painted a spine-chilling picture of a future world, in which extreme polarization has driven class distinction beyond social and political and became biological.

By mid-20th century, science fiction was well ahead of academic inquiry in dealing with catastrophic environmental collapse. British science fiction writer John Brunner (1934-1995) wrote his innovative yet poignant 1968 novel *Stand on Zanzibar*, the title figuratively depicting a projected 7 billion global population in 2010 standing shoulder to shoulder on the island of Zanzibar, in east Africa. The horrifying prospect of a world vastly overpopulated was there for all to see.

Many readers would have heard of, if not actually seen, the 1968 movie *2001: A Space Odyssey*, hailed as both a motion picture and science fiction classic, and based on a short story by the British science fiction writer Arthur C. Clarke. Clarke is a master of speculation with his many science fiction stories, but when it comes to how to do it, the most thoughtful and inspiring work has to be his non-fiction writing in *Profiles of the Future: An Inquiry into the Limits of the Possible* (1962). Clarke pointed out in this book two pitfalls in forecasting the future: a Failure of Nerve and a Failure of Imagination.

The failure of nerve renders bold predictions unacceptable, and history is full of such examples:

• Scientists in early 19th century still found the notion that rocks falling from space (meteorites) too bizarre to believe;

• In 1895 British scientist Lord Kelvin (1824-1907) proclaimed "I can state flatly that heavier-than-air flying machines are impossible". The Wright brothers proved him wrong eight years year;

• Einstein would not believe in 1934 that a controlled release of atomic energy was possible. Eight years later this was achieved by Enrico Fermi and others in Chicago;

• A mere ten years before Apollo 11, most people dismissed landing a man on the Moon as a 'pie in the sky' fantasy.

The above instances are examples of our collective 'failure of nerve' in refusing to accept the possibility of new ideas becoming reality, even recoiling in horror at the logical endpoints of new developments. In the last chapter we have seen how linear extrapolation, aka the "persistence" method in tropical cyclone forecast works, but even with such a crude method, many people still refuse to accept the conclusion.

Contemporary examples of our collective failure of nerve, with global repercussions, can include our stubborn refusal to contemplate the possibility of a global financial meltdown before 2008, although there were loads of evidence pointing in that direction; the unsustainable nature of compound economic growth; and runaway global warming pushing the world and humanity to the brink of calamity. People who hold that space travel beyond the Solar System to the distant stars will never be possible, or computers becoming conscious (albeit a highly controversial development), or *a technological singularity*, also count as failures of nerve.

Next, instances of a 'failure of imagination':

• French philosopher Auguste Comte, in his 1835 work *The Course on Positive Philosophy*, said humankind would never know the chemical composition of stars. Within the next half century astronomers and physicists have begun analysing stellar spectra to find that out.

• Toward the end of the 19th century people began to worry as horse-drawn carriages increased, London roads might soon be buried under mountains of horse dung, not expecting that the newly invented automobile was already poised to take over roads in London and everywhere else.

• As the telephone became a household and business must-have, and its network expanded, people predicted that soon the world would run short of copper metal and its price would skyrocket. The invention and commercialisation of the optic fibre cable not only replaced copper as the material of choice, it also opened up a whole new vista of cabling a global communication network.

• In 1943, when asked about the future prospect of the computer industry, Thomas Watson, president of IBM replied, "I think there is a world market for maybe five computers."

• When personal computers first came on the scene, many forecast that non-English speaking peoples would be entirely left out of this technological revolution, because computers could only handle English. Nowadays, computers could not just handle English, but are able to translate between different languages.

Laugh as we might, we are no better when we are asked to contemplate future development of our modern-day society. Take the concepts of garbage and trash as waste, which is essentially a product of the industrial society. Left on its own, Nature generates no waste: everything is recycled. Can this be achieved in the human society as well? This is the central idea of the "Zero-to-Landfill Initiative" or "Cradle-to-Cradle Economy." Yet most people would think not. Again, a failure of imagination.

Failure of nerve and failure of imagination are not mutually exclusive. There is an overlap between the two. Both serve as a stark reminder that we should always keep an open mind, and avoid writing off something new as impossible. American literary critic and philosopher Fredric Jameson once said, "It is now easier to imagine the end of the world than an end to capitalism." Viewed in the light of the current state of global affairs, Jameson's poignant remark is a vivid description of a combined collective failure of nerve and imagination of humanity.

Clarke, in his *Profiles of the Future*, also put forward his famous Three Laws:

1. When a distinguished but elderly scientist states that something is possible, they are almost certainly right. When they state that something is impossible, they are very probably wrong.

2. The only way to discover the limits of the possible is to venture past them into the realm of the impossible.

3. Any sufficiently advanced technology is indistinguishable from magic.

It is also worth noting this other quote from Clarke: "We tend to over-forecast in the short term, and under-forecast in the long term." The reason behind this is not hard to understand. Changes take time but when we are confronted with something novel and exciting, we often forget this, and come up with over-optimistic forecasts. On the contrary, due to our limited life experience - mostly under a century - we are not able to conceive changes that could be achieved in the long term. Hence the tendency to under-forecast.

Isaac Asimov, the prolific American science fiction writer and a contemporary of Clarke, once said, "What is really amazing, and frustrating, is mankind's habit of refusing to see the obvious and inevitable until it is there, and then muttering about unforeseen catastrophes." (*Asimov on Science Fiction,* 1981). There is no better summing up of human ineptitude when confronted by technological, social, and historical changes.

Readers are exhorted to keep in mind the wise words of Asimov and Clarke when we attempt to predict the future of humanity.

8

2070 – 50 Years into the Future (1)

8.1 History Past and
Future

An Outline of History written by English writer and social critic H.G. Wells was published in 1920, just a few years after the end of World War I. In the Introduction, Wells wrote "There can be no peace now, we realize, but a common peace in all the world; no prosperity but a general prosperity. But *there can be no common peace and prosperity without common historical ideas*. Without such ideas to hold them together in harmonious co-operation, with nothing but narrow, selfish, and conflicting nationalist traditions, races and peoples are bound to drift towards conflict and destruction."

Wells' words echoed the horror that was World War I. More than a century later, his observation has become even more pertinent to the times. Like it or not, the world is now locked in the embrace of a common fate, after having gone through more than half a century of relentless globalization. No country can stand aloof and expect others to deal with global issues such as climate change, ecological collapse, the rising sea level, global pandemic, trade wars, financial crises, recessions, social upheaval, influx of refugees, all-pervasive network surveillance, rise of artificial intelligence, terrorism, resurgence of fascism... The list goes on.

With this situation as a given, let us try to speculate what the world will become 50 years from now (2020). [The Chinese edition of this book was published in early 2020, and this English edition was published in 2023. While updates to the contents have been made throughout the book to reflect important developments since 2020, the following chapters will continue to adopt 2020 as the starting point for the 50 and 500 years projections.]

How long is 50 years? To an individual, 50 years is the better part of his/her life. A young person aged 20 will be an old person in 50 years.

In terms of the thousands even tens of thousands of years of human history, 50 years is a short time. The Old Kingdom period in ancient Egypt lasted 800 years, the Shang dynasty in ancient China 600 years. To these histories, 50 years is a short time.

But when it comes to modern and contemporary history, 50 years can be an interestingly long time. Take the half century from 1770 to 1820: America became independent, France had a revolution, the Napoleonic wars were fought, the steam engine invented, and the Industrial Revolution took off. Another even more interesting half century, this one from 1900 to 1950: a major recession, two world wars, invention of nuclear weapon and the electronic computer, establishment of the United Nations, independence of India, and the rise of the People's Republic of China, among other events big and small. Yet another illustration of the accelerating pace of civilisation mentioned...

As I explained at the very beginning, just as a long jump athlete requires a sprint to jump far, and an archer drawing back the bow in order to shoot the arrow, we need to look back in order to look forward. So, for heuristic purpose, with 2020 as our origin, let us look back 50, 100, and 150 years at the world in 1970, 1920 and 1870, respectively.

By 1970 humans has already landed on the Moon (1969). Starting with the May 1968 college student protests in France, Western countries witnessed large scale anti-war and counter-culture campus protests. Laser was invented 12 years ago, the integrated circuit (IC) 11 years ago, and the hydrogen bomb 18 years ago. 1970 was also the year just before the U.S. dollar was unpegged from the price of gold, when the horror of the Vietnam war, where the sky rained Agent Orange or incendiary bombs, was brought for all to see on the TV screen, while not far away in China, an equally tragic human madness was unfolding behind a Bamboo Curtain in the form of the Cultural Revolution. Computers, although in widespread use, still operated with magnetic tape and punch cards, and personal computing, electronic mail (email), internet and smart phones were still at least two decades away in the future. But eight years later, in 1978, the first baby fertilized *in vitro* (aka test tube baby) was born. It is also worth noting that, back then, the atmospheric concentration of carbon dioxide was just 325 parts per million, or ppm. (By 2020 it has gone up to 415ppm)

Go back further, to 1920. It was the year after the May Fourth Movement in Republican China, 2 years after the end of World War I, the year after the Treaty of

Versailles was signed and the League of Nations established. Women in America had just won the right to vote (women in Britain achieved it slightly earlier, in 1918, but was restricted to those aged 30 or older and herself or her husband owning property). The U.S. Federal Reserve system, operating as a central bank, was in its eighth year of operation. The Ku Klux Klan ran rampant in parts of the continental U.S. Civil aviation took off, only 17 years after the first powered aircraft took flight. The first radio broadcast was made, but the moving picture has yet to grow a voice. The telephone and television have yet to be widely adopted. The first ever antibiotic, Penicillin, was eight years in the future. The atmospheric concentration of CO_2 was 300 ppm.

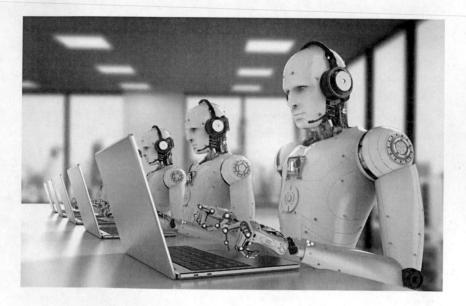

What about 1870? It was four years after Alfred Nobel invented dynamite, and seven years after the emancipation of African American slave labour. Meanwhile, on the other side of the world, the Meiji Restoration in Japan had gone on to its third year, the Self-Strengthening Movement in China its tenth. India became part of the British Empire 12 years before, Hong Kong had been her colony for 28 years, and it would seem 'the sun never set' anywhere within her Dominion. Charles Darwin published his *On the Origin of Species* in 1859, Karl Marx his 3-volume *Das Kapital* from 1867 to 1883. Gas light was still the most advanced form of outdoor public lighting in Western countries and Japan, and horse-drawn carriages plied the mostly unpaved city streets:

the electric light and automobile, as we know them, had yet to be invented. Wireless telegraphy is 30 years in the future. Women worldwide did not have the right to vote. Atmospheric CO_2 concentration was only 285 ppm.

Having read through the previous paragraphs, it is clear that any historian or science fiction writer bold enough to try to sketch an imaginary world of 2070 would be facing a daunting - if not impossible - task. It would not be wrong to say, just as someone living in 1870 would find it next to impossible to imagine a world in 1920, and just as impossible for someone in 1920 to imagine the world in 1970, we in 2020 would find it just as much an impossible mission to imagine the world of 2070.

If imagining the world 50 years from now is so impossible, does it mean we should not bother? Of course not! And that is exactly why I write this book. To those in posterity, 50 years from now, what I have written may look childish and naïve, but not without meaning or a purpose. We may be unable to foresee everything, but at least we can make projections from what is here and now and extrapolate from what we know. The main purpose is reveal dangerous trends, and put up signs of "don't go this way!" As long as we approach this challenge with our best imagination and a dose of humility, bearing in mind constantly that which ultimately matters are probably things we are completely ignorant of, we will not be too far off the mark.

Knowing What
Questions to Ask

While science is often seen as an activity focussing on finding answers to the "mysteries of the Universe," Sir Arthur S. Eddington, famous English astronomer of the early 20th century who helped to prove the validity of Einstein's General Theory of Relativity, once said "When it comes to scientific inquiry, asking questions is often more important than looking for answers." The simple truth is that if we don't know what pertinent questions to ask in the first place, how would we be able to seek for the answers? As a matter of fact, the Chinese word for 'knowledge' already embodies this concept as it comprises two characters which translate to "learning to" "ask."

British physicist Lord Kelvin (1824-1907) also said, "When you can measure what you are speaking about, and express it in numbers, you know something about it; but when you cannot measure it, when you cannot express it in numbers, your knowledge is of a meagre and unsatisfactory kind…"

Guided by such wisdom, I have listed twenty questions all of which require a number as answer. These answers will give useful hints how the world might look like in 2070.

1. What will the atmospheric concentration of CO_2 be?

2. What will the per capita CO_2 emission be?

3. How much higher would the mean sea level be compared to today?

4. How many climate refugees would there be worldwide?

5. By how much had wildlife been (diversity as well as quantity) reduced compared to the early 21st century?

6. What is the world population?

7. What is the average human lifespan?

8. What is the average retirement age?

9. What is the world's per capita GDP?

10. How much is the disparity between the rich and the poor (the Gini coefficient)?

11. How many people (and in terms of percentage of world population) are living below the poverty line/threshold?

12. What is the total global debt?

13. How many countries are there in the world?

14. How many permanent member states make up the United Nations Security Council?

15. How many countries possess nuclear weapons?

16. How many ICBMs with nuclear warheads are there in the world?

17. How many countries allow their people to elect the head of state by universal suffrage?

18. What is the maximum operating speed of computers? Or does the Moore's Law, which predicts a doubling in computer operating speed every two years, still apply?

19. What is the maximum information storage density?

20. What is the length of the average working week?

The list can go on: how many cars in the world, how many flights per day, how many nuclear power plants in the world, how many robot domestic helpers each household owns..., and what is the acidity/alkalinity of the oceans, and the demographic percentages of university graduates, internet usage, employed in manufacturing, vegans...etc.

While many more questions could certainly be asked, I do believe that answers to the above twenty questions can already outline what kind of a future will be waiting for us.

Instead of dealing with each question in their order, I propose to group them in order of relatedness for discussion and analysis.

I regard the questions 1 to 5 to be of crucial importance to any future world, so I would leave them to the next chapter/section.

I shall deal with those questions about world population.

World population increased from 1.6 billion in 1900 to 6 billion in 2000. The 3.75-fold increase in just 100 hundred years is unprecedented in human history. Demographers have estimated that the total number of people alive within this 100 years has exceeded the total number of people that had ever existed in the last million years up to 1900. By the end of 2022, the United Nations announced that the global population has already reached the 8-billion mark. While population growth is expected to slow down, it is still expected to reach 9.8 billion by 2050, and to 11.2 billion by 2100. This means that by our target year of 2070, the world population might well have exceeded the 10 billion mark.

For those who are accustomed to huge numbers (think of the 1.9 trillion dollars of the US Covid-19 recovery package), this 2 billion increase may not seem much. The truth is that this increase of 2 billion people from now till 2070 is larger than the size of the world population in 1900, and in a world much impoverished and vulnerable than the one in 1900. Note that the birth rate in developed nations has for a long time been close to zero, meaning that the growth in world population would come predominantly from Third World countries, with all that that entails.

In addition, leaving aside any humanitarian disaster - and wars - brought about by a complete collapse of the natural environment, people in rich nations and poor are going to live longer, thanks to improvement in public hygiene and advance in medicine. In particular, people living in affluence would probably achieve a lifespan of more than 100, or even 120 years. Centenarians would become the expected norm, and there would be an increasing number of super- and ultracentenarians.

While the lengthening of the average human lifespan is something to be celebrated, it does pose a problem to public spending: how would society pay for the ever-increasing cost of retirement income and age care? Would people in the future agree to lifting the legal retirement age in step with the lengthening of lifespan, so as to prevent the working population from shrinking? (Imagine having to work when you are 80 or 90 years old…) Would younger people be worse off in jobs and career advancement opportunities if more and more people worked until a much older age? In short, are we prepared for - and would we want - a super-geriatric society? (Like it or not this trend might already have begun, with the incumbent president of the U.S.A. Joe Biden inaugurated at 78, and the comeback of the former Malaysian president Mahathir bin Mohamad even older at 94!)

Quite aside from the quantity of life - lifespan - what about the quality of life, especially in the last decades of a supercentenarian?

Society would be subject to an even greater burden, if some, or most, supercentenarians had lost their self-care capability and had to spend their final decades in intensive care.

Problems caused by an aging society, already evident in many developed countries, are expected to worsen in future. Left unsolved, the double whammy of a lengthening lifespan coupled with a low (even close to zero) birth rate would be disastrous to the economy, and to the future of humanity at large. In a capitalist economy, a dwindling labour force with demand exceeding supply would push up wages. At the same time, an older population tends to spend less. Both spell grave troubles to the *modus operandi* of capitalism.

From a long-term biological perspective, economic crisis would be the least of our concern because with death rate exceeding birth rate, the logical outcome is extinction of the human species.

The good news is, among the many difficult problems we are facing, the problem of an aging society is the easiest one to solve. An average birth rate of two per couple, otherwise known as the 'replacement level' birth rate, is all it takes to avoid either a population explosion or implosion. Demographers would suggest an actual practical number of 2.1 children per couple, taking into account factors such as celibacy, homosexuality, infertility and infant mortality.

On a global scale, United Nations experts have predicted that, as the consistently high birth rate in Third World countries becomes offset by a low birth rate in developed nations, world population would likely stabilize at about 12 billion at the beginning of the next century. This is no cause of celebration though, for between now and then, overpopulation and an aging society would continue to cause serious problems. In particular, the practice by affluent nations to help raise productivity with migrant labour will continue to create social tension. There are also problems caused by climate and war refugees.

What will the population scene be like in 2070? In a most ideal scenario, a replacement level birth rate is achieved in good time and maintained across the globe, the world population stabilizing at a manageable size, thus reducing regional tension and conflict as a result of overpopulation and massive involuntary movement of people. Replacement level birth rate ought to become basic knowledge worldwide, to be embraced as indispensable commonsense just like washing one's hand before eating.

The next question, 'What is the world's per capita GDP,' tests not only our optimism or otherwise toward the future of economy. It also requires our forecasting to go beyond the bounds of traditional economic inquiry, to encompass a study of the state of nature. Like it or not, future economists need to equip themselves with knowledge on how well, if at all, the environment is coping with human activities - if they would not want to risk becoming irrelevant.

Per capita values can be deceptive. One does not have to be a major in statistics to know that there can be an abysmal gap between the incomes of individuals and of nations. The next two questions therefore, the ones on the Gini coefficient and number of people living below the poverty threshold, can actually be rolled into one: 'would the world fifty years in the future be a more equal one, or one in which the rich and poor have moved even further apart, with more and more wealth in fewer and fewer hands?'

The United Nations announced its 15 Millennium Development Goals (MDGs) at the start of the century, hoping to achieve sweeping results principally in the global eradication of poverty and hunger by 2015. Having failed to meet many of these goals, the UN revamped the list and launched the SDGs - Sustainable Development Goals - in the same year, this time all 17 of them, to be achieved by 2030:

1. End poverty in all its forms everywhere.

2. End hunger, achieve food security and improved nutrition, and promote sustainable agriculture.

3. Ensure healthy lives and promote well-being for all at all ages.

4. Ensure inclusive and equitable quality education and promote lifelong learning opportunities for all.

5. Achieve gender equality and empower all women and girls.

6. Ensure availability and sustainable management of water and sanitation for all.

7. Ensure access to affordable, reliable, sustainable, and modern energy for all.

8. Promote sustained, inclusive, and sustainable economic growth, full and productive employment, and decent work for all.

9. Build resilient infrastructure, promote inclusive and sustainable industrialization, and foster innovation.

10. Reduce income inequality within and among countries.

11. Make cities and human settlements inclusive, safe, resilient, and sustainable.

12. Ensure sustainable consumption and production patterns.

13. Take urgent action to combat climate change and its impacts by regulating emissions and promoting developments in renewable energy.

14. Conserve and sustainably use the oceans, seas and marine resources for sustainable development.

15. Protect, restore and promote sustainable use of terrestrial ecosystems, sustainably manage forests, combat desertification, and halt and reverse land degradation and halt biodiversity loss.

16. Promote peaceful and inclusive societies for sustainable development, provide access to justice for all and build effective, accountable, and inclusive institutions at all levels.

17. Strengthen the means of implementation and revitalize the global partnership for sustainable development.

Will any of these 17 SDGs be met by 2030? What about by 2070? If so, would the world then be a much more equal and therefore safer place?

Achieving any one of these Goals is a Herculean task, let alone all 17 of them. It would involve complex political manoeuvring, careful economic planning, and comprehensive social re-engineering within national borders, with close coordination and cooperation beyond. Given the vast amount of entrenched interests operating in the global capitalist economy, a powerful pushback to necessary changes would be expected. One is hard pressed to be optimistic.

Next, we come to the question on the size of the global debt. This really is a question to challenge readers to envisage how the current over-financialization of our economy and the rise of Debt Civilization will pan out in the next 50 years. From another angle, we could ask how many more financial upheavals and recessions/depressions will the world experience from now till 2070 - even with the lessons we had learnt from the 2008 global meltdown? From yet another angle, we would like to know how big would the flow of "hot money" circulating around the globe be by 2070, especially in comparison with the global GDP? And what will be the outcome between the lure of "leveraging" and the call for "deleveraging"? An even more pertinent question is whether the American dollar hegemony would still hold sway, or would there be other international currencies that supplant - at least partially - its predominance? For the more pragmatic-minded investors, the most sought-after answers would be the values of key indices such as the Dow Jones or Nasdaq, or the price of cryptocurrencies, gold, and petroleum - or as depicted in science fiction stories - the price of clean air and clean water.

Needless to say, all investors (read everyone) would love to know the answers to these "trillion-dollar questions." If history is our best guide to the future, what lessons could we learn from what had transpired during the 50-year period from 1970 to 2020?

For all that talk about debt and finance, I personally find this next question vastly more interesting: '*How many countries are there in the world?*' My guess is most readers will gloss over this question thinking "it'd be more or less like today, wouldn't it? How else could it be?"

Looking back on the political history of the world in the half century from 1920 to 1970, the number of countries increased twofold, largely as a result of former colonies gaining independence. There is no foreseeable historic moment like this in the near future, but to think that the number of countries remaining the same for any lengthy period of time is naïve. Don't forget that Sikkim was once a sovereign country, but was subsumed into India in 1975, and Russia annexed Crimea from Ukraine in 2014. And the time of writing, the Russia invasion of Ukraine has been going on for over a year, with Russian vowing to "return Ukraine to the Motherland." With enormous bloodshed from both sides, the final outcome has yet to be settled.

On the contrary, the number of states could multiply. Think of the dissolution of the U.S.S.R. in 1992, creating some fifteen independent states; and Yugoslavia, breaking up into 5 countries. There may be states in the making too. Catalans, the people native to Catalonia in Spain, are still fighting for independence. So are the Kurds in the middle east. As of today, the United Nations has 193 member states but recognize 197. I am confident that these numbers would have changed in 50 years' time. Would you wage a bet? But I wouldn't be around in 50 years' time so win or lose…

It is even more interesting to ponder over the next question, "How many permanent member states make up the United Nations Security Council." As we all know that number has remained five (China, Britain, America, France, and Russia) since the end of WWII and the establishment of the United Nations, and the only five countries possessing the power to veto any resolution tabled at Council sessions. Needless to say, this current arrangement does not help in the least in advancing the cause of the United Nations, whose job has long been made harder by the confrontation between America and Russia, and more recently between America and China.

Neither is the General Assembly, nominally the highest authority in the United Nations hierarchy, any easier to work with. With 193 member states, it is virtually impossible to reach a consensus on any issue of global significance. Nor is the voting right accorded to each and every member state at the General Assembly convincingly democratic. States, regardless of their size and population, all have one vote each.

[Hong Kong, where I am from, boasts a population of 7,500,000, and Hong Kong is just a city. There are many sovereign states with populations much smaller than that of Hong Kong.] For example: Iceland's population is 300,000. Yet when it's time to vote at the General Assembly, Iceland's vote is the same as China's, with a population of 1.4 billion. This is not how the majority rule works.

To deal with global issues we need global leadership, and this is best performed by the United Nations. To make the United Nations work more effectively, it must be accorded the requisite authority. One approach is to review the Security Council membership to become truly representative. Adopting the list of member countries comprising the G20, made up of countries according to their economic performance and geopolitical influence, is a good start.

My following suggestions may appear to be far-fetched to the worldly-wise. However, they each has its own rationale. To further strengthen representation, I suggest adding three countries from the top ten list by population, which are not already in the G20 group of nations: Pakistan, Nigeria, and Bangladesh. Given Pakistan already has nuclear weapons, it is reasonable to add Israel - although never having admitted to owning nuclear weapons - to the Security Council membership, together with Israel's sworn foe, Iran, ranked 18th by order of population, and 25th on GDP.

I believe increasing the UN Security Council membership this way to 25, representing two-thirds of the world population, and with a two-thirds majority, i.e., 17 votes, carrying any motion, would make it so much more representative of the wishes of the world, and effective in tackling global challenges. No longer would any bloc of states, be it led by China, Russia, or America, be able to sway the Security Council, or for that matter the UN General Assembly, to their advantage. (The current practice of inviting non-permanent members from time to time as observers only without voting rights should of course be continued)

The next two questions (15 and 16) deal with nuclear-armed countries and nuclear armament, both requiring our urgent attention, and imperative of a solution. Global de-nuclearization is imperative. The future of humanity is at stake. In an all-out nuclear conflict, everyone's a loser. Current membership of the global Nuclear Club stands at nine: America, Russia, China, Britain, France, India, Pakistan, Israel, and North Korea. Yet there have been signs nuclear weapons are proliferating, and the risk of a nuclear war increasing. A reformed Security Council should put nuclear disarmament first on its agenda.

Question 17 looks at the state of health of democracy worldwide. In asking 'how many countries allow their people to elect the head of state by universal suffrage' I want to know if, in a world fifty years from now, democracy is alive and strong, or weakened and defeated. Has the sort of autocratic world portrayed in the novel *1984* come true? As we've seen in Chapter 5, regression in democracy across many regions and countries in the past two decades is deeply worrying. In half a century, if that regressive trend is not arrested, would autocracy take an even stronger hold on more states? Would there be a 'world dictatorship'? Would military strongmen now wielding unchecked influence in many parts of the world give rise to 'warlord states'? We shall come back to this discussion in a later section.

The next two questions, 18 and 19, have to do with computers. In trying to answer these questions we must visualize the possibilities afforded us by fifty years' worth of advancement in computing science and technology, such as optical and quantum computing. We would be curious about a future computer's capability: have they surpassed humanity, such that, for example, the affairs of the U.N. Security Council can be managed by an AI-algorithm armed with nothing but the most benign intentions toward humanity. (This future scenario was actually described by the American science fiction writer Isaac Asimov in *The Evitable Conflict*, published in 1950) Has the AI acquired consciousness? Would we be able to upload our minds to a machine? Would the "Technological Singularity" so eagerly waited for by some enthusiasts become reality? And even if it is, what percentage of the world's population will thus be uploaded? And what would be the relationship between these "immortals" and those left behind?

Returning to a much more mundane level, my last question is 'what would be the length of an average working week' by 2070. This question may seem trivial but is also profound. Let us look back at the past. The week is a relatively recent invention, having originated from the Jewish Sabbath. Our distant ancestors worked almost all year round. They had neither the 'week' in their calendar, nor had rest days regularly, apart from seasonal festivities and ancestral obligations. For example, it wasn't until 1929 that the Americans began to enjoy a 5-day working week. In the developed world, it is now universal practice to work 5 or 6 days a week a vast improvement from ancient times (although 'voluntary overtime work' is becoming more and more commonplace under the onslaught of neoliberalism and globalization).

Or is it? Anthropologists and archaeologists have found that our ancestors did not actually work more than we, even when they did not enjoy a regular day or two off, or take vacation leave. True, ancient people generally work through the day and rest during hours of darkness, but work and break weren't that strictly demarcated. They were their own masters with work and rest, somewhat like what a lot of us experienced working from home in Covid lockdowns. Even now, in many countries, people still practise the siesta and take a nap after lunch and during the hottest time of the day. (The Chinese government legislated to abolish this practice as a custom only in the 1980s, when the country opened up for economic development)

There is yet another finding which points to the leisurely lifestyle of ancient humans. In gathering-hunting societies as studied by anthropologists over the past two centuries, people need only to spend four to five hours each day hunting prey or gathering food to sustain themselves. They spend the rest of the day socializing and caring for family. Compare this with a modern-day professional person working ten or more hours a day - and bringing work home too. Our lifestyle may well be modern, but it can hardly be called 'progress.'

An even shorter working week might well be on the agenda, but not because this will give us more free time. Some researchers believe, as robots and AI become more and more common in the workplace, the remaining manual work ought to be shared by workers made jobless by automation. This would alleviate the social dislocation resulting from mass unemployment. A shorter working week might also put a brake on economic activity in general, reducing carbon emission, and hence environmental degradation, in the process.

At the time of writing, 4-day week pilot programmes are set to start in the US and Ireland, with more planned for Canada, Australia, and New Zealand. It awaits to be seen if this would catch on to become the new normal.

All in all, the way we approach and answer the questions posed in this chapter reveal our hopes and fears about the future. Now that we have gone through the last 15 questions, it is time we return to the first five, which I consider the most important, as the future - or otherwise - of humanity hangs on those answers.

8.3 ▶ Nature's
Red Card

To gauge what the world would be like in 2070, the 5 environment-related questions I have drawn up are:

1. What is the atmospheric CO_2 concentration by then?

2. What is the per capita CO_2 emission by then?

3. How much higher is the mean sea level compared to today?

4. How many climate refugees are there worldwide?

5. How much less wildlife is there compared to early 21st century?

Imminent collapse of the environment/ecology is a problem we have come across many times in the first half of this book. Here I shall reword this problem simply as: what is the atmospheric CO_2 concentration in 50 years' time?

In early 2023, atmospheric CO_2 concentration is close to 420 ppm, an increase of about 50% from the 280ppm in 1850, the early days of the Industrial Revolution. Scientists have estimated once atmospheric CO_2 concentration exceeded 450ppm, the rise in global average temperature would also exceed the dangerous threshold of 2°C, initiating numerus feedback loops in Nature and causing extensive environmental degradation and calamities. The most horrific nightmare is the large-scale thawing of the permafrost in Siberia, Alaska, and Tibetan Plateau, thus releasing huge amounts of methane, another highly potent greenhouse gas. The greenhouse effect would thus be pushed into overdrive, and global warming would enter a runaway phase.

A warming of 2°C, as it turned out, is way over the safety limit. Most recent research has shown that a threshold of 1.5°C must not be breached if we do not want the 'permafrost time bomb' to go off releasing methane and aggravating global warming. At the current rate of warming, this 1.5°C threshold would be reached by 2030 latest. Humanity has less than 10 years left to take decisive and drastic action to halt warming dead in the track, or risk plunging the entire world into a climatic maelstrom.

The sad reality is that bold and swift actions are still absent from the agenda of the world's governments. As such, the global average temperature in 2070 could be as much as 3°C to 4°C above that of 1850 - and this is a conservative estimate. Humanity collectively would be locked in a climate meltdown with no prospect of being arrested let alone reversed. The planet's ecology would be devastated. Food production would stall. Epidemics would run rampant.

Calculations have also shown that, to keep the rise in global average temperature under the 1.5°C threshold, humanity must, by 2030, bring the total carbon emission down to half the current level, and to further reduce it to absolute zero by 2050. The answer to the second question, in other words the per capita carbon emission in 2070, should ideally be zero.

How does humanity get to a per capita carbon emission of zero by 2050? The logical answer is a complete phasing out of all fossil fuels including coal, gas, and oil, with a corresponding upscaling of carbon-free renewable energy such as solar, wind, wave, geothermal, and some degree of nuclear energy to satisfy all energy needs. This will require as much as 30 times more generating capacity from renewable than they do today. For countries and regions which have yet to embark on the path to renewable energy, it would be an even more monumental task.

On the other hand, if the answer to question 2 turns out to be 'a much higher per capita carbon emission than today', or 'more or less the same as now', then humanity is doomed. We would have to deal with frequent and murderous heat waves, unextinguishable raging wildfires, prolonged periods of drought, super hurricanes/ typhoons, ravaging floods, an increasingly acidic ocean environment, more critical shortage of food and water, frequent and virulent epidemics…More than a few scientists have pointed out that in this global calamity, it would be the people of the Third World contributing the least to the cause yet suffering the worst of the consequence. This is the spectre of 'climate injustice,' a challenge often raised in international forums on climate change.

Question 3 poses the prospect of an even more severe impact. Over the past hundred years, the expansion of sea water under warming, and the melting of the Greenland ice shelf and glaciers around the world have together raised the mean sea level by more than 20 cm. Here it must be noted that the melting of floating ice packs, for instance, in the Arctic Ocean, does not raise the mean sea level, as the ice is floating on the water surface. The ice sheet over Greenland is another matter. It is calculated that if all the ice over Greenland melt, sea level the world over will rise by 7 meters.

Let us not forget that all the water in the world's oceans act as a gigantic heat sink, storing a vast amount of heat. Even if by a stroke of miracle, carbon emission can be halted abruptly tomorrow, heat released by the oceans will continue to raise global temperatures and in turn cause more sea level rise. This is estimated optimistically at a further 20 to 30 cm.

But what if we cannot halt our carbon emission, at all? While the latest Assessment Report No. 6 (AR6) released by the UN's Intergovernmental Panel on Climate Change (IPCC) in 2021 puts the rise at around 1 meter by 2100 in their "worst-case scenario" (in terms of unabated carbon emission), many scientists view this as too conservative. A 2-meter rise is deemed a more likely outcome. If that is the case, the mean sea level could well be a whole meter above the current level by 2070. Needless to say, all coastal population centres would be severely affected, with the likes of Miami and Venice inundated for most time of the year. Some scientists projected that up to 2 billion people could be displaced by the end of this century and become climate refugees. Depending on our answer to question 4, we are painfully reminded that in comparison, Europe's refugee problem today might very likely just be a pale shadow of the true calamity to come.

As a matter of fact, the melting of the polar ice caps in the last few decades has caught scientists by surprise. With average temperatures well below freezing all year round, the increase since 1850 of 1.2°C in global average temperature should not have much effect on polar ice. However, average temperature rise can be misleading. Over high latitude regions, such as the polar regions, temperatures can rise much more than at lower latitudes. (one reason is the Albedo Effect when loss of snow and ice cover leads to greater absorption of more solar radiation and hence more melting...) One example was found in Greenland, where the average ground temperature there has risen by as much as 4°C in the past century.

Around the Antarctic continent, ocean currents warm the ice shelves around the edge of the continent, causing them to melt rapidly. These ice shelves sit on top of the Antarctic landmass and extends out to the surrounding ocean floating on water. If, as scientists project, one of the major ice shelves, the West Antarctic Ice Shelf, was to melt completely, the immense amount of water will raise the sea surface by 23 meters.

It must be pointed out that sea level rise would not happen overnight. Whether it turns out to be 7 or 23 meters, the scenario depicted in scientific studies would be a gradual process lasting decades or even centuries. Sure, there would be time to act. But would we be able to turn it around?

While the sea surface would not rise abruptly overnight, there might be another time bomb which could detonate any time now. That which has caused scientists much anguish and concern is the melting of the permafrost, exposing ancient animal remains such as the mammoths which had hitherto been buried for thousands of years, and hidden latent in these partially putrefied remains bacteria and virus coming back to life once exposed. The possibility is all too real of these ancient pathogens, totally unrecognisable to our immune system and causing entirely unknown reactions and novel diseases. The ensuing pandemic would be too catastrophic to contemplate.

Which brings us to question 5, the one about the health of the ecology. The conclusion may sound tragic: unless humanity manages to arrest the current trend and turn things around, the prospect of a Sixth Extinction occurring in the Anthropocene, causing widespread human suffering and the dying off of vast number of animal and plant species, is unavoidable.

Faced with the likelihood of the collapse of the ecology, and of civilization, seed vaults - a modern day Noah's Ark - have been constructed in several locations, with the Svalbard Global Seed Vault the most notable. With the subterranean vault built into the geological inert and stable island landmass of Spitsbergen, Norway, it came as a striking blow of irony when, in October 2016, melt and rain water caused by unusually warm weather and high rainfall seeped 15 meters into the access tunnel. The seed storage area was luckily not affected but the fickle nature of global warming was there for all to see.

Is global warming all that bad? Should we not expect warming to be beneficial? It is true there may be benefits. A higher atmospheric concentration of carbon dioxide will speed up photosynthesis in plants and so increase crop growth. A generally warmer climate will reduce the fatalities associated with cold weather, such as hypothermia or accidents in a snowy environment. Countries fringing the Arctic Ocean may also benefit from the melting of polar ice, freeing up long hoped-for maritime passages and vastly improving access to resource exploitation, such as undersea oil and gas. Russia and Canada may set to reap the greatest benefit from global warming, as they would suddenly find a lot more freeze-free land available for agriculture. Siberia and the Canadian provinces of Yukon, Northwest Territory and Nunavut might well become future food baskets to the world.

And yet, all these as yet unrealised benefits, would in all probability be more than offset by the world wide devastation wrought by global warming.

The history of humankind has entered a highly critical phase. If civilization could be compared to sailing down a river, humanity has entered a section of angry torrents and treacherous rapids, and if we want to pass through this treacherous stretch of water intact and unharmed - at least relatively so - we together would have to summon our most profound wisdom, our greatest courage, and our strongest determination. Should humanity prove it is not up to the challenge, civilization would be ripped up going through the rapids, and countless lives would perish as a result.

It is worth repeating a passage I wrote in Chapter 3.2 about the human predicament. The 21st century will definitely be a 'bottleneck' in human history, and civilisation will reach, within this century, a big turning point. However, it makes a world of difference, and of life and death, between taking the bull by the horns in a deliberate, purposeful, and knowledgeable mobilisation and transformation process, or being forced to endure the destruction and misery when everything come crashing down.

How could it be explained then, that in the face of imminent disaster, the majority of us still do not feel a sense of urgency? One explanation has to do with our inability to grasp the true power of compound growth. Visualize duckweed growing in a large pond, doubling its coverage of the pond's water surface every day. Now imagine you were the gardener looking after this pond. Seeing that half the pond was already covered, you reassured yourself that there would still be days before the duckweed covered the pond completely, and you would not need to deal with it yet, only to find, on the very next day, and to your utter dismay, that the duckweed had covered the entire surface of the pond, and the fish, plus whatever creatures living in the pond, had all been suffocated to death. All of us humans are both the gardener tasked with looking after the pond, and the creatures living in it.

Scaremongering you will say. True, and it is only fair for the average people on the street to assume, on a day-to-day basis, that tomorrow will not be so different from today. How else would we lead our lives if every other day turns out to be an upheaval of the previous? Given this popular mindset, it is no wonder that warnings of 'imminent drastic changes' are dismissed as scaremongering. "We still have time to tackle this" is what most people think.

Psychologists also explain this complacency as one's natural desire and tendency to seek and remain in one's "comfort zone," and to be made to leave one's comfort zone is something utterly dreaded. The good news is that in recent years, the threat of climate change has finally entered the mainstream news, and none other than the UN Secretary-General Antonio Guterres and Pope Francis have repeatedly made a call for action, with world leaders at least paying lip service. The bad news is that people are still more concerned about the "clear and present dangers" of inflation, fuel shortages, the Ukrainian war, return of the pandemic, banking collapse, refugees, and terrorism etc. Fighting climate change just has to take the back-seat in face of such turmoils.

So, what do we do? There is some good news, and bad. Let me share with you the good news first: our civilization CAN continue WITHOUT consuming any more fossil fuels.

It is a long and widely held misconception that a world powered by 100% renewable energy is sheer fantasy. Science shows, however, that the total solar energy falling on the Earth's surface is 8000 times what we need to power the entire world. Or, if we managed to capture all that energy for an hour or two, that would be sufficient for all our energy need for a year. In the Sahara Desert, where the Sun shines fiercely from sunset to sundown, an area 600 kilometres on each side is all that would be needed to capture solar energy to power the whole world.

Solar energy can be captured directly with so-called photovoltaic panels, large arrays of connected semiconducting material sandwiched between glass plates which converts sunlight into electricity. Solar energy can also be harvested from wind and wave, both driven by the Sun's heating effect on the air in the atmosphere, and the water in the sea. No wonder that an environmentalist proclaimed, "if the 21st century does not become the solar energy century, it will become humanity's last century!"

Yet another source of energy is geothermal, which is entirely different from solar energy. This is heat dissipated from deep underground and caused by the decay of radioactive elements. Scientists believe harnessing geothermal energy on a global scale with currently available technology is more than sufficient to satisfy the energy need of the entire world.

But is this happening? Like it or not, the bad news is: NO! The explanation? Such drastic revamping of the power industry would be too disruptive, not economically 'cost-effective' and therefore not in the best interest of the 'market' so say politicians and some economists. Needless to say, Big Oil and Big Coal are fighting the change all the way, and have been spreading misinformation with astronomical amounts of money. A still very much unshakeable blind faith in the market under corporate brainwashing has led humanity down this ridiculous road to ruin.

Experts across many disciplines have long since argued, save having to go into a global mobilisation mode with rationing such as in a time of war (such as what took place in the US after the Pearl Harbour attack), a carbon tax is the most effective and practical way to curb carbon emission. This carbon tax is to be adjusted upward annually, in step with the ramping up of renewable energy supply, to achieve a complete phasing out of fossil fuels over time. At the same time, governments are to facilitate the growth and adoption of renewable energy sources with financial assistance and tax concession, creating an unambiguous signal to the market that fossil fuel is a sunset industry and investing in renewables is the right and financially sound way forward. In the process energy price could go up, and it is here that carbon tax revenue should be used to relieve low-income household of a higher cost of living.

This scheme of things is not new, but after having been put forward more than two decades ago it is still, especially for those power-hungry and emission intensive economic powerhouses such as China, the U.S., India, Russia, Japan, and Germany, not in the pipe-line. As a sad example, the traditionally fossil-fuel driven Australian economy garnered a global first when a carbon tax was implemented in July 2012 by the Gillard Labor government. However, it was repealed as soon as the pro-fossil fuel Liberal-National coalition government returned to power in the September 2013 federal election, making it possibly the shortest-lived carbon tax regime in human history.

Let us return to the projection for 2070. Would it be a time when the carbon tax has accomplished its mission of winding back global carbon emission to zero? Or one in which we are forced into rationing of emission quotas under martial law…because humanity has run out of options?

My guess is that by 2070, the global situation had become so dire, and the environment on the brink of collapse, that humanity had no alternative but to resort to the highly controversial, and as of to date as yet unproven, suite of geoengineering technologies to try save themself from eventual demise. One such proposal is to put up gigantic parasols or sunshields in orbit around the Earth, to block or reflect incoming solar energy thus reducing its heating effect on land, water, and air. Another equally challenging idea is to inject huge amounts of airborne particles in the form of sulphate aerosols, also to reflect and scatter sunlight coming in from space. Huge fleets of aircrafts will have to be employed and the injection will have to be repeated at regular (say yearly) intervals.

These technologies do not however address the root cause of global warming which is a runaway greenhouse effect caused by carbon emission from human activities. Although advocates of geoengineering claim the technologies could reduce warming to give humanity a badly needed breathing space, it is the consensus of the science community that this approach amounts to giving up humanity's control on his carbon emission, and the consequent and increasingly rapid rise of atmospheric carbon dioxide. In any event, risky as it is to try solving a proven problem (global warming) with an unproven solution (geoengineering), by 2070 we might have no more options open to us.

An optimistic scenario is one in which, not only had we managed to curb all carbon emission, we had also scrubbed the atmosphere of carbon dioxide. Of course, this would mean not only a complete replacing of fossil fuel with renewable to power the world, but renewables generating such surplus energy as to enable CO_2 scrubbing to take place. Still, this scenario leaves us with the problem of how, and where, to dispose of the scrubbed CO_2, which process would also add to power consumption.

In 2020, famous science fiction Kim Stanley Robinson published a novel called *The Ministry for the Future*, in which he laid out in frightening detail humankind's gargantuan and arduous efforts in fighting climate catastrophe within the 21st century. Although a work of fiction, this is highly worth reading to understand the dire choices in front of us.

It was James Hansen, when he was a NASA climate scientist, who argued in 2007 that an atmospheric CO_2 concentration of at most 350 ppm (350 parts per million) is one to keep "if humanity wishes to preserve a planet similar to that on which civilization developed and to which life on Earth is adapted." In other words, 350 ppm is the threshold which humanity shall strive at all costs not to cross. History shows the preindustrial CO_2 level was 280ppm. At the time James Hansen sounded his warning the CO_2 level was already at 385 ppm. It is now well above 420 ppm. Even under the most optimistic scenario, Hansen's goal would not be realised in several hundred years' time.

The dumping of vast amounts of carbon dioxide into the atmosphere continues, even in the three years of the global pandemic. The rise of that ppm number seems unstoppable. In fact, nothing seems to slow, let alone arrest, its upward trend. Not international conferences hosted by none other than the United Nations. Not grass root activists such as the U.S. based Avaaz and 350.org, or Swedish student turned environmental activist Greta Thunberg (who founded the School Strike for Climate movement in 2018). Not the global movement Extinction Rebellion with their campaigns of civil disobedience and aggressive ways of protest. Not even massive loss of life and livelihood in climate disasters such as the Pakistan floods of 2022, when a whole one-third of the country was submerged by heavier than usual monsoon rains and water from melting glaciers.

In one of her many speeches, Thunberg said "I don't want your hope. I want you to panic, as if your house is on fire...... The eyes of future generations are upon us. And if you choose to fail us, we will never forgive you."

Environmentalist Tanya Steele highlighted the stark reality thus: "We are the first generation to know we are destroying the planet, and the last one that can do anything about it." Unfortunately, the "window of opportunity" for any effective actions is closing fast.

Amidst the horrendous record-breaking heat waves and wild fires of summer 2023, UN Secretary General Antonio Guterres proclaimed that the age of Global Warming had come to an end, because we had already entered the era of Global Boiling. Is this enough to jolt humankind out of their stupor? No one knows. As in a game of soccer, Nature has already shown us the yellow card countless times. Humanity has been booked for foul play. If we continue to ignore the warnings, it will be game over when Nature has had enough and shows us the red card of expulsion.

8.4 ▷ The End of Growth

So, is blaming everything on fossil fuels then taking it out of the equation the answer to all ills? No! *Limits to Growth*, released in 1972, did not include global warming as a growth-limiting factor. Subsequent work by United Nations expert panels resulted in the 2005 release of the *Millennium Ecosystem Assessment* and the 2019 *Global Assessment Report on Biodiversity and Ecosystem Services*, both reports ringing alarm bells loudly on environmental degradation and loss of biodiversity. Simply put, the combined impact of human activity and anthropogenic climate change has far exceeded Nature's capacity to cope.

The simple truth is that human consumption has already exceeded our planet's total carrying capacity. Basic number crunching will show that if everyone in the world lives the way of a typical American, 5 planet Earth's resources is required to support such a lifestyle. This is simply impossible. And yet, this is exactly the aspiration of most if not all of the world's developing nations, which make up two-thirds of the global population.

In Part III we have looked at how compound growth leads to all sorts of problems. The inescapable conclusion therefore: the way economic growth has been managed for the past century and longer must change.

At long last, we come to a crucial and most difficult question, which boils down to simple numbers. It is so very important I have chosen to leave it out until now.

What would the rate of growth be in 2070?

Zero. It has to be. (Maybe not exactly zero but certainly less than 1%, as the doubling period at 1% growth rate is 72 years, and at 2% it is 35 years…)

But wait. What about the developing nations, especially those still struggling to lift themselves out of poverty? To leave them with room to grow, economically and otherwise, the rate of growth of *developed* nations has to become negative by 2070.

Any decent mainstream economist will denounce this line of reasoning as ludicrous nonsense. My response is this famous quote from Sir Arthur Conan Doyle's just as famous fictional detective Mr Sherlock Holmes: "When you have eliminated all which is impossible, then whatever remains, however improbable, must be the truth."

Actually, problems caused by unlimited and unchecked economic growth have long since caught the attention of men of insight and foresight. The year after the Limits to Growth report was released, E. F. Schumacher (1911-1977), British economist and advisor to the British National Coal Board, published *Small is Beautiful* pointing out the dead-end nature of unbridled economic growth. (It is worth noting the subtitle of the book is *A Study of Economics as if People Mattered*) American ecologist and economist Herman E. Daly, in his 1977 work *Steady-state Economics*, fleshed out the concept with sound and detailed proposals on how to arrest endless growth.

Unsurprisingly, mainstream economists turned a blind eye and deaf ear to these pleas for change. Came the 21st century, similar pleas were repeated in British economist Tim Jackson's 2009 book *Prosperity without Growth*, American journalist Richard Heinberg's *The End of Growth* (2011), and *The Great Disruption* (2011) by Australian environmentalist Paul Gilding, amongst others.

Mainstream economists, on their part, chose to pretend to have fallen asleep. This in itself is unfortunate enough, but more so because 'growth' is the central tenet of capitalist production, and to those economists brought up on the 'growth' dogma, an economy without growth is simply unthinkable. American author Richard M Mosey (1950-2014) wrote in *2030 the Coming Tumult: Unlimited Growth on a Finite Planet* (2009), "If the economy stops growing, capitalism dies; if the economy keeps growing, nature dies. This is a fight where only one remains." It summarised the conundrum perfectly.

To a classically trained economist, zero growth spells untold disaster, and must be avoided at all cost. This is utter nonsense, especially so when viewed against the living world. Every single one of us, having reached adulthood, goes into a steady state of zero growth. Growth does not only mean growing taller and bigger. Growth can, and does, continue in the form of a more mature personality, sharper wits, and more profound life experience. On the other hand, it is uncontrolled growth that spells disaster for a biological organism. We have a name for it: cancer.

When it is the economy, what we want to see is *zero-growth prosperity*. Here, zero growth applies only to material or physical growth. A mature economy, indeed, any mature society, sets no limit on other forms of growth: intellectual, moral, cultural, spiritual. These are the forms of growth that ought to be encouraged and nurtured.

Does it belong to the realm of dreams in the mind of an idealist, who knows next to nothing about the complexity of economic management? British economist John Maynard Keynes (1883-1946), widely regarded as the greatest economist of the 20th century, once said, "The day is not far off when the economic problem will take the back seat where it belongs, and the arena of the heart and the head will be occupied or reoccupied, by our real problems — the problems of life and of human relations, of creation and behaviour and religion." In other words, economic growth would no longer be the Holy Grail to die for (pun intended).

But even a grand master as Keynes failed to take into full account 'the urge of capital,' rendering his vision wishful thinking. To achieve zero-growth prosperity, we must upend the current mode of capitalist production. It requires a declaration of war on the endless "accumulation of capital," and by implication the agents of that accumulation, namely the rich and the powerful. No more, no less.

Needless to say, the rich and powerful will fight back, and with the full force of the law enforcement, maybe even the national security, machinery, aka police and army, upfront. This was how the French government dealt with the *Mouvement des gilets jaunes* (Yellow Vest Protests), and governments elsewhere with similar protest movements, with varying degrees of severity.

In the short term, the super-elites might shield themselves from the impacts of environmental collapse via gated communities and stockpiles of food and water, and the impacts of social upheaval via guns and mercenaries. In his book *Survival of the Richest* (2022), American writer Douglas Rushkoff explored the mindset of the super-

---

J. Maynard Keynes, *First Annual Report of the Arts Council* (1945-1946) elites who are planning to survive the Armageddon that they had created. Yet, as the social activist Susan George so astutely observed, "Some of us may be travelling first class and some in the bottom bunks, in the end we are all onboard the same Titanic." The conclusion of Rushkoff is that creating a fairer world is actually the most surefire way to avert global catastrophe, and hence ensuring the survival of the richest.

One point, often made by those concerned about the environment, needs addressing before closing this chapter: the suggestion to reduce the world's population at least by half to avert an environmental catastrophe.

Runaway population growth, so some people suggest, as in the case of some Third World countries, is a major factor in environmental degradation. Halving it, therefore, might solve the problem. Or so they believe. But they never go further to think, let alone spell it out, how this could possibly be achieved - in a humane way. History shows that World War II killed 3.5% of the world's population. The latest global pandemic, Covid-19, killed less than 0.1%. A 50% reduction of the global population due to similar or any other causes would be an unprecedented and unimaginable humanitarian calamity. Surely, no one would want their loved ones to be among those 'halved.' The planet might be saved, but humanity is not redeemed.

Advocates of such extreme measures may also have missed one crucial fact: that even if the global population was halved, those left behind would still require 2.5 Earths' worth of resources to support them. In fact, the Global Footprint Network has shown that the U.S.A. alone has a much bigger footprint than many other countries combined, developed, or developing on a per head basis 1.5 times that of Denmark, 2.2 times that of Spain, 2.4 times that of China, and 7 times that of India and 10 times Congo, an indisputable example of severely uneven distribution of resources and extreme inequity. If we are to eliminate half of humankind, should we first eliminate the super-consumers like Americans, or the under-consumers like Congolese? The answer is painfully obvious.

The fact is that if we were to distribute and make use of available natural resources sensibly, the Earth could have easily supported 10 billion, without a single person going hungry. Mah tm Gandhi summed it up well, "Earth provides enough to satisfy every man's needs, but not every man's greed."

In defence of her neoliberal economic policies, Margaret Thatcher famously said, "There is no alternative!" Faced with present day developments, I shall borrow Thatcher's rhetoric and adapt it to become one on the future survival of humankind. We must dispel the curse of economic growth because There Is No Alternative.

9

2070 – 50 Years into the Future (2)

Changes Beyond
Numbers

In the previous chapter we came across numbers which are critical in understanding and solving the problems confronting humanity. However, not all critical problems can be reduced to a numerical quantity.

Leaving aside almost unpredictable events which could have profound and planet-wide repercussions, such as impact by a celestial body with catastrophic consequences on the scale of the extinction of the dinosaurs or worse, or coming into contact with an alien civilisation, or a technology which will rewrite the world order - let's say production of unlimited energy accessible to anyone, what questions are there still for us to ask, about what the world will be like in 2070, just 50 years from now?

I would say the list is long. So, I am going to suggest the following, while you may want to add some more of your own.

In the year 2070,

1. Have we achieved permanent settlement of the Moon?

2. Have we landed on Mars?

3. Have we found life, albeit in primitive form, elsewhere in the Solar System?

4. Have we achieved controlled nuclear fusion and in the process averted any more energy crisis?

5. Have advances in computer technology made the keyboard and monitor obsolete? Will we have microchips implanted into our brain stem?

6. Have virtual entities imbued with artificial intelligence become our best friends, especially to elderly people living alone? (aka the science fiction movie *Her*, 2013)

7. Are robots helping in almost every household as domestic servants? What about robot soldiers?

8. Are nano machines monitoring our health from within, circulating in our bloodstream?

9. Has the world experienced financial collapse or economic recession worse than the one in 2008?

10. Has the permafrost all melted?

11. Has the world had another global pandemic?

12. Has the private sector taken over from national governments as the driving force in space exploration? And is space travel therefore more accessible to ordinary people?

13. Has the Outer Space Treaty, which came into force in 1967, been reduced to empty words, ever since the pace of militarization of space picked up again with, for example, U.S. President Donald Trump's establishment of a Space Force in 2019, and commercial plans for asteroid mining by companies such as TransAstra?

14. Has the United Nations become stronger or weaker (and hence more irrelevant) than it is today?

15. Has World War III occurred, leaving the ruins of a world strewn with rubble and radioactive fallout?

16. Has the global network of computers or the internet awakened? Did it turn out to be friendly or deadly?

17. Has the Technological Singularity arrived, with human minds being uploaded and merging with the internet?

18. Which country/sovereign political entity has the highest GDP? Or has GDP been dropped/superseded as an indicator of the economic well-being of a society?

19. Which country has the largest military budget?

20. Has a universal currency replaced the hegemonic America dollar?

21. Has humanity's war on cancer been won?

22. Has dementia be cured?

23. Has human rejuvenation technology, capable of reversing the aging process, become reality? Will a 120-year old person be inhabiting a body physiologically at 60 or even younger?

24. Has advances in medicine and human biology been applied to raise human intelligence? Could an IQ of 150 become the norm for most of humanity?

25. Has similar advances been applied to higher mammals such as apes, dolphins, and man's best friend the dog?

The list can go on, but these are more than enough to show how very different and interesting (or frightening, depending on your point of view) the world of 2070 can be.

Instead of me examining and then answering these questions, I would let you the reader to take up the challenge. You might want to invite those around you who are

228

just as concerned about the future of humanity, making this a brainstorming exercise. If only high school teachers and college professors were to do the same with their students, the prospect of a brighter future might just be that much higher...

If I may throw a hint or two, controlled nuclear fusion in question 4 would remain in the foreseeable future be exorbitantly expensive and complicated, which would of course make it not the 'unlimited energy accessible to everyone'. In the same vein, rejuvenation technology at question 22, accessible only to a select few due to its prohibitively high cost, would only aggravate the already abysmal gap/social polarization between the haves and have-nots, further weakening social stability.

On question 11, the threat of lethal and highly contagious man-made pathogens is the stuff of nightmares. While the international bioweapon arms race is the main source of this threat, with the rapid advance in genetic engineering, it would become relatively easy for any decently-equipped laboratory to concoct a deadly virus which could escape – either through negligence or malice – into the environment.

The most immediate concern to humanity would of course be questions 10 and 14. In particular, if the latter question were to come true, and World War III was fought as an all out war with thermonuclear weapons, the entire world and humanity with it would become so unrecognizable that any further discussion on our future is meaningless.

9.2 Will There Be a
WWIII?

The United and States and the People's Republic of China are the two most powerful states in today's world. Most political commentators believe the rise China and its challenge to U.S. global hegemony will be the main theme of 21st century history. Some scholars have described the current predicament of these two powerful states as a modern day case of the Thucydides Trap (so named after the ancient Greek historian and general Thucydides, who also wrote the *History of the Peloponnesian War*), in which the dominating status of Spartacus was challenged by the rise of Greek city state of Athens, resulting in war and the mutual destruction and decline. As the Chinese saying goes, "two tigers cannot both reside in the same mountain," so if history is any guide, an everything-or-nothing all-out war between America and China looks inevitable. (There is another equally pertinent Chinese saying, which best describe Russia's position in this U.S.-China stare down, "sitting up on the hill watching the tigers fight it out." There is also the Chinese fable "The Fight between the Snipe and the Clam" , in which the fisherman eventually came and take both animals back for dinner.)

Yet I am cautiously optimistic, and my answer to the question, "is it likely the U.S. and China will fight to their death" is "No," or "the likelihood of it happening is less than 50%". I shall explain why.

The unparalleled power of total devastation is what makes people think twice about fighting a nuclear war. Even if a country succeeded in launching a sneak attack in the form of a pre-emptive strike, and managed to wipe out 90% of the nuclear arsenal of the foe, the 10% left, on mobile launchers on trains and trailers, in missile silos deep underground, or on nuclear submarines, were more than sufficient for a lethal retaliatory strike and achieve a near-total wipe-out of the attacker.

The one characteristic of nuclear weapons which make it so different from conventional weaponry is its long after-effects. Radioactive fallout from a nuclear detonation can disperse in the atmosphere and spread across the globe, eventually precipitating, and getting into land and sea, contaminating all personnel as well as foodstocks. If this was not bad enough, dust and soot from a nuclear explosion and the large scale fires it generated would be discharged into the atmosphere, and stay in the stratosphere where little or no vertical circulation occurred. This will lead to a block-out of sunlight for months or years on end, thus plunging the world into a long, cold, dark man-made Nuclear Winter. Without sunlight, plants and crops died, and then animals that feed on them. The food chain would collapse. The world would be doomed.

According to the palaeontologists, this was exactly what happened 65 million years ago, when an asteroid smashed into our Earth from outer space and brought the dinosaurs to eventual extinction.

A nuclear war will have no winners. If this line of thinking holds, countries will be highly deterred from launching a nuclear strike, reducing greatly the likelihood of a global war. Of course, the implicit assumption is that leaders behave rationally, but as the German poet Friedrich von Schiller wrote in 1801, "Against stupidity the very gods themselves contend in vain," it might be that human folly will triumph and will push humanity over the edge.

Nuclear war might not happen on a global scale, but regional conflicts fought out with conventional weaponry might well become a frequent occurrence. The adoption by technologically advanced states of autonomous offensive weaponry or killer robots, which could increase the likelihood of armed conflicts, has raised worldwide concern. There is also the likelihood of aggravation in cyber warfare and assaults on state and corporate finance, both being fought in cyberspace, but with the worst possible outcome being global financial collapse and regression to a pre-internet age. Though there might not be a massive direct physical casualty, the resulting global upheaval and destruction of world order leading to loss of life is just as dismal a prospect as any war.

Permafrost
Timebomb
Triggered?

While I am cautiously optimistic about the unlikelihood of an all-out nuclear World War III, I am pessimistic about the second life-and-death question confronting the human race: will the permafrost have melted completely by 2070? I have reason to believe there is a higher than 50% chance the permafrost disappear entirely in the next half century. By 2070, were this to happen, humankind might have no other option than to embark on emergency geoengineering, widely discredited by most scientists today, as being too reckless and highly capricious. There might be no other way to save our environment from total collapse.

We have seen earlier how, when permafrost thaws, large quantities of methane will be released into the atmosphere. Methane, being a greenhouse gas many times more potent in trapping heat than carbon dioxide, will ensure that the rise in global average temperature exceeds the 4 to 5 degrees Celsius predicted by the IPCC scientists, by as much as 2 to 3 degrees more. Global temperature rise in this magnitude will render entire regions uninhabitable, and the resulting rise in sea level will drive massive influx of coastal population inland.

A most optimistic projection out of this very depressing scenario of the consequences of a complete melting of permafrost is that this might serve as a rude awakening to world leaders, jolting them out of the current stupor into decisive action, albeit late but better than none, in a last bid to save the human habitat. It will be no different to a wartime mobilization of everyone and everything, with rationing being the policy mainstay. Drastic as it may seem, it has happened before. Drawn into World War II by the Japanese attack on Pearl Harbor, America mobilized like never before, rationing strategic supplies such as gasoline and precious metals, and civil manufacturing capabilities were requisitioned to produce military equipment. Instead of cars, production lines rolled out armoured cars and tanks.

A pessimistic projection, however, will see humanity going about their business-as-usual ways until the eleventh hour, without accepting the fact that catastrophe is around the corner. Our Earth's natural environment began to disintegrate more and more rapidly. Food supply becomes scarce. International and domestic order began to unravel. Social instability gave way to armed conflicts then wars, until what was left of the world, and humanity, became dominated by a handful of strongmen, oligarchs, and warlords. A post-apocalyptic Dark Age thus created.

It has been said that civilization is only nine meals away from barbarism. Many writers have tried their hand at depicting such a post-apocalyptic, barbaric world order, created not necessarily by runaway climate change but also other causes. One example is the novel *Nightfall*, co-authored by science fiction writers Isaac Asimov and Robert Silverberg in 1990, and developed from a novelette by the same name written by Asimov in 1941. Another example is Frank Herbert's (Yes! You're correct. He is the author of *Dune.*) *The White Plague* (1982). In movie form, there is *Mad Max: Beyond Thunderdome* (1985), and its newer 2015 rendition *Mad Max: Fury Road. The Postman* (1997) and *The Road* (2009) are two other examples.

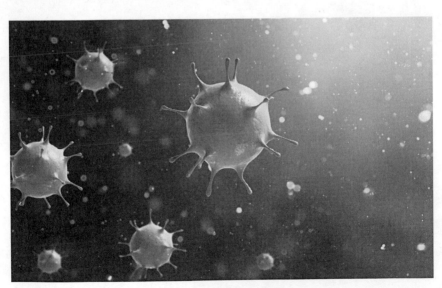

We often say that fact is stranger than fiction. I can assure you that when the end of the world is upon us, it will be no less graphic but vastly more horrible than any movie depiction (such as that of human cannibalism in *The Road*) of a post-apocalypse world.

"Humankind will go extinct!" is a warning often heard, but I believe in the resilience of the human race as a biological species that this warning will never come true. What will be extinguished though is the civilisation and global order that the human race has built. The post-apocalyptic world will be one of barbarism, with a remnant population barely surviving...

In chapter 7, we saw that the future is undetermined. But just as the opening of the Pandora's Box in Greek mythology, even if humankind is at wit's end, there is always hope. And it is exactly hope that will motivates us to examine, in the following chapters, what we together can do to bring about a better 2070.

9.4 ▶ From Political Democracy to Economic Democracy

Time and again, history has shown that power begets more power, and wealth begets more wealth. Sociologists call this positive feedback mechanism the Matthew Effect, so named because of this passage in the Gospel of Matthew, "For to everyone who has will more be given, and he will have abundance; but from him who has not, even what he has will be taken away." *Matthew 25:29 RSV.*

There are bound to be winners and losers in any game. In the social game, the winner eventually makes his way to the top, and gets to rewrite the rules of the game to ensure, among other things, that the rules reinforce his control over how the game plays out. If there was an *immutable law* of history, this is it.

The first major assault on this *immutable law* of history came with the end of the dynastic monarchy and the advent of representative democracy. The rules of the game in democracy ensure that in principle, every civilian - instead of a member of the aristocracy - has a chance of being elected to become the top leader of a country. While it is undoubtedly a great triumph to be celebrated (apart from the dictators who still shun democracy in the 21ˢᵗ century, that is) it could be argued that in modern democracies still adhering to the capitalistic mode of production, political power is only delegated so that economic power could be further strengthened, and wealth more concentrated in a few, without the risk of peasant uprising or a bloody workers' revolution. Many have said that capitalism is a friend of democracy, but seen in such a light, it is more appropriate to say that democracy is a friend of capitalism. Marx famously described democratic elections in capitalistic countries thus: "The oppressed are allowed once every few years to decide which representative of the oppressing class are to repress them."

Let's delve deeper into this twin phenomena of "Power begetting wealth" and "Wealth begetting power." In the past, political and economic power has always been the two sides of the same coin. The monarch wields absolute authority, and owns everything - and sometimes everyone - within his domain.

Wealth, on the other hand, confers substantial political influence on the owner. The House of Medici, an Italian banking family in Florence that came to prominence in 15th century Europe, and the Rothschild family in 18th century Frankfurt, Germany, are representative of wealthy merchant houses wielding significant political influence. The exception is in imperial China, where wealth did not bring on political status, and those in power were always wary of the wealthy, and farmers and scholars have long been held in higher regard than merchants.

In modern societies, the "power begetting wealth" part of the equation has been rejected. While a democratically elected president or prime minister is expected to enjoy certain privileges during their terms of office, they are not expected to amass any great wealth due to their position, apart from the salaries they received. And yet, while it is no longer *legitimate* to use one's political influence to get rich and thereby acquire economic influence (this of course does not mean illegitimate corruption has disappeared), wielding one's wealth to influence political processes has become an accepted practice, with the foremost capitalist country of the United States being the prime example. Washington D.C. alone boasts more than a hundred thousand lobbyists, registered or otherwise, racking up tens of billions of dollars worth of business. This in turn is dwarfed a hundred or a thousand-fold by political donations, especially before and during election campaigns. Although controversial, and indeed contested in court, the right of corporations (as legal persons) to fund campaigns of federal candidates was upheld by the U.S. Supreme Court in 2010. It is not without basis that the form of government in the US is called a "plutocracy." "Wealth begetting power" has trumped "Power begetting wealth," at least in modern democracies.

The rich and powerful manipulates and controls the mass constantly. Dispersing protesters and suppressing riots require the baton and tear gas, but this is required only rarely. More often it is something much more insidious and pervasive: advertisement. Just as drug addicts are under the control of traffickers, we the people are controlled by the ruling class with something which has become part of ourselves: Lifestyle. More precisely, the consumption-oriented kind of lifestyle in which "I spend therefore I am." Each year, hundreds of billions of dollar are spent by businesses big and small on advertising, cunningly devised by top-notch psychologists to brainwash all of us to live the way they want us to. From the environmental point of view, the entire advertising industry is one gigantic waste of valuable resources. The result is mountains of trash and severe pollution.

Two things work together in a democracy as check-and-balance on the exercise of political power: an independent media, and public opinion. With economic power, this important function is often weakened, even annulled, all under the excuses of 'business considerations' and 'commercial in confidence.' Worse, truly independent - and fearless - media with quality is fast becoming an endangered species in the wild jungle of media enterprise. Big corporations dominate the media scene these days, and some have not only dominated but become domineering, such as the News Corporation owned by the Rupert Murdoch family.

If nothing else works, vested interests in the economy always have a last resort. All that Big Corp needs to do is to issue a threat to divest (*capital flight* in Marxist terminology), and politicians will see to it that no reform on the tax regime, industrial relations, or environmental protection, just to name a few, will ever come to fruition. Big Corp's interests will continue to be served at whatever cost to society and humanity. Unless you are a dyed-in-the-wool cynic, you would reckon that such abuse of economic power is a frontal attack on the core values of modern society.

To ensure the continued functioning of our liberal democracy, at the same time tackling global issues such as climate change and environmental degradation, we must clamp down on Big Corp's growing influence in the political arena. The fact remains, however, that the rising trend of neoliberal politics in the past few decades have widened the wealth gap substantially, with poverty becoming ever more entrenched, and harder to eradicate. French economist Thomas Piketty, in his 2013 *magnum opus Capital in the Twenty-First Century*, demonstrated the relationship between capitalism and the consequent wealth and income inequality that we see around the world today. Before him, American economist, and Nobel Laureate Joseph Stiglitz, in his 2010 book commissioned by the United Nations General Assembly *The Stiglitz Report: Reforming the International Monetary and Financial Systems in the Wake of the Global Crisis*, pointed at the unprecedented wealth gap and concentration as the primary cause of 2008 Global Financial Meltdown. He came up with a list of concrete recommendations to close this gap and reduce the risk of future financial catastrophes. Most if not all of them fell on deaf ears.

Meanwhile, two British scientists set out to study the social consequences of inequality. Epidemiologists Kate Pickett and Richard Wilkinson published their findings in *The Spirit Level: Why More Equal Societies Almost Always Do Better* (2009, revised 2010 with subtitle *Why Equality is Better for Everyone*). Based on a wealth of socioeconomic data, they pointed out that social problems of all kinds, such as physical and mental health, juvenile delinquency, teenage pregnancy, school absenteeism, domestic violence, drug abuse, alcoholism, and obesity etc are significantly worse in countries where inequality is severe and entrenched, *regardless* if these countries themselves are rich or relatively poor. (Countries under extreme poverty are another matter.) It follows, therefore, that the solution is not in pursuing blindly the goal of 'economic development,' but in building an egalitarian society.

It should now be clear that be it for saving the environment, our liberal democracy, or creating a safe and harmonious world, it is necessary to 'regulate capital' (the words of Dr Sun Yat-sen, the founding father of modern China, in his political theory *Three Principles of the People*). English politician and historian Lord Acton (1834-1902) famously said, "Power corrupts, and absolute power corrupts absolutely." So does wealth. It is time to promote a similar idea of "Wealth corrupts, and huge wealth corrupts absolutely." Immense private wealth poses more problem to society than it's worth. No one would argue against the imperative need to eradicate poverty. I see no reason why limiting wealth should not be part of our future endeavour.

The conventional way to limit wealth is through high progressive taxation, which has been a long-standing tax policy particularly in the social democratic Nordic countries. However, as things stand at this point in the 21st century, concentration of wealth has become more than a traditional 'high tax, broad welfare' policy can handle. More effective taxation regimes and public policies need to be devised and implemented. Here are just several of many such proposals:

• A comprehensive financial transaction tax;

• Implement the Tobin tax (named after American economist and Nobel Laureate James Tobin 1918-2002) on all foreign exchange spot transactions, to reduce speculation;

• Substantial reduction of the legal privileges of Corporate Personhood;

• Strict enforcement of anti-trust regulations;

• Abolition of tax havens such as the Cayman Islands, British Virgin Islands, Bermuda Islands, together with money-laundry countries like Switzerland, Luxembourg, Panama, and Hong Kong;

• Ban all political donations by individuals or corporations, and regulate election-related expenses as public spending;

• Abolish, beyond a reasonable value, the inheritance of a deceased person's estate.

Each of these proposals would merit a book of its own, but let's examine in brief the first and last ones.

Firstly, not all supporters of the financial transaction tax are left-leaning. Support for this tax has also come from several of the wealthiest people in the world, namely Bill Gates, Warren Buffett, George Soros, together with politicians like former British Prime Minister Gordon Brown, former French President Nicholas Sarkozy, U.S. Congressman Bernie Sanders, as well as prominent American economist Joseph Stiglitz and Jeffrey Sachs, and British sociologist Anthony Giddens. They are all for this so-called 'Robin Hood tax' to become reality.

The numbers tell the story: a relatively small 0.05% rate will generate a global tax revenue of at least US$ 100 billion every year, or 1 trillion dollars in ten years' time, for the benefit of all humankind. If you want to know how this is to be achieved, I could heartily recommend the book *How To Spend a Trillion - The 10 Global Problems We Could Actually Fix*, which is written by Rowan Hooper and published in 2021. Bear in mind though that entrenched and powerful institutional resistance has not been fully dealt with is this optimistic treatise.

In the same vein, the proposal of setting a limit on how much of a deceased's estate one is allowed to inherit, would be met with strong and vehement resistance. However, just as we can no longer accept the inheriting of political power along family lines in modern societies (which has been the norm for several thousand years), wealth inheritance may well be heading the way of the rubbish bin of history. As well it should, as inheriting economic power is no longer in line with the core values of a modern civilization. British philosopher Bertrand Russell once said, "Economic power that can be used to manipulate others shall not belong to anyone. Personal wealth that does not come with such a power can be kept." I dare add that the elimination of wealth inheritance is a necessary step toward a more mature human civilization.

Sceptics will point out that the rich, with immense wealth at their disposal, surely would find a way to circumvent any legal restriction on the acquisition and accumulation of wealth, or find loopholes in the legislation, trust funds and foundations being just two more common among the many complicated schemes. But this pitfall applies to all forms of taxation. Just as we will not stop taxing income and profit because there are legislative loopholes, we should not give up on the policy to limit the amount of inherited wealth.

The picture could not have been clearer. Political democracy, albeit a dazzling achievement in human civilization, is only half the goal accomplished. The other half, an economic democracy, must be firmly established before a genuine Deep Democracy can take the pride of place in human civilization.

Of course, Economic Democracy should not simply stop short at limiting (the acquisition and accumulation of) wealth. More importantly, poverty eradication should be the intermediate goal, with achieving moderate prosperity for all being the final one.

Easier said than done! The United Nations, charged with maintaining world peace as its primary task, is also expected to work towards the elimination of poverty around the world. Yet more than 70 years after its formation, global poverty is far from being eliminated. In fact, in terms of the absolute number (instead of percentage) of people living under poverty, the problem has gotten worse. In the meantime, gross global wealth has increased manyfold. So has productivity worldwide. Nowadays, governments around the world baulk at the goal of "poverty eradication" instead of "poverty alleviation." "The poor will always be with us." is still the adage peddled. Isn't this the most damning criticism of the model of economic development which has dominated the world?

Some people warned that the development and adoption of artificial intelligence will result in massive unemployment and social unrest. This well-intended warning, however, is founded on a false premise. As we have seen in Ch 7.1, improvements in technology, such as the adoption of robots and artificial intelligence, should bring about a corresponding improvement to the quality of life of workers, an increase in leisure time being one such improvement. Unemployment should not be a prime concern, unless of course when we are living under capitalism.

We've all been brought up to think we need a job. What we need, in truth, is an income. Just as artificial intelligence can eventually alleviate drudgery at laborious tasks, it is also capable of creating unprecedented wealth. As such, we would no longer need to work our lives away just to make a living. Instead, we could all be paid a basic income from the wealth generated by AI-driven production. This income is known as Universal, or Unconditional, Basic Income (both abbreviated as UBI) or simply BI.

The idea of UBI is not exactly new, and has been around for several decades. To those supporting this idea, the basic premise is that in this day and age of unprecedented material wealth and productivity, a society which cannot provide for the basic needs for all its people - without the duress of working on several jobs, worrying for the next bill, and the stigma of being "on the dole" - is morally untenable. On the last point, it is true that many countries nowadays operate social welfare programmes for the poor and the needy. However, the many restrictions imposed and the complexity and tediousness during the application, together with the social stigma that accompanies it means that a lot of people choose rather to endure daily hardship and etch a living from hand to mouth rather than becoming a recipient. What is more, the level of assistance offered is generally not sufficient for the recipient to lead a dignified social life. To have a glean on the ordeal of those who tried to live under this system, I recommend all to watch the British movie *I Am Blake* (2016).

The proposed Universal Basic Income would solve all the above problems in one go. It is a stipend which will be given unconditionally - non-means tested in the technical jargon - to every citizen (at a lower rate for those under 18 years of age) on a regular basis throughout their lives. It does not matter whether the person is working or not, the level of income if they are working, or the amount of wealth they possess. While it is true that a billionaire (or their children) who has no need for this income will receive the same stipend as a janitor, this affront to our sense of fairness is a very small price to pay for the huge benefits that would be brought by such a scheme. No more will there be any social stigma for the recipients, and the mountains of administrative tasks in operating the old welfare system - both by the government and by the applicants - will disappear overnight.

What needs to be pointed out is that unlike the "negative income tax" once proposed by the economist Milton Friedman in the 1970s, implementation of the UBI will just replace all "direct transfer payments", and will not replace the other basic welfare institutions such as child care, public education, medical services, and elderly services etc.

Needless to say, such a proposal has met with strong opposition and criticisms, not the least from the economists. The first question is "Where would the money come from?." Following hot the on heels will be the criticism that this is tantamount to increasing the money supply without restraint, and the resulting inflation will largely annul the gains made by the poor and the needy. On another level, it is feared that such a hand-out will make people lazy hence leading to a shortage of manpower. It will also encourage the appearance of many more parasitic "welfare queens" who just take from society but contribute nothing in return.

In recent years, many scholars have undertaken extensive and rigorous studies of the above issues. Their overall conclusion is that the benefits would outweigh the drawbacks. As such, it is a scheme that should be seriously considered, and be included in our political agenda. (In the US presidential election of 2022, the Chinese-American independent candidate Andrew Yang had included UBI as part of his campaign pledges. Although he did not make it to the final round, this may be the first time the proposal becomes part of a presidential campaign)

Owing to the lack of space, I could not go into the detailed analyses of the pros and cons of UBI, but would recommend readers to the books *Raising the Floor* (2016) written by Andy Stern, and *Basic Income - A Guide for the Open-minded* (2017) written by Guy Standing. On the all-important problem of whence come the money, new income generated by the "Robinhood Tax" described earlier (Tobin tax, financial transaction tax, inheritance tax etc.) could be used to foot the bill. On a more radical level, a school of thought called New Monetary Theory contends that money could just be created for the purpose. While creating money out of thin air may sound outlandish, don't forget that the trillions of dollars created overnight to bail out the banks via multiple rounds of "Quantitative Easings" are just that, no matter how nicely the scheme is wrapped out in the sophisticated parlance of High Finance. Readers are invited to read the book *The Deficit Myth* (2020) written by Stephanie Kelton, and to decide whether the argument is convincing or not.

Still, the proof of the pudding is in the eating. No matter how nice it looks on paper, it is the real-world implementation that counts. Unluckily, this scheme has not yet been adopted by any country on a permanent basis so far. There have been quite a number of pilot programmes throughout the years, in developed countries such as Finland, Canada and the US, and in developing countries such as India. Although results from such pilots are mostly positive, the limited durations of these experiments means that their validity - especially in terms of the behavioural changes of the recipients - is open to question. Still, a general observation is that the contention that a basic income will encourage laziness have not been borne out. Yes, some of the recipients will reduce their amount of worktime or even drop out of work. But these are mostly cases where mothers choose to spend full-time looking after their kids, or people taking up courses and training programmes to upgrade their knowledge and skills, which they have no chance of doing in the past.

A historical referendum on whether to roll out a UBI was held in Switzerland on June 28, 2016. While only 23% of the Swiss population supported the proposal, this in itself was not an insignificant number, with Switzerland being the first country ever to put the UBI issue to a nation-wide polling. An opinion poll conducted among EU countries in 2022 reveals that the support for UBI is gaining momentum, with Germany (55%), Spain (53%), Italy (52%) and UK (48%) leading the way. It is hoped that given time, the support of the populace will translate into policies by the government. A worldwide implementation of UBI will bring humankind one big step forward in "Making poverty history!"

An economic democracy doesn't stop at limiting wealth and eliminating poverty. Thorough reforms would also be needed to the following:

• The promotion, through tax concessions and other policy measures, of Social Enterprises (SE) which put the creation of "social values" (benefits to the staff, the customers and to society as a whole) ahead of profits for their "shareholders." (Under capitalistic logic, "corporate social responsibilities" (CSR) and the three bottom-lines (3BL) of "People, Planet, Profit" would forever remain empty words in traditional profit-maximizing enterprise);

• Promote "worker ownership scheme" and "democratic management" of enterprises, with worker cooperatives being the ultimate goal of enterprise evolution. (An example of a successful cooperative is the 80,000-staff strong Mondragon Corporation in Spain)

- Phasing out transnational banks which are 'too big to fail,' to be replaced by regional non-listed banks, at the same time separating commercial banks (dealing mainly in lending) from investment banks (investing, and sometimes speculation). Such a separation was put in place in the U.S., in the form of the Banking Act of 1933, known popularly as the Glass-Steagall legislation. It was repealed in 1999, at a time when neoliberalism was ascendent;

- Cap the bank interest rate at a blanket 15% on all loans and credit, including such fees and charges as late payment surcharge;

- Interest-free money to be issued directly from the government. This concept was first promoted by German architect and environmentalist Margrit Kennedy (1939-2013) in her book *Interest and Inflation Free Money: Creating an Exchange Medium That Works for Everybody and Protects the Earth*, first published in 1987 and updated repeatedly afterward. A popular introduction can be found in her 2011 book *Occupy Money*;

- Set an expiry date or a half-life for all currencies. For example, the face value will be halved in 12 months and again in another 12. This could even be an automatic feature of electronic currencies such as the Bitcoin.

As always, there are plenty of workable solutions to the money and income problem. While there is the real issue of "cognitive capture" where most people (including the experts) could not imagine otherwise, American mathematician, philosopher, and advocate for economic democracy David Schweickart astutely pointed out that "Capitalism continues to dominate our world not because it is the best system we humble humans are capable of coming up with, but because it is a system supporting huge vested interests, and is in turn supported by them."

Worshippers of a free market economy will no doubt criticize the above as anti-market heresy. I shall respond thus: firstly, free market economies exist only in an economics textbook; secondly, markets are tools, not a sacred cow. Just as American physicist and energy policy commentator Amory Lovins said, "Markets are only tools. They make a good servant but a bad master and a worse religion."

Albert Einstein said, "A problem could not be solved by the same level of thinking that created it in the first place." American environmentalist Paul Hawken said this to a youth group, "Civilization needs a new operating system. You are the programmers, and we need it within a few decades."

Saving the world begins with the re-imagining of both the social order and the economic model. This is the simple truth. If I am to put a name to the world that we should be striving for, I would call it "Democratic Market Eco-Socialism," or DMES for short. The four pillars of democracy, market, a sustainable environment, and social justice are all indispensable. Take one away, and this future world will crumble to ruins.

Is all of this just a utopian *somniloquy*? Irish poet and playwright Oscar Wilde has this to say, "A map of the world that does not include Utopia is not worth even glancing at, for it leaves out the one country at which Humanity is always landing. And when Humanity lands there, it looks out, and, seeing a better country, sets sail. Progress is the realisation of Utopias.

World Government
a Reality?

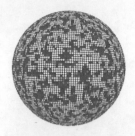

To tackle issues that are global in nature, we need a coordinated global effort. Policies such as the introduction of carbon tax, the Tobin tax and the abolition of tax havens etc. could not be accomplished by a single country. As long as there are other countries with lax or no regulations, trans-national corporations and their capital will flee to those countries. Implementation and enforcement of the regulations by a central authority is much needed for such regulations to work. Nothing less will do.

So, is a world government possible? It certainly sounds utopian, and to hope that the forerunner of a world governing body to be in place in fifty years' time, wholly unthinkable to most worldly-wise experts. Yet come to think of it, would it be more inconceivable to the people living in early 1914 that the world would be engulfed in two World Wars in the next 40 years? Or to the people in the throes of the Second World War in 1944 that all European countries will be united under a European Union by 1994, and that a common currency will be adopted? What if a time traveller could go back to 1987, and tell the people living under the Soviet Union that the regime that had ruled their lives for more than 70 years will be no more in less than 5 years' time?

Rhetorical arguments aside, we do need to explore in greater detail how a world government or at least a world council with substantial power could come into being. The first step is the full realization that humankind is already on the brink, and that only a central authority over and above the sovereignty of individual nation-states could overcome the logic of "The Tragedy of the Commons" and "The Prisoners' Dilemma," and pull us back from the edge of the precipice.

Institutionally, the United Nations set up after the Second World War is the logical candidate as a forerunner of this central authority. As pointed out in the previous chapter, however, in order to vastly strengthen the role of UN, radical reform in its structure and *modus operandi* - to the Security Council in particular - is required. At the same time, three other existing organizations wielding powerful influence on the global economy would also require drastic reforms: the World Bank, the International Monetary Fund, and the World Trade Organization. These organisations would be best subsumed under the UN umbrella, preferably supervised directly by the Security Council.

In these day and age of intense geopolitical struggle, such suggestions may seem overly idealistic and naïve. But what is the alternative? Even if we could avoid a Third World War fought with thermonuclear weapons, impacts of extreme weather (heat waves, forest fires, floods, droughts, and super-storms) would lead to the eventual collapse of our food production systems both on land and in the sea, as well as acute shortages of potable water. Coupled this with more frequent and virulent pandemics and rising sea level world-wide, and the resultant surge in climate refugees, would any country be able to shield itself from catastrophe or even total break-down?

Letting countries mind their own business and going their own diverse ways is no way forward, for it would be too late to turn things around when calamity strikes, and collapse of civilisation is imminent. Business-as-usual is just not a viable option.

For the sake of our future together, we must strive to pave our way forward by (1) sticking together, for this is the only way to stop us going over the precipice; and (2) coming to the realisation that we are not in a zero-sum game. In this Age of Abundance and Post-Scarcity Society (especially with the advent of AI), we possess more than sufficient knowledge and resources to create a better world, with everyone living in decency and sufficiency.

Not possible? Nelson Mandela (1918-2013), who fought successfully against apartheid in South Africa and became its first president, once said, "It always seems impossible until it is done."

There is another possibility though. As the saying goes: Be careful what you wish for! While I envisage a world government as something necessary and desirable, it is based on the assumption that it would be a benevolent one respecting human rights and dignity. What if it is a malevolent one? A tumultuous world like ours in the 21st century is a hotbed for power-hungry dictators. A world government might emerge, not from international negotiation and consensus, but from the iron fist of a world-conquering military strongman, having defeated challengers, crushed any residual resistance, and silenced any remaining dissent. Imagine Nazi Germany instead of America dropping the world's first atomic bomb, thereby changing the entire course of WWII, and of global geopolitics thereafter. The world would be one, but one in which every single person is placed under constant surveillance by a global dictatorship. Instead of an idealist's Utopia, we would find ourselves in a nightmarish Dystopia. History has proven time and again that it is full of surprises.

A sobering fact is that nearly a fifth of the world's population is already living in such a state. The People's Republic of China (PRC) ostensibly upholds universal values such as freedom, democracy and rule of law, and slogans can be seen everywhere promoting these 'socialist core values.' And yet anyone living there knows how intolerant the regime is towards any form of dissent, not to say attempts to promote democracy and the sharing of power with the ruling Chinese Communist Party (CCP). To compound the irony, the PRC is a signatory to the United Nations International Covenant on Civil and Political Rights, (as of September 2019 the PRC has yet to ratify this Covenant) and its own constitution confers on its citizens the 'freedom of speech, publication, assembly, association, protest and demonstration'. In real life though, these freedoms are severely curtailed by the state, and basic human rights more often than not trampled upon.

That China is the world's largest single autocracy, unprecedented in human history, is beyond any doubt. Its population of 1.4 billion is equal to the population of the world in 1880, when an imperial China was outgunned by much smaller Western, and one Asian (namely, Japan), colonial powers, intent on splitting up the vast country into spheres of interest for their own gain. Since the overthrowing of the Qing Dynasty in 1911 and the formation of the Republic of China (ROC) , China has since gone from turmoil after turmoil, until the Opening and Reform Policy introduced by Deng Xiaoping in the 1980s. Since then, by turning the country into a "World Factory," the government has raised the living standard of its people immensely, but at the same time exacting a severe toll on the freedom of expression, on the ecology, and on social equity on which the Chinese Communist Party had once placed great emphasis.

Many observers hoped that "economic liberalization" in China would eventually lead to "political liberalization," and that joining the WTO would expose China to outside influence and hence engender positive changes. Sadly, such hopes turned into the greatest disillusionment in history. Beginning with the Tiananmen Massacre of 1989 and its subsequent crackdown, China has gone backwards spiritually more than its gain in material progress. While its GDP has overtaken Germany and Japan and is second only to America, on the World Happiness Index released by UN in 2023, China ranked 82nd among the 156 countries surveyed, placing it on par with some of the worst examples in the Third World. Decency has become a joke. Corruption has become rampant. Dissent is quashed. Human rights are not recognised. Take the example of Liu Xiaobo (1955-2017), writer, human rights activist. While he was awarded the Nobel Peace Prize in 2010, he was kept detained in prison and could not attend the Award ceremony in person. He eventually died from wilful neglect by the Chinese authority to his terminal illness in Beijing, after which his body was hurriedly cremated to stop him being mourned as a martyr. His painter and poet wife Liu Xia was placed under house arrest after his death, until July 2018 when she finally departed China for Germany, allegedly on compassionate grounds so she could seek medical treatment abroad, and yet dared not to speak out afterwards, for fear of endangering friends and relatives still living in China. This kind of persecution is just the tip of the iceberg. Countless other instances of human rights abuse in China either went unreported or unresolved even after coming to worldwide attention.

In his famous dystopian novel *1984*, George Orwell invented the concepts of Newspeak and Doublethink, with the slogan "Big Brother is Watching You!" and "War is Peace, Freedom is Slavery, Ignorance is Strength". While the target of his satire - the Soviet Union - has gone down in history, his predictions live on in Russia under Vladimir Putin and in China under Xi Jinping. So does his projections about global geopolitics with transnational power blocs vying for power.

Why such focus on China in a book about the future of humankind, especially when the latest statistics shows that India has just overtaken China in terms of population? The reason is simple. Both in terms of economic clout and military might, China - and not India - is considered the only country that could challenge the global hegemony of the United States. It has been said not long after WWII that when Uncle Sam sneezes (especially when in Wall Street), the world will get a cold. It would not be long when something similar could also be said about China. With its global influence on the rise, very few doubt that China will be playing a pivotal role in the future history of humankind.

While China-bashing could be sneered as a Western ploy to suppress the rise of a great nation, China would do herself - and the world - a great service if she could embark, and stay unswervingly, on a road of reform to democracy, at the same time evolving institutions superior to, and immune from the ills of currently practised capitalist economy. The "Beijing Consensus" is moot if it is based on deprivation of the basic political rights of its own people. On the other hand, if China embraces democracy and other core values of modern civilization, she could become a true leader of the Third World championing global justice and the formation of a New Global Order.

In particular, China could rise to the challenge of pushing through long overdue reforms of the United Nations and to transform it into a representative and effective forum capable of countering the self-interest of Western superpowers, rallying all Third World nations to this cause in the process. At the same time, she should lead the fight against climate change and environmental degradation by achieving zero-emission of greenhouse gases as soon as possible, and help promote the transition to clean, renewable energies in other countries. She could also pioneer the move beyond capitalism by introducing Universal Basic Income and the abolition of the inheritance of wealth.

Han Yuhai, Chinese writer and long-time critic of neoliberalism, had this to say in his 2010 work *China and the World in the past 500 years*, "China can only be truly reborn if the world is reborn. If the world is not reborn, there is no hope for a Chinese revival." I would hasten to add this, "The world can only be truly reborn if China is reborn. If China is not reborn, there is no hope for a world revival."

We have yet to see any real prospect of the PRC becoming a democracy. At the same time, the West - American in particular - is still at the risk of being taken over by the extreme right (otherwise known as the alt-right). At the time of writing, Donald Trump is staging a comeback in the 2024 election. A few years before her death in 2022, former US Secretary of State Madeleine Albright published a book titled *Fascism - A Warning* (2018). In 2021, famous British journalist and social commentator Paul Mason also published a book called *How To Stop Fascism*. White supremacy, Christian fundamentalism, sexism, militarism…. We have once thought that humankind has put these all behind him. Development in the past two decades speaks otherwise. While Bolsonaro was replaced by Lula de Silva in Brazil, giving some respite to the well-being of the Amazon rainforest, Netanyahu and his far-right cabinet has made a comeback in Israel, and pushing for a constitutional reform that vastly weakens democracy. The battle is still being fought in every corners of the world, and the outcome is not yet certain.

Will Fascism win the day? The dystopian movie *V for Vendetta* released in 2005 depicted such a nightmarish future coming true in Britain. Its symbol - the Guy Fawkes mask worn by the disfigured protagonist V - has endured amongst countless frontline activists, adopted by them universally in defiance against tyranny of all kinds.

Instead of symbolism, how about technology against tyranny? Will technology make it easier to stage an uprising or revolution? Will it be a tool of liberation, giving people more freedom? Or will it be a force of oppression, increasing the control by the ruler over the ruled? With the rise of ubiquitous electronic surveillance and the use of big data and AI, the latter possibility looks more likely than ever.

A bit of consolation may be gained by looking at Chinese history through the ages. The first emperor in Chinese history, Shi Huangdi, who united a war-torn country through military conquest and founded the Qin dynasty some 22 centuries ago, decreed the confiscation of all forms of armament and weaponry and to have them melted and cast into twelve gigantic statues, to thwart any attempts of insurgency. One thousand years later, when China came under the rule of the Mongols, the Yuan court used a similar counter-insurgent measure: one chopping knife for every ten households. Notwithstanding, the Qin dynasty lasted only 15 years, the Yuan barely 100.

Since those times, technology has come a long way. Yet it remains a double-edged sword. Fast forward to the end of 2010, when the people of Tunisia came together in protest against corruption and inequality, an act of civil resistance in what is now called the Jasmine Revolution, sparking similar large-scale protests that rippled through Arabic speaking countries in the Middle East and North Africa. To this day it remains a matter of debate as to the role of social media in this so-called Arab Spring movement. The sad fact, however, is that the aspiration of the people is until these days mostly unfulfilled.

Turning to the Far East, millions of Hong Kong people took to the street from mid-2019, in protest of the Extradition Law Amendment Bill. Two online applications featured prominently in this mass movement which did not have a central coordinating body: LIHKG, an online forum, and Telegram the cross-platform instant messaging service, which together took on the combined role of a discussion and debate facilitator as well as encrypted messaging among protestors. And yet at the end of the day, these were no match to tear gas, baton, and rubber bullets.

"Political power comes from the barrel of a gun," said Mao Zedong, late chairman of the Chinese Communist Party. A dictatorship keeping its people under constant watch with surveillance technology that permeates into all aspects of life would appear to be undefeatable. Yet history has shown that time and again, tyrants were overthrown, and dictatorships came to an end. Whether it be in the "far, far future" of the *Star Wars* saga, or the near-future of *Hunger Games* movie series (2008-2010), defiance will persist. The Death Star will not remain forever impregnable.

Looking around the world today, governments large and small are arming themselves with greater powers, eroding civil rights in the process and further tightening the stranglehold on people's freedoms. We stand to lose everything we hold as good and true if we don't come together and stem this insidious tide of tyranny. Parliamentary struggle and street protests are still our best weapons so far against batons and bullets. Fifty years is just a blip in human history, and we can't afford to wait. The time to act is now.

9.6 — A New Renaissance and
Rebuilding Civilization

We have looked toward the future in an attempt to find out what our word would be like in 2070. I believe I have listed enough reasons to make you feel pessimistic. Likewise, I have also listed reasons to harbour hope. It's your choice. And if you happened to feel pessimistic, how about this line from the 2009 documentary *Home*, "It's too late to be pessimistic."

Perseverance is the best of the human spirit. Chinese Confucianist will say 'do the impossible,' and, if all else fails, 'die an upright man.'

British philosopher Mary Midgley (1919-2018) once said, "All around us, we can see people trying to solve by logical arguments, or by the acquiring of information, problems that can only be dealt with by a change of heart."

In this last section, I shall explore what Midgley described as 'change of heart.'

The most often quoted sentence in *The Communist Manifesto*, published in 1848, is 'all that solid melts into air'. What it refers to is that, under the hard logic of industrialism and capitalism, traditional institutions are subjected to the constant assault from the insatiable forces of profit making and market efficiency. Culture, moral values, beliefs, even personal interaction in daily life, have been severely corrupted so much so individuals have lost their physical and spiritual anchorage.

Eleven years later, in 1859, Darwin published his theory of biological evolution. Darwin argued that human beings are, after all, an animal, albeit a highly evolved one. Western civilization, with the Christian faith as the backbone, was dealt a severe blow, one much more traumatizing than the Copernican theory that the Sun is the centre of the Universe. For many, total refutation of Darwin's theory was the only way out. But for intellectuals of the day, a respect for academic rigor required that they attempt to reconcile Darwin with the long-held view that Man was created by God and was special, a seemingly futile effort which continues to this day.

Austrian neurologist Sigmund Freud (1856-1939) founded the clinical method of psychoanalysis in the early 20th century, damaging the supremacy of human beings further. It was discovered that our subconsciousness was a powerful force in shaping the way we think, without ourselves being aware of it. Rationality, love, beauty, values that we cherish and upheld as good, are simply the superficial manifestation of desires and urges hidden deep in the dark corners of our consciousness. Exhortations and sound arguments are nothing but our rationalizing those subconscious desires and urges.

Simply put, humankind transitioned from being in the bliss of ignorance to the pain of knowing, all in a matter of 200 years.

Swiss psychiatrist and psychoanalyst Carl Gustav Jung (1875-1961) has this to say in his 1933 anthology *Modern Man in Search of a Soul*, "[The modern man] is the man who stands upon a peak, or at the very edge of the world, the abyss of the future before him, above him the heavens, and below him the whole of mankind with a history that disappears in primeval mists." Viewed as such, modern man is lonely and lost. Jung exhorted us to search for our soul exactly because our soul has gone missing.

Modern man's anxiety and loss is also starkly reflected in the works of Irish novelist and playwright Samuel Beckett (1906-1989). His 1953 existential play *Waiting for Godot* featured characters waiting for something or someone throughout the entirety of the performance, only to be left at the end of it, as is the audience, none the wiser about what they are waiting for.

The anxiety, loss, and pondering suffered by modern man are mainly caused by events in recent history. The scientific revolution, enlightenment, secularization, industrial revolution, urbanization, marketization, and globalization have swept away traditional world views and values, without a new set of world view and ethics - or so it is believed - to take their place. An empty soul and a hollow spirit has become the hallmark of modern man. And in craving for a substitute, we have turned toward traditional religious faiths, defying Bertrand Russell's prediction that advances in science will displace religion. Spiritual movements have popped up everywhere to fill the vacuum, from the New Age movement in the West, to Falun Gong the pseudo-religion which is banned as a heretic cult in China.

I believe if we take a much broader view of our history, this sense of loss is just a transient pain in the process of humankind becoming mature. Our future poses an immense challenge, and humankind cannot afford to be mired in constant pain. We must resolve to rid ourselves of this pain before we could tackle with experience and wisdom the challenge of the future. I believe the crucial thing to do is for the human spirit to embrace the spirit of science.

English scholar Charles P. Snow (1905-1980) was the first to point out in 1959 the breakdown in communication between the scholars in the humanities and the sciences. Snow, himself a physical chemist by training, argued that this breakdown into 'Two Cultures,' in which men of letters and men of science held dear only their respective world views and values, is a malaise of modern civilization, and posed a major barrier to solving the world's problems.

Simply put, scientists and literary intellectuals live in two separate and distinct worlds. They speak differently, think differently, and observe the workings of the world differently, so much so they found themselves unable to communicate meaningfully with one another.

Worse than not talking to each other is the mutual disrespect, despise, and the occasional antagonism. In the eyes of a literary intellectual, science is devoid of feelings, cold, mechanical, and unhuman. To them, science has displaced God, robbed everything spiritual of meaning, and destroyed traditional qualities such as virtue and morality. The pursuit of science has left the human world without faith or feelings. And just as in a machine which functions on logic, numbers and settings, the human component no longer counts. Culture is dead, so is the human spirit. It has been said that while we have become a "scientific giant," we have also become a "spiritual dwarf." To save the world - so claimed literary intellectuals - we must stop science dead in its track.

On the other hand, there are more than a few scientists who would look down on these self-important, egoistic, and ill-informed - at least in matters of science - men of letters as 'eggheads,' shut away in ivory towers and far removed from the real world.

Literary classics, so say some scientists, are nothing but endlessly repeated pining and whining about nothing.

Other works such as abstract paintings fetching sky-high bids at an auction are just sensational pieces without substance. Men of letters occupy high places yet are ignorant of what actually goes on in the real world, so much so that almost all the problems plaguing the world - climate change included - should be blamed on them, especially when they or their students become politicians.

That's not the end of it. Both scientists and humanities scholars believe without a doubt that they are the true torch-bearer of civilization and the human spirit. Scientists would say that professors in the humanities are wasting taxpayer's money, and humanities scholars would say scientists are a threat to culture and civilization (in addition to stealing the lion's share in university fundings), so that either side regards their opposite numbers entirely dispensable.

I might have exaggerated it somewhat. Many scholars in fact have passionate knowledge of both the arts and the sciences, the great physicist Albert Einstein who was a consummate player of the violin is just one example among many. However, Snow's description of the two cultures is a valid picture of the modern world after all, and to some extent scientists have themselves to blame. Logical positivism in the 20th century held high the principle of verification, in which anything that is not verifiable or reduced to an equation - and this would include attributes such as desire, emotion, love, hate, fortitude, aesthetics, and a sense of the mystique - be precluded from the pursuit of knowledge. Elevating science to an absolute apex turned it into an unchallengeable "Scientism," to the dismay and disdain of many.

We must also take into account the immense 'service' that science has rendered in the last two centuries to capitalists and consumerism. Science and technology have given capitalists powerful means of control and exploitation of labour, at the same time increasing the seduction to the spending public to spend even more on gadgets and stuff. The public at large does not know that capitalism is the root cause of the evil, so science has become the scapegoat.

However, on the other hand, humanities scholars are also to blame. To them, scientists are always objective, rational, rigorous, and as much as possible impersonal in academic inquiry, without realizing that scientists are just as much motivated by a strong curiosity, a passionate perseverance, and the rewarding ecstasy when they make a discovery. What is more, humanities scholars fail to fully appreciate that such discoveries have brought about a much deeper understanding of the evolution of human beings, human nature, the human mind, and the development of feelings, desires, and beliefs, which are also the pursuit of the humanities.

As we all know, science is a great achievement in terms of the material civilization of humankind. Yet, most people do not realize that, on a more important level, science is an outstanding achievement in the spiritual civilization of humankind.

In fact, reason and emotion are the two sides of the coin that is human nature. Reason dries up without the motivation of emotion, and emotion runs wild without reason reining it in. Like the Ying and Yang symbol in Daoism (Taoism), reason and emotion complements each other.

What has this got to do with the future of humankind? It has, and a lot!

American biologist Edward O. Wilson (1929-2021) pointed out that today's problems arise from the fact that 'We have paleolithic emotions, medieval institutions, and god-like technology.' To achieve the 'a change of heart' advocated by the philosopher Mary Midgley, we must first raise our awareness and mental outlook to another level. We have seen before that the spirits of science and democracy are highly integrated. Taking a wider perspective, the scientific and humanitarian spirits are also highly congenial. To raise humankind's mentality, the crucial first step is to realize the unity between the sciences and the humanities.

In 1998, Wilson published his *Consilience - The Unity of Knowledge* as an initial effort in realizing this integration. In the past two decades, many prescient scholars have followed in his footsteps.

My own attempts to promote such a perspective began more than two decades ago. In my view, a philosophy which I called "Scientific Humanism" or "Consilient Humanism" in which the sciences and the humanities are embraced as an integrated whole is indispensable to genuine human flourishing and happiness. Science, far from being the archenemy of the humanities, ought to be and in fact is the most dependable ally. Man will forever be denied true happiness as long as he fails to achieve a consilience of mind, body, and spirit. On the contrary, if he was to embark on his quest with an open spirit and unbiased mind, he is more the wiser, kinder, and human.

Viewed against this light, the Enlightenment movement which began in the 17th and 18th century is still a work-in-progress, and hence an unfinished project. In the intervening centuries, humankind has experienced many cultural shocks. Baptised first by the theories of Darwin, Marx, and Freud, then given a shocking revelation of the dark side of human nature through the exploits of Nazism, Fascism, and communism, followed by insight from the study of genetics, paleoanthropology, evolutionary psychology, sociology, and neuroscience, we must take to our road ahead with courage, lest we stand in shame to the Enlightenment pioneers. To draw a distinction from the historical Enlightenment, we may call this new movement in the 21st century the New Enlightenment.

One of the starting points of this New Enlightenment is the dual nature of the controversial concept of modernity. Modernity has as its ingredients the spirits of rationalism, humanism, and democracy. It is however also rooted in the Janus-face of capitalism, which champions profit-making and ever-increasing efficiency, both dehumanizing qualities. Just as we deal with any traditional culture and heritage, we need to extract its best and remove the worst. Don't throw out the baby with the bath water.

At the beginning of this book, we called the Great Axial Age more than 2,000 years ago the First Enlightenment. The Second Enlightenment, therefore, would be the one in 17th and 18th century Europe. The one I am advocating now would become the third and the New Enlightenment.

The New Enlightenment faces many daunting challenges: neoliberalist domination of political, economic and cultural thinking in the West, the return to Oriental despotism in Russia and China, resurgence of racist and extreme rightist ideology, terrorism driven by fanatical religious ideology, waves of climate refugee caused by global warming, regional and global geopolitical tension verging on war, deeply entrenched vested interests (think Big Coal, Big Oil and Wall Street) standing in the way of meaningful change...In the face of all this, humankind finds no safe haven. We either charge forward and bring about the dawn of a new golden age, or throw our hands up in resignation and despair and let the darkness engulf us. The choice is ours.

Is all this talk about a New Golden Age just hot air? No! Humankind now has in his possession three overriding advantages like never before. First, global productivity under automation/AI/nanotechnology is now more than sufficient to satisfy the material needs of every single human being on this planet. Second, the internet makes direct democracy possible in which everyone can participate and interact in real time. And third - which I deem the most important of all - our understanding of ourselves, from our biological origin, nature and goals through evolutionary biology, our fears and desires and frailty and foibles through psychology and neuroscience, and how to co-exist in harmony with others through social psychology, history, political science, and game theory, has all reached an unprecedented level.

Some may consider the last item too abstract or academic. This could not be further from the truth. In his book *The Philosophy of Civilization* (1949), Albert Schweitzer proclaimed that "All human progress depends on progress in its theory of the universe, whilst conversely, decadence is conditioned by a similar decadence in this theory." We often say maturing is a process of understanding. While this statement certainly applies to an individual, then why not the entire human race? Based on this ever-deepening understanding, coupled with the non-zero-sum game principle expounded in game theory, we would be able to design social institutions fit for human nature, and political institutions promising a win-win outcome for the international community.

More than a century ago, in the early days of the Republic of China, philosopher and public intellectual Zhang Dongsun (1886-1973) wrote about his outlook on the future of civilization. His 1919 essay *The Third Civilization*, published in the journal *Liberation and Reconstruction* which he had founded in Peking (now Beijing), argued that human civilization developed in three stages. The first stage, which Zhang called "Religious Civilization," is founded on superstitious beliefs and traditional cultural practices. The second stage is one founded on freedom and competition, which he called "Individualist and Nationalist Civilization." "Socialist and Universalist Civilization" is the third stage, with mutual aid and collaboration as the foundation. Zhang argued that humankind was still in the second stage, and progress must be made to attain the third stage for any future to be hopeful. Viewed in the light of history in the last hundred years, one must admire at the lofty foresight of Zhang's analysis.

A similar plea was made in the 20th century by the great philosopher Bertrand Russell. While Russell's liberal and cosmopolitan views are at loggerhead to Marxist-Soviet dialectical historicism, he insisted that only by looking beyond nationalism and coming together in a rational and embracing mindset, would there be any hope of creating a true World Government, thereby ensuring a bright future for humankind.

Into the 21st century, Canadian-American cognitive psychologist Steven Pinker put forward his case for a bright future for humanity in his 2018 work *Enlightenment Now - The Case for Reason, Science, Humanism and Progress*. Pinker argued, with the support of voluminous data, that thanks to the so-called Enlightenment values, progress in many areas of human society, such as health, prosperity, safety, peace, and happiness, has been made, notwithstanding various deteriorating trends occurring worldwide. In short, the world as a whole has been getting better, according to Pinker, and as such, we shall not become pessimistic and lose hope. Pinker's plea to humankind to embark on a new Enlightenment is clear.

However, Pinker failed to take into account the crucial roles that capitalism and neocolonialism play in social change, in particular the inherent logic of "capital accumulation," and its destructive effect on the environment. In his 2021 book *The Nutmeg's Curse: Parables for a Planet in Crisis*, Indian writer Amitav Ghosh convincingly argued that the current climate crisis has its deep origin in the colonial conquests of the West, and could never be solved under the prevalent paradigm of global capitalism and neocolonialism.

For readers who sincerely wish to devote themselves to a meaningful course of action, I strongly recommend the following books as additional required reading: *Utopia for Realists* (2014) by Rutger Bregman and *Clear, Bright Future: A Radical Defence of the Human Being* (2019) by Paul Mason, being analyses more from a socialist perspective.

In terms of government policy, U.S. Congresswoman Alexandria Ocasio-Cortez submitted her Green New Deal bill in February 2019 but did not make it past the U.S. Senate. The substance of the bill is modelled on Franklin D. Roosevelt's New Deal in the 1930s, difference being instead of simply salvaging the national economy, the Green New Deal is aimed as well at improving social justice and saving the environment, on top of revitalizing U.S. economy with substantial investment in job-creating green enterprise. By way of background information, read *On Fire - The Burning Case for a Green New Deal* (2019) by Naomi Klein, and *The Global Green New Deal* (2010) by Edward Barbier. If the Democratic Party managed to win the coming US presidential election of 2024, there is a slight possibility of the GND moving forward. In case it loses, the prospect is dim indeed. (In July 2020, the Korean government announced its Korean New Deal, which aims to transform the economy

- among other goals - to make it greener. It awaits to be seen how successful this initiative will turn out.)

To sum up, our first and foremost task is to arrest the current trend of development and growth, one which completely ignores sustainability. Next, we need to liberate ourselves from the old mindset and start thinking innovatively, and to build a new social order in which wealth is created together and shared together and nobody is left out. Only then can harmony be restored: harmony with others, harmony with nature, and harmony within ourselves.

In the environmental movement, the 3Rs of "recycle, reuse, reduce" has in recent years been extended to the 5Rs of "Refuse, Reduce, Reuse, Repurpose, Recycle". From a much broader perspective, the most important Rs in my view are "Reimagine" and "Reinvent," and these including our political, economic, and financial institutions. Overcoming our "failure of nerve" and "failure of imagination," of all the slogans chanted at social justice movements, this is the most resounding of all, "Another World is Possible!"

In a way, I do envy the younger generation of today. Yes, the challenges they are facing are daunting. As the future of humankind hangs in the balance, however, they have no choice but to meet the challenges head on, and hence have the chance of rebuilding civilization, and ushering in a new era of human history. Whether that era will be the dark ages of barbaric warlordism, or the New Golden Age of super-abundance and social harmony, the choice is theirs to make. We harbour no illusion that this will not be a titanic and uphill battle, but the rewards would be great. No superhero will come and save us. You are the ones you have been waiting for.

To conclude, let me share one of my favourite quotes, this one from American anthropologist Margaret Mead: "Never doubt that a small group of thoughtful, committed citizens can change the world; indeed, it's the only thing that ever has."

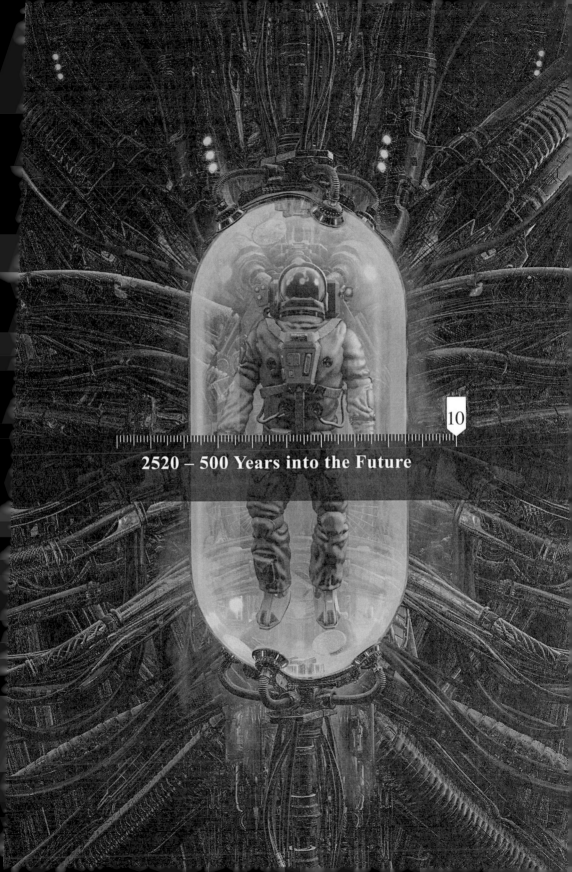

2520 – 500 Years into the Future

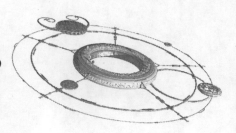

10.1 How long is 500 Years?

We have tried to look into a future 50 years from now. Let us now cast our sight and mind even farther, into a future 500 years from now.

Everything is relative. Compared to the typical human lifespan, 500 years is an immeasurably long time. Compared to the several thousand years of human civilisation, 500 years is neither immense nor insignificant. Compared to the several million years of human evolution, 500 years is just an instant.

How long is 500 years? Take the typical average lifespan of a person in a developed country, which is 85 years. In 500 years, a person would have lived his or her life 6 times over. If it takes 25 years on average for a generation turnover, then in 500 years there will be 20 generations. 500 years is also 1.8 times the duration of the Ming dynasty in China (1368-1644), or about twice the time from James Watt's much improved steam engine (1776) kickstarting the Industrial Revolution to the present.

How short is 500 years? It is a mere one fifth of the time from the time when Confucius was active to the present; one tenth from when the Great Pyramids were built; one twenty-fourth from the Agriculture revolution; a thousandth from the first fire lit by our distant ancestors.

Looking back 500 and 1000 years, let us see what exactly there were in that distant past. Notable historical landmarks and events around the year **1520** include:

• the fall of the Byzantine Empire, also called the Eastern Roman Empire, 67 years earlier in 1453;

• death of Leonardo da Vinci, a year earlier;

• publication, in 23 years' time, of the *De Revolutionibus Orbium Coelestium (On the Revolutions of the Heavenly Spheres* 1543) by Polish scientist Nicholaus Copernicus

(1473-1543), the seminal work championing the revolutionary Heliocentric Theory;

• the Ottoman Empire at its apogee;

• Treasure Fleet dispatched by the Chinese Ming dynasty imperial court, under the captaincy of Muslim Admiral Zheng He (1371-1433), concluded its seventh and last maritime expedition 87 years earlier;

• 28 years earlier, Italian explorer and navigator Christopher Columbus (1451-1506) became the first European to reach the Americas when his fleet made landfall in the Bahamas in 1492;

• the Aztec and Inca civilisations in Central and South America would soon be driven to extinction by Spanish conquistados;

• the fastest a man could travel was at a speed of about 50km per hour on a galloping horse;

• primitive firearms already in use;

• the world has yet to wait for the invention of the telescope and the microscope;

• world population was 500 million i.e. one sixteenth that of today.

Going back 500 years more, we found in the world of **1020**:

• the centre of the civilised world in the East was the cosmopolitan city of Bianliang (present day Kaifeng city in the Henan Province PRC), imperial capital of the Northern Song Dynasty (960-1127), with a population of some 440,000; its Western counterpart was Cordoba in present-day Spain, then a centre of culture and learning established at the western end of the Muslim world during the heydays of the Islamic Golden Age, when the rest of Europe in the Middle Ages was in relative decline;

• the modern day decimal numeral system, otherwise known as Arabic numeral as was first named by Europeans, was introduced around this time by Muslim scholars into Europe, the system having been invented over time in India in the 5th and 6th centuries;

- the most advanced weapons were the bow and arrow and sword and sabre (although gunpowder was first used in the battle field by the Chinese in 904 CE, it took more than five centuries for artillery to become a mainstay in warfare);

- world population was 300 million.

With these historical events in mind, and armed with discussions and analysis before this, let us begin our attempt to look into a future 500 years from now.

10.2 Longevity and
Immortality

Similar to the way we set about examining a world 50 years from now, I have listed the following questions to help forecast the shape of things to come in **2520**:

1. Has the human race destroyed itself? If so, who, or what has taken his place?

2. What is the average human lifespan? Or has immortality been achieved?

3. Have we acquired the Midas touch, i.e., the transmutation of elements?

4. Is there a world government?

5. Has strong AI become reality? Is it recognised as a citizen i.e., gaining legal personhood?

6. Has the technological singularity (uploading of the human mind) occurred?

7. Has the human race been genetically reengineered? Are there superhumans? If so, do they come in different species?

8. Is there a limit to how much we can know? Have we come to that limit?

9. Are humans everywhere in the Solar System? Have we transformed planets and satellites by planetary engineering, such as enriching the atmosphere of Mars, cooling down Venus, aerating the surface of the Moon, and hollowing out asteroids and use them as habitats or spaceships?

10. Are there more people living off-planet than on Earth?

11. Has faster-than-light space travel been achieved? If so, how much faster?

12. Is *interstellar* space exploration being undertaken, with colonization of planets orbiting other suns?

13. How much of planet Earth has been re-wilded? Simply put, what is the forest cover percentage of the planet compared to that of today?

14. Have humankind turned other species on Earth - chimpanzees and dolphins or even our beloved cats and dogs - into our true companions via intelligence/ cerebral-enhancement techniques?

15. Have we already encountered aliens, or at least detected their presence?

Question 1 is the most important, as it prefaces all other questions. The destruction of the human race, brought about either by himself or other agents, will render all subsequent questions superfluous and meaningless. Science fiction enthusiasts though will still be curious as to who, or what, will succeed humanity as the dominant species on Earth. Will this world be taken over by an artificial intelligence? Or by another biological species? If the latter, will they be able to evolve to become intelligent? Or will the world go back to a pre-human primal state?

If humans were still around, the question that follows is: how long will they live? 200? 300? 500? Or forever? Longevity, or near-immortality, can be achieved in two ways. First, continual advances in medical biology might extend the human lifespan enormously. But it might be more likely that through integrating the biological human organism with mechanical and electronic software and hardware, to become a 'cybernetic organism,' or 'cyborg' in short. The ultimate cyborg would be a mechanical body coupled to and containing a human brain and spinal cord as the control and command centre, as depicted in the movies *Robocop* (1987/2014) and *Alita* (2019). The mind might grow old. The mechanical body wouldn't. Enhancements and regular upgrades would come as part of the package. For those who believe in the singularity, immortality comes from the uploading of the human mind to the ubiquitous computer network - probably an internet spanning the whole solar system. (The speed of light - unless somehow overcome - would however set a limit to the viability of a solar-system-spanning consciousness)

Super-longevity, of course, affects not just the individual. If it happened, the social impact, let alone the associated economical and political ones, would be profound.

Imagine how it will mean to familial and matrimonial bonds, to retirement age and upward mobility of the younger generations, to the consumption of natural resources, and to the stagnation of culture and the human mind etc . Are you going to bet that we would get much wiser as we get to live that much longer, or that human society would become a collection of senile derelicts?

Since this is such an important question, let's look at it in greater detail. Owing to resource constraints, a society with near-zero mortality would entail a near-zero birth-rate. As a result, it's a society mostly devoid of baby woos and cries, and the brashness and laughter of teenagers. Such a gloomy scenario is depicted in the science fiction movie *Children of Men* (2006), only in this situation, it is a result of an unknown plague, to which no cure could be found.

We are all familiar with the wise exhortation "Seize the day?," especially for the younger generation. And yet when one could live virtually forever, there would not be any urgency to any matter that requires our attention. What is left undone today could always be deferred to tomorrow, and there are endless tomorrows ahead of us. For those preferring to take things easy, procrastination would become the order of the day. What this would do to the human spirit is anybody's guess, but one is inclined to be pessimistic.

In a similar vein, to the potential immortals, death by accident would be their worst nightmare. As a result, they would be risk-averse to the extreme. As the saying goes, nothing venture, nothing gain. To these immortals, no gain would justify the colossal loss. Throughout history, there had been those who were willing to sacrifice themselves for the betterment of their fellowmen, as in uprisings against tyrannical rule. Such noble sentiments and heroic deeds would all become a thing of the past. The decline and disappearance of the spirit of adventure might also be an answer to the famous Fermi's Paradox - the reason why no signs of advanced alien civilizations are found so far is that all such civilizations descend into adventure-averse conservatism because of immortality.

Old age could lead to wisdom, but could equally lead to super-conservatism and petrification of the mind. With old age running into centuries, the latter would become more and more likely. Advances in civilization are often the results of young minds defying the "wisdom" of the older generation, and the courage to try out new things and venture into unknown directions. Take artistic creations for example. No matter how great and ground-breaking a composer Beethoven is, could you imagine him - if he lives until now - turning out works in the wonderful styles of Debussy, Bartok, Gershwin and Shostakovitch? Or Shakespeare producing works like Kafka's *Castle* or James Joyce's *Ulysses*? An inescapable conclusion is that a race of immortals will be locked into a culture of stagnation and putrefaction.

By now you may begin to realize how immortality or even super-longevity could be a curse in the disguise of a blessing. As to be discussed in the next section, it my well be that humankind will spread out among the stars, and resource restrictions will be a thing of the past. If we focus our attention to our home planet, however, those rare individuals born there from time to time would surely leave this geriatric planet as soon as they could. As the human society on Earth gets older and older, it might withdraw itself entirely unto itself, and shut itself off from the outside world… Earth would become the ultimate Cosmic Elderly's Home.

10.3 The Midas
Touch?

Looking back at Question 3 in the previous chapter, we now move on to the level of control, or manipulation over matter possibly achieved by human science and technology 500 years in the future.

The physical world is made up of space, time, matter, and energy. It has been shown by physicists in the early 20th century that space and time are two sides of the same coin. Instead of space and time being unconnected and independent of each other, our world is actually a "4-dimensional space-time continuum". Matter and energy, on the other hand, are transmutable. Hence the four fundamental elements of existence have now been replaced by matter-energy and spacetime, a parsimony achieved through the insight of science.

Let us now deal with humanity's control over matter-energy, and leave the aspect of the control over space-time to a later section.

The scale of humanity is so miniscule when set against the Universe as a whole, that even our Sun is less significant than a speck of dust floating about in the vast expanse of the St. Peter's Basilica in the Vatican. The sum total of energy produced in the Universe far exceeds the meagre needs of humanity by any stretch of the imagination. Our Sun alone emits enough energy to power the entire world 2 billion times over. If humanity ever ran out of energy, it can only be due to our own ineptitude and hubris, not in the least reinforced by our addictive dependence on fossil fuels. This can and will be overcome. There will in principle never be another 'energy crisis.'

Energy, however, is a double-edged sword. Will humanity unleash a more horrible monster than nuclear energy? I am afraid I have to say 'yes.' It is my prediction that in 500 years' time, it is highly likely humankind comes to wield a much more powerful form of energy. It is just as likely this new energy be turned into a weapon of destruction. And it has, at least in science fiction: the Death Star, portrayed in the *Star Wars* movie series, is a mobile battle station the size of a planetoid capable of blowing up a real - and inhabited - planet with an energy blast (the Planet Buster). Unless forever forbidden by the limit set by the speed of light, interstellar warfare will be more destructive than that imagined in any science fiction story.

The control of energy is one thing. The control and manipulation of matter is quite another. We might have an endless supply of energy at our disposal, but this does not mean we would also have the means to create at will any of the known elements in the Periodic Table (such as gold or uranium), or the chemical compounds formed from these elements, many of which are essential to humanity, such as food and medicine.

Large scale conflicts sparked by a scramble for energy sources, mainly that of oil which only came into widespread use in the early 20th century, are a recent occurrence. It used to be physical matter, not energy, that people fought over, examples of which include gold, iron, diamonds, spice, sugar, tobacco, fur, timber, rubber or even guano (bird droppings).

In principle, transmutation of the elements - the dream of the alchemists - has already been achieved in the 20th century using huge particle accelerators. However, the astronomical cost involved even for a miniscule amount means no practical application could result from this process.

And yet we are talking about 500 years in the future, when the super-science of the time might look just like magic to us here in the 21st century. Would cheap and large-scale transmutation technology, coupled with unlimited energy supply and the capability to synthesize materials, propel humanity from a transitional post-scarcity era into an Age of Super-Abundance? Under such a scenario, there would be no more need to fight over material resources, and human history would enter a whole new era.

There is no way to predict whether this rosy picture of a future would ever come to pass. In the famous science fiction novel *Dune* (written by Frank Herbert in 1965, and twice turned into movies since), the whole story revolves around the spice melange, which could only be found on the planet Arrakis. The premise is that even in the distant future portrayed in the story, there are still substances that could not be synthesised at will. Contrast this with the replicator in the Star Trek TV series which could replicate anything we want (most often seen in Captain Pickard's Ready

Room), which is only 200 years or so into our future. Whether the optimists or the pessimists will be vindicated would have a huge impact on the future of humankind. If the pessimists won out, the fight for scarce or precious resources will go on. If the optimists won, both interstellar trade and warfare would become the laughable prehistory of the human race.

There is yet another question. Even with complete mastery over matter and energy, who is going to do the chores? Me? Or my robot? If it is the latter, will we all turn into the lazy and obese boys and girls onboard the spaceship *Axiom* as depicted in the 2008 Walt Disney animation movie *Wall-E*?

We have seen earlier that with the advance in artificial intelligence, computers and robots will one day acquire the ability to replicate and improve themselves in the process. Hungarian-American mathematician and physicist John von Neumann first proved the theoretical possibility of a self-replicating machine (which he called the universal constructor, later became widely known as 'von Neumann machines') in the 1940s, paving the way to later study and advances in computing, artificial intelligence, and genetics. The opening question thus becomes: 'will von Neumann machines be in widespread use in 500 years?' Bearing in mind if that was the case, every step in the production of anything, from acquiring raw materials, fabricating the necessary tools and machinery, to the final finishing, would all be carried out with zero human input.

I believe the answer is 'yes,' and I say this with 99.99% certainty. The premise is of course that humankind has not destroyed itself - on the civilizational level and not the biological level - before he acquired that capability.

We will shortly see that answers to the questions in this section are closely tied to the possibility of an "Alien invasion" aka *War of the Worlds* (1898) in literature, or *Independence Day* (1996) on the big screen.

10.4 Withering of the Nations?

We have touched on the prospect of a world government in our forecast for the next 50 years. My belief is that while the prospect of humanity achieving world government in the next 50 years remains slim, achieving world government within the next 500 years appears very likely. In the popular media two works on the silver screen, both big and small, have become household names. It so happened they both featured a world government in their imagined universes: American screenwriter and producer Gene Roddenberry's (1921-1991) creation *Star Trek* in the 1960's, and American film director George Lucas' *Star Wars* movie series since 1977.

Star Trek's world of the future has little place for traditional nation state. Instead, humanity pledges collective allegiance to the United Federation of Planets. Note that the date set in the opening television series, when the starship *USS Enterprise* began its "5 year mission, to explore strange new worlds, to seek out new life and new civilization" under the newly appointed Captain James T. Kirk, and to *"boldly go where no man has gone before"* was in 2258, a mere two centuries and a bit in the future or halfway between now and 2520. Roddenberry could be derided as overly optimistic, especially during the Cold War era, to have made that prediction. How about giving it 260 years more, bringing it to our projected time of 500 years from now?

We shall leave the remote possibility of a Galactic Empire to the *Star Wars* movies, all of which opens with the words "a long time ago, in a galaxy far, far away..." and turn our attention instead on what might happen in the Solar System in several hundred years' time.

Five hundred years can be a long time, the human society might have gone through divisions and reunions, and at levels unimaginable to us in the present. Mars, uninhabited for now, might have become a settlement independent of Earth, in more ways than one. Humans might even have managed to settle the asteroids, some the size of a mini planet but many much smaller, and come to form a loose-knit union of sorts, and broke off entirely with their home planet. Our only natural satellite the Moon, though, does not enjoy the protection of distance and so lunar settlers could only but pledge their continual allegiance to mother Earth. This, a Solar System colonized by humans, is the backdrop against which drama in the American science fiction television series *The Expanse* (2015-2022) is played out. As with *Star Trek*, it was set in a relatively near future of about two hundred years and well before 2520.

The demise of the sovereign state as a political institution has been the subject of at least two academic discussions in the past. Karl Marx and Friedrich Engels' dialectical historicism held the view that capitalism was already in decline, and hypothesized that after going through the transitional stage of revolutions and socialism, human society will become communist. By then, the state machinery, which according to Marx and Engels, was merely a tool of class oppression, having served its historical purpose, would have no place in human society and withered. It followed therefore, in a world united under communism, there would be no more need for a sovereign state.

So far, Marx and Engels' prediction remains just that, a prediction. Others, however, have been making attempts over the years, via different ways and means, to make it happen. Globalisation was all the craze in the 1990s, and with the inception of the World Trade Organisation in 1995, talk of the demise of the sovereign state came to the forefront again.

According to some, conventional sovereign states would eventually be replaced by a whole host of international bodies such as the World Trade Organisation, the International Monetary Fund, the World Bank...etc. together with transnational corporations. History has turned out otherwise, and with the cooling off and reversal of globalisation after the 2008 global financial crisis, sovereign states remain the single dominant force in both domestic and world politics.

One historical fact could invalidate *Star Trek*'s prediction on the future of human society's political structure: the age of sovereign states. Countries, just like human beings, can be young or old. Up to the year 2020, Israel is only 74, Singapore slightly younger at 57; but countries with an imperial past, such as Russia and France, are hundreds of years old, whereas China and Iran are thousands of years old. To have set a time a mere two hundred or so years in the future when states/countries no longer existed might be stretching it too far, with due respect my much beloved Gene Roddenberry.

But hang on! Neither the creators of *Star Trek* the television series or the subsequent movies made it explicit that there were no longer individual sovereign states on Earth. In fact, nothing on this point was specified one way or the other. It might well be possible, in a *Star Trek*-esque future, sovereign states still existed but were all subsumed under an umbrella organisation such as a federation or commonwealth of planetary systems, akin to the present day European Union where member states still retain their sovereignty but have agreed to and adopted a common and unified currency, tariffs and trade practice, and migration/border control.

We have earlier examined the possibility of the European Union becoming/being adopted in future as a model for a global human society. I was not too hopeful about this happening in the next 50 years but what about the next 500?

On another level, it is interesting to note that in the first ever *Star Trek* television series (fans call it *TOS - The Original Series*), the use of cash or money in any other form was never seen or mentioned, nor was there advertisement or commercial promotion. And there was no talk of corporations, the stock market and speculative finance…

Even more interesting is the fact that for decades, millions of viewers who have grown up watching *Star Trek* have never found this state of affairs ridiculous, impossible, or objectionable. While my guess is that very few of them would have put it in these terms, it is as if they have tacitly accepted that a future society based on socialism (almost a dirty word in the US of A) is a natural progression of things, and capitalism would have become a thing of the past.

Such socialist ideals is of course nothing new. More than 2500 years ago, Confucius had portrayed such a condition which he named *Da Tong* (the Great Harmony). True, this remains today an ideal, a distant dream. And yet this ideal is still spurring countless people on their quest for a just society, where oppression and exploitation have been abolished.

If Confucius can be called an idealist, then Marx is a romanticist. Marx held the view that, with advances in science and technology, humankind would eventually break free from the curse of material scarcity, and transitioned from the Realm of Necessity to the Realm of Freedom, by which time it is possible for one "to hunt in the morning, fish in the afternoon, rear cattle in the evening, criticize after dinner, without ever becoming hunter, fisherman, shepherd or critic."

But Marx was only referring to the Freedom after breaking free from the drudgery of production. The biggest threat to the freedom of humankind remains that of a madman hell bent on world conquest and domination, driven by a desire not just for material wealth, but out of megalomania. In Chapter 5 I have pointed out it is too early to say if the world of the future would be one of progress and democracy, or of stasis and despotism. As a hardcore fan of American science fiction writer Isaac Asimov, I found his idea of a Galactic Empire preposterous when I first read his *Foundation* trilogy (written in the late 1940s) in junior high school. I could not help but wondered, if humankind in the distant future was well on the way to prosperity, abundance, and peaceful coexistence, why would we have relapsed politically to imperial rule? Sad to say, having seen so much and personally lived through so many episodes of human folly, I am not as confident now.

So, *Star Trek* says the future is socialist, while *Star Wars* says it is imperialist. Which would be closer to the mark? Take your pick.

10.5 Humanity's Interstellar Diaspora

I have touched on the possibility of a civilization-wide collapse happening within this century, which may cause those of you with children - or even grandchildren - considerable anxiety and anguish. The human toll of such a collapse is simply far too devastating to contemplate. But if we were able to look at it from a detached point of view, we might want to know if, in the event of the human society surviving a worldwide collapse of civilization, how long would it take to rebuild and recover?

To the citizens of the Western Roman Empire, its collapse in 476 would be no different from the end of the world. Likewise, the fall of Constantinople in 1453, spelling the end of the Eastern Roman Empire, would be the end of the world to its citizens. Viewed in the broad context of human civilization, these events were merely points on the long timeline of history. If it had happened in the past, it might happen again in the future; and if human society had risen from ruins so many times in the past there is no reason to doubt that it would not again in the future. Of course, it took Europe close to a thousand years to come through the so- called Dark Ages (some historians do find this description of the Middle Ages exaggerating), so it might take just as long or even longer than until 2520 for humanity to recover from a modern-day collapse.

Remember this as well: whereas historic collapse of civilization had been regional in scale, today's would be global, with what humankind has been doing to the environment and the climate. Scientists have pointed out that the effects of climate change will last for hundreds of years, that being the longevity of carbon dioxide in the atmosphere. If, for an added stroke of misfortune, a global nuclear war broke out as well, the lethal consequences of worldwide radioactive fallout together with human habitat degradation by climate change would turn our Earth into a hostile environment for life. Seen in such light, the post-apocalyptic world as depicted in the 2015 movie *Z is for Zachariah* was way too idyllic, and the much grimmer world of the 2009 movie *The Road*, with cannibalism rampant, a much likelier outcome.

Rebuilding a post-apocalyptic civilization has always been a major theme in science fiction. The two representative classics are John Wyndham's (1903-1969) 1955 *Chrysalids*, which described a post-apocalyptic world where all mental and physical abnormalities are to be ritualistically purged, and American science fiction writer Walter M. Miller Jr.'s (1923-1996) 1959 novel *A Canticle for Leibowitz*, where Catholic monks helped rebuild human civilization over a period of thousands of years.

Let us allow ourselves the highest degree of optimism and assume that either humankind missed a global collapse by a whisker, or rebounded swiftly after one. In either of such futures, would we see human societies littered across the length and breadth of the Solar System, and beyond?

A quick review of the current state of space flight technology is helpful. Unmanned space probes sent from Earth have reached and operated on or around many Solar System destinations: the Moon, major and minor planets or asteroids, comets, and the interplanetary environment including the solar atmosphere. A few have travelled far beyond the bounds of the Solar System and remained operational well beyond their designed and expected lifespan. Note however that these are all unmanned. The requirements of sustaining a human pilot or passengers over a vast distance in the hostile environment of outer space complicate the design of a space vehicle exponentially. The timescale of interplanetary flight, within our Solar System, is measured in years, for say a return voyage to Mars or the Asteroid Belt. For destinations even farther away, it would be measured in decades.

But we are predicting it happening by 2520, 500 years in future. I am convinced, unless human civilization suffered a severe setback or a complete collapse which would interrupt the pace of exploration, humankind would have travelled far and wide in space, and would have settled on some of the less hostile environments in the Solar System. Imagine cities on the Moon, Mars, or Mercury. Imagine rocky asteroids converted into itinerant habitats or interplanetary cruise ships. Imagine *terraforming* Venus to make it inhabitable.

Sceptics and naysayers will dismiss the idea of a Martian city as ludicrous and pure fantasy. But ask Columbus in 1492 just after he landed on the Bahamas if he could imagine a city the size of New York in 500 years' time, could he? American science fiction writer Kim Stanley Robinson's 2012 novel *2312*, started on a city on Mercury, the planet closest to the Sun, and extended to colonies on the satellites of Saturn, at the distance ten times the separation between the Sun and the Earth.

Once we enter the realm of boundless space *beyond* the Solar System, however, it is a totally different story.

The highest speed humankind can possibly achieve in theory is the speed of light. At this speed of 299,792.458 km per hour, the Earth can be circled 7½ times in 1 second. Space is simply so vast, though, even light from the Sun takes a little over 8 minutes to reach Earth and over 5 hours to reach Pluto. Travelling at the speed of light - which may not be technically feasible as we shall see later - even getting to the nearest star, Alpha Centauri in the southern constellation of Centaurus (the half-human, half-horse creature from Greek mythology), will take more than 4 years. For that matter, other well known bright stars in the northern sky are even farther away and take years more to reach, even at the speed of light. Sirius the brightest star in the constellation Canis Major (the Big Dog) is 8.7 years away at the speed of light - or, as the astronomer say it, 8.7 light-years away; Altair in the constellation Aquila (the Eagle) is 16.7 light-years away; and Vega in the constellation Lyra (the Lyre) is 25 light-years away. Compared to these relative neighbours, the remaining dots of light in the night sky, bright or dim, are stars much farther away that their light takes decades, centuries, or millennia to reach Earth. And yet all these stars near and far are merely one component in a conglomeration of stars, planets, dust, and gas, which stretches 100,000 light-years from one side to the other, in a grand assembly called the Milky Way galaxy. *Imagine having to cover that distance, even at the speed of light!*

Albert Einstein's Theory of Special Relativity reminds us that as we approach the speed of light, mass increases, and thus requiring an ever increasing force to propel it. In this light, the most human technology might come to is about 90% of light speed. Travelling to a star 100 light-years away will then take about 110 years. Even if the average human lifespan had been extended to 200 years, who would volunteer to undertake such a one-way trip just to squander half of his/her life in space?

But some scientists find that too optimistic. Getting to half the speed of light is already incredible, according to them, let alone achieving 90% speed of light. Assuming, rather arbitrarily, a one-way journey outward to the stars was capped at 30 years, with the support of "artificial hibernation/suspended animation" technology to both lessen consumption of life-sustaining essentials and avoid boredom and the risk of mental breakdown. Travelling at half the speed of light, this means the Sphere of Humanity would be restricted to within 15 light years in diameter, or a volume with less than 50 stars according to astronomers. This would be the spatial extent of the future Commonwealth of the Stars.

This Commonwealth could be substantially enlarged if we adopt the ideas of 'multi-generational starships', or the practice of just sending frozen human embryos, which would only be revived and nurtured to adulthood by robots some twenty years or so prior to the arrival at the destination. However, both 'solutions' pose thorny ethical questions.

What if we somehow managed to break the physical barrier that is the speed of light? Here again, science fiction writer's boundless imagination has come to our help. Faster-than-light spaceflight - or superluminal propulsion - forms the indispensable backbone of both *Star Trek* and *Star Wars* stories. However, it was only in *Star Trek* that a quasi-technological description has been given of how fast a starship could travel on the so-called 'warp drive': from the speed of light at Warp 1, to 1500 times light speed at Warp 9 which was the maximum. Using this daringly imagined device to warp across *interstellar* space, it would still take a solid year to reach a star 1500 light years from Earth at top speed, and 123 years to cross the Milky Way galaxy from one side to the other.

Yet another means of traversing the immense distance in space is the so-called 'worm hole,' technically an 'Einstein-Rosen bridge,' a speculative structure supposedly connecting two disparate points in the spacetime fabric of the Universe. That one actually exists has never been demonstrated let alone proved, but that has not stopped writers and filmmakers from making use of it to take a flight of fancy, the latest attempt being the 2014 movie *Interstellar*, in which the protagonists travelled through a worm hole to a distant galaxy in a bid to save Earth's human society from eventual demise.

Worm hole or not, the speed of light need not be a barrier to a future interstellar human diaspora. Just as it had been on Earth, the human diaspora can take the form of ripples radiating out from multiple origins. From the cosmic perspective, the whole Milky Way Galaxy could actually be colonized in a relatively short time-span. Imagine we were to launch, in a century's time (2120), humanity's first ever manned interstellar flight capable of a maximum speed of 0.5c (c being the symbol for the speed of light). A star 10 light years away would be reached in 20 years (2140). Assuming that it would take 100 years for the pioneer settlers to establish their presence and develop indigenous facilities to fabricate and launch (in 2120 + 20 + 100 = 2240) two interstellar spacecrafts, also capable of a top speed of 0.5c. These will travel to two other star systems, also 10 light years away from them. After these two spacecrafts - barring any accidents - arrived at their respective destinations (2260) the above process was repeated, resulting in the launch (2360) of 4 interstellar spacecrafts reaching 4 other stars also 10 light years away (2380). The upshot is that this "ripple" will be expanding at a rate of 10 light years in 120 years' time, with the number of stellar systems colonized by humankind doubling in the same period. 120 years may look like a long time, but the diameter of the Milky Way Galaxy will thus be traversed in 10,000 years, a mere eye blink in the history of the Universe. It takes 150,000 years for our ancestors coming out of East Africa to people every corners of the Earth. It may take less than one-tenth of the time to people every corners of the Galaxy. A sobering thought indeed.

An even more sobering thought is that the above could be achieved without any humans leaving the Solar System at all. What with the advances in AI and self-replicating Von Neumann probes, everything could be done by machines. In the first movie based on the *Star Trek* franchise (*Star Trek: the Motion Picture*, 1979), Earth is visited by such a machine intelligence. The question that naturally arises is that unless humankind is the first intelligent species to appear in the Galaxy, should the Galaxy - including the Earth - not be colonised by some elderly alien species already? This is the famous Fermi's Paradox, which we will explore in greater detail in a later section.

Coming back to humankind's expansion into space, knowing the spirit of adventure innate to the human psyche, would you bet that we would leave the exploration of the Universe all to the machines? George Mallory is famously quoted as having replied to the question, "Why did you want to climb Mount Everest?" with the retort, "Because it's there". Would this not be the same reason that would propel humans outward into the interstellar void?

With this in mind, let's come to the question of whether a day will come when the number of people living off Earth will exceed those remaining. To a large extent, this would depend on how many Earth-like worlds we will be able to find out there. To date, scientists have discovered some 4900 planets circling other stars, with several dozens of these extrasolar planets, or exoplanets in short, orbiting within a habitable zone around its parent star. Life as we know it - ourselves included - may find the environment on such planets welcoming. Research has since shown that, in our Milky Way galaxy of 300 billion stars, there could be over 10 billion potentially habitable Earth-sized planets, and this is just a conservative estimate. All these 'Earth 2.0' could one day become humanity's "home away from home." In the longer term, descendants of such worlds may find "Earth" to be a romantic myth lost in the early pre-history of the human race.

On the other hand, "Earth 2.0" may forever be a utopian dream, and we may not be able to find another planet half as congenial as our home planet. This is the pessimistic premise of the 2015 novel *Aurora* written by science fiction writer Kim Stanley Robinson. But even if this is the case, large number of people may still choose to live in space habitats within the Solar System, following the ideas as propounded by the scientist Gerald O'Neil. A typical design is a rotating cylinder nearly 50 kilometres long and 10 kilometres in diameter. The inner wall of the cylinder will provide living space for thousands with simulated gravity. There will be farms, hills, forests, rivers, lakes, as well as clouds and local weather. How many people will eventually live in such space cities? Only time will tell.

If I were forced to place a bet, I would venture that 500 years is too short for off-Earth population to exceed that of Earth's. Given a few more centuries, however, the answer may well be different.

Humankind Beyond
Recognition?

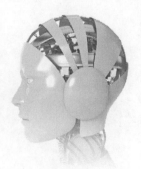

Our discussions so far have been premised on the assumption that the human race remains more or less the same in 500 years' time. But what if human beings have transformed itself beyond recognition by then?

From an evolutionary perspective, 500 years is of course too short a period for significant biological changes, either physical or mental. Imagine we brought two persons from the past, from 500 and 5000 years ago respectively, and showed them the present-day world. They would be bedazzled, bewildered, and the one from 5000 years ago might just exclaimed, that this world was "beyond recognition!" Yet the more they saw, and the longer they stayed with us - and assuming, most importantly, they were as wise as we - they would eventually understand how things worked and how the contemporary human society operated, amazing and somewhat incomprehensible though they might have appeared to them initially. Finally, these persons from the past would settle down and blend in with the rest of us, sighing in relief - and in disappointment - that although things looked different on the surface, deep down, human nature, *especially the dark side of it* (selfish and self-centred, lazy, and slack, greedy for power and wealth), remained the same.

True, set against the vast backdrop of human history, 500 years may not be ample time for human nature to change. But do not forget that in a compound growth situation - of which humanity's onward development is one - the exponential curve rises sharply in due time. The "Great Acceleration" which started less than 200 years ago means that we might just be at this stage. Will the human race - with the help of genetic engineering and advanced biomedical technology - change beyond recognition 500 years from now?

We have examined the possibility of 'man-machine amalgamation' in *Chapter 10.2*, so let us move on to the next questions:

5. Has strong AI become reality? Is it recognised as a citizen, or gaining personhood?

6. Has the technological singularity (uploading of the human mind) occurred?

7. Has the human race been genetically reengineered? Are there superhumans? If so, do they come in different species?

Should there be a 'yes' to any of the above questions, it will certainly spell a major upheaval to the human condition.

Humankind has been the sole intelligent species dominating the Earth for millions of years. The appearance of strong AI, one that ranks equal to if not above humans in intelligence and level of consciousness, will pose an unprecedented challenge to the human race. What sort of relationship would there be between them and us? Would an AI which had acquired a consciousness still be our willing servant? Would an AI with superior intelligence look down upon us as weaklings, as we on other animals? Or as their pets, to be cared for but not concerned about in any serious ways?

Another possible outcome is the union of humans and AI, in which ultimately the two become one. The melding of two intelligent minds might well make humanity's dream of immortality come true. Imagine our individual memory, experience and consciousness could be uploaded and multiple backup files of ourselves were made. In the event something was to go wrong - highly unlikely given the advanced technology we are imagining - simply upload a backup file and everything would be as good as new. Is this how one secures eternal existence? Or is a new 'me' born every time a backup file is uploaded? Who will then be the real "me"? Some might find this philosophical quandary too much to contemplate.

How would supporters of post-humanism rise to this challenge? I know not what their answers will be, but for myself, I could only aspire to the Buddhist concept of Nirvana, where one is released from the endless cycling of birth, death and rebirth, and all sorts of mundane sufferings, with the self being extinguished in the process. To be incorporated into a super-consciousness which transcends life, death, space, and time, the loss of the self may be something worthy of celebration, rather than a cause for consternation.

But let us leave the realm of mysticism and come back to reality - or the reality in 2520 a mere five centuries from now. Has humanity almost completely re-engineered himself to beyond recognizable? Fish-like, so they can now live in the oceans, or plant-like because their skin cells contain chlorophyll for photosynthesis, bird-like with hollow bones and much stronger breast muscles powering wings so they can fly, or at least glide? Or so modified that they can live in the vacuum of space or the lunar surface, or on Mars? And what about the mind? Telepathy? Mind-meld? Will scenes as depicted in the 1968 film *Barbarella* come true? In one of scenes, all one needs to do in making love is touching the other's hand, achieving sensual and emotional satisfaction well beyond the raw orgasm of physical copulation.

The total re-engineering of humans has been given a name "pantropy" by the American science fiction writer James Blish. In his collection of stories *The Seedling Stars* (1957), he postulated that as humans spread out to the stars, they would re-engineer themselves in myriad ways to suit the conditions of different planetary surfaces. In the classic story *Surface Tension* (1952), humans have been reduced to the size of tiny tadpoles living under water, and the surface tension of water becomes so great a barrier to break through that the world of air above is a realm unknown to them, or at most the stuff of myths and legends.

Coming back to Earth, it is obvious that any design to enhance human capabilities must involve a substantial sharpening of the wit and senses. These superhuman 'post-humans' would possess a much more powerful perception and higher intelligence than we. To us, they might be incomprehensible, just as us to our clever pet. As posed at the beginning of the 1935 science fiction novel *Odd John* by Olaf Stapledon: "No matter how clever a cat, could it ever understand what is crossing the mind of the King who is holding him?".

One way to achieve an enhanced perception and intelligence is for humans to evolve a Hive Mind or Gestalt Intelligence, in which multiple minds and consciousness are linked as one single but powerful entity. This idea remains in the realm of science fiction, exemplified by the 1953 science fiction novel *More Than Human* by Theodore Sturgeon, in which individual minds were linked by telepathy to form a super-consciousness. In future, it might more likely be achieved through hardware, through man-machine amalgamation. By then, not only would we each have a unique and autonomous 'self,' we would also be part of a larger 'collective self' comprising dozens or even thousands individuals or groups.

Having done with ourselves, would we apply the same on lesser creatures? Would we raise the intelligence of cats and dogs and dolphins and apes to make them our true companions in our cosmic adventure? Should we? If so, a robot and a super chimpanzee might well make the best company on a long and lonesome space flight.

Be it machine or monkey, once made more intelligent by us, might they not turn round and find fault with their once human master now human companion? Conflict and all-out wars with such man-made creations have been a recurrent theme in science fiction and many such stories have been written and movies made. Among them are the movies *Terminator* (1984), *Matrix* (1999), *Rise of the Planet of the Apes* (2011) and their sequels. While imagined, the scenarios depicted in these movies becoming real cannot be entirely dismissed.

On a more romantic note, American science fiction writer Clifford D. Simak described in his novel *City* (1952) a future where humans have all gone into space, leaving robots and intelligent, talking dogs as the custodians of planet Earth.

What if humans are the loser? Who, or what, will replace humankind? British science fiction writer Arthur C. Clarke once said "No individual exists forever, why should we expect our species to be otherwise. Man, said Nietzsche, is a rope stretching between the animal and the superhuman - a rope across the abyss. That will be a noble purpose to have served." Words of a true visionary, just that we have no idea if, at the other end of the chain, would be Nietzsche's superman, or something beyond his wildest dreams.

Of the 14 questions I have listed, three remain unanswered:

8. Has the quest for knowledge reached its limit?

13. Has humankind repaired the natural environment on a global scale, including the 're-wilding' of Earth?

15. Have we encountered aliens?

Of the three, question 13 is the easiest to tackle. Assuming humankind managed to avert all catastrophic disasters - or managed to rebuild after one or more such catastrophes - a reformed global human society would have - so it is hoped - dutifully repaired Earth and restored the natural environment to her former glory. Forests and wetlands would be put back in their rightful place, as well as coral reefs and kelp forests in the oceans, together with their animal inhabitants, lovingly nurtured by human custodians. Plant and animal species which had unfortunately been driven to extinction would be brought back to life through genetic engineering using seeds or remnant genetic material from museum specimens, followed by a carefully planned and controlled release back into the wild. Many environmentalists have been advocating this idea of 're-wilding' the Earth, and I am hopeful it will happen, if not in the next 50 then in the next 500 years.

In other words, if we were to be put in a state of induced hibernation and set to wake up in the year 2520, the vista greeting us would be one of primeval wilderness, not a high tech megalopolis of the future. People in this future would be living the simple, leisurely, laid-back lifestyle of a village. Such a future world was depicted in British writer H.G. Wells' 1895 work of science fiction *The Time Machine*, but instead of a future society of Elois served by the subterranean Morlocks, a hideous - and carnivorous - species of mutated human slaves providing the Elois with their daily needs, ours would be 'staffed' by eternally functioning and forever vigilant Von Neumann robots.

Incidentally, one future scenario of which the re-wilding of nature is but an ironic outcome, would be the self-destruction of the human race. Left unimpeded and undisturbed, Nature proceeds to take over the entire planet once again. This has happened, though on a much smaller and restricted scale, in and around Chernobyl the ill-fated city in Ukraine, after the majority of its 17,000 population was forced to flee the nuclear power plant meltdown in April 1986.

I dare say by way of prediction, that by 2520 - assuming human society had not destroyed itself, or, having suffered a cataclysmic setback but was able to bounce back and recover fully - the human society as a whole would have stopped killing animals for their meat. The days of a meat-eating humankind would be looked upon as a stage of infancy and barbarism, and regarded either in disdain, or immense compassion. As to whether this is a required step in the progress to Buddhahood, I dare not say. Yet I am as sure that humans would continue to enjoy a bite of succulent, albeit cloned and lab-grown, meat.

10.7 We Are Not Alone,
or Are We?

Of the two remaining questions, readers may find the one on the limit of knowledge (Q8) a tough one while the other, the one about encountering aliens, easy. Anyway the two do not seem to be connected in any way. In fact, not only are these questions closely connected, one informs the other on the respective predictions.

Despite the hype created by Eric Von Daniken in his work *Chariots of the Gods* (book in 1968, movie in 1970), there is so far no evidence that the Earth, and the human race, have ever been visited by any alien civilization from outer space. Were such an alien civilization to exist, and be capable of traversing vast distances in the Universe, there is nothing to stop them - or it - from dropping by at any moment in time past, present, or future. On the cosmic timescale, the chance of this happening - or not - should be not much different whether we cast our eyes to 50 or 500 years into the future. In short, it could happen tomorrow, or not in a thousand years.

That is true if humanity was to just sit tight and wait to be visited. It would be different though in 500 years, at which time we would have mastered much more advanced means of detection (of intelligent signals from outer space) and of space travel (on the scale of star systems and at much higher speed, both manned and unmanned), significantly increasing the chance of coming into contact with an alien race. And don't forget: this alien race can be anything from being unimaginably more advanced than us, on par, or vastly behind us. Imagine our interstellar probe landing on a world inhabited by beings at a stage of development similar to the Peking Man who lived 500,000 years ago and already using fire. Isn't this not an alien encounter all the same?

Next let us examine the likelihood of invasion, colonisation, and destruction by the arrival of an extraterrestrial race.

We now know that the Universe came into being 13.8 billion years ago, and the Earth 4.6 billions years ago. Dinosaurs ruled the Earth for nearly 150 million years, but became extinction around 65 million years ago. The evolutionary split between our primate ancestors and that of our closest relative the chimpanzee took place around 7 million years ago, and we began to walk on two legs around 4 millions ago. During all these unimaginably long spans of time, human civilization has a history of just over 10 thousand years, a mere blink on the cosmic timescale. While modern science arose some 400 years ago, and the Industrial Revolution some 200 years ago, it is only during the last hundred years that humankind took to the sky in planes, fathomed the ocean depths in submarines and broke out into space with rockets. The Nuclear Age, Space Age and Computer Age are all less than a century old. I have pointed out earlier that intelligent species in outer space could be more backward than us, like the fire-using Peking Man. On the other hand, they could in all likelihood be more advanced than us. Now the question is, under the second scenario, how advanced would they be if their science and technology are 100 hundred years, 500 years, or 1,000 years ahead of us?

Just spend a second to contemplate this, and you would realize that even if they are just 100 years ahead of us, their technology will be so much more advanced that if they decide to invade us, the chance of us putting up any effective form of resistance is virtually zero. So much for the heroism as depicted in the Hollywood blockbuster *Independence Day* (1996).

This brings us to the vital question "Is there a limit to knowledge?" and "Has this limit been reached 500 years from now?" This is pertinent to the question of "alien invasion" because if there is no limit to knowledge, the conclusion above will be inevitable. Humankind will not stand a chance if any civilization more advanced than us decides to subjugate us. On the other hand, if there is a limit to knowledge, AND that this limit has been reached by us in 500 years' time, than no matter the alien civilization is 1,000 or 100,000 years more advanced than us in terms of technological development (say, 1,000 years has passed since the splitting of the atom), we would be roughly at a par with them in terms of technological prowess, and resistance to their invasion would still be possible.

Try putting this question of "limit of knowledge" to a hundred top scientists at the forefront of their respective fields of research, I dare say not one will concede that there is a limit to knowledge (you may call that romantic faith). And yet, science historians have pointed out a slowing down in the pace of new discoveries and a reduction in the number of breakthroughs over the past half century. This is especially so in several areas of basic scientific inquiry, such as the relativity theory, quantum mechanics, the origin of the Universe, chaos theory and genetics. Apart from the much-anticipated unification of the theories of relativity and quantum mechanics (more specifically the emergence of a theory of "quantum gravity"), we may not witness another heroic age of scientific discovery as exciting as the 20th century.

Is our collective "failure of nerve" and "failure of imagination" to blame, making us too conservative or even pessimistic about the prospect of a continual and unlimited advance in knowledge? Or is there really a limit to what we can know, one which we cannot deny *a priori*? No one can tell.

Looked at from another angle, why should we need to worry about being invaded by aliens from outer space? A strong argument could be made that extraterrestrial beings that possess the means to travel between the stars would be so far ahead of us in their technology that they would have no need for anything from our world. Imagine an alien race from a post-scarcity world living a lifestyle of abundance, with an unlimited supply of energy at their disposal, possessing the Midas touch, and served in all their needs and wants by armies of Von Neumann machines. Why would they want to take over our planet and drive us to extinction?

Some would further argue that alien civilisations much more technologically advanced than us, with a lethal arsenal of mass destruction at their disposal, would have to be as well developed in their morals. If that was not the case, so the argument goes, these aliens would have long since blown themselves up. Our fear of an alien invasion and plundering is but a reflection of humanity's innate and immature insecurity complex.

In truth, these analyses are all conjectural. The optimistic arguments above have not precluded the portrayal of aliens in popular literature as evil and aggressive. In his science fiction magnum opus the *Three Bodies* Trilogy (2008 - 2010), Chinese writer Liu Cixin put forward the 'Laws of the Dark Forest'. The underlying argument is that alien species by definition possess alien values and motivations, and even if one out of a thousand such species has a sadistic urge to snuff out other intelligent species whenever possible, the logic of explosive technological growth means that any species slightly technologically inferior will have their fates sealed. The only course of action open to any up-and-coming intelligent species is therefore try to conceal your existence as much as possible, and if once discovered, destroy the other species given the first opportunity. This is one of the darkest thesis ever propounded with regard to extraterrestrial intelligence.

There are scientists who would readily agree, including ones as prominent as the physicist Stephen Hawking (1942-2018), who warned in 2010 that humans should avoid making contact with aliens that he thought almost certainly exist, adding "the outcome (of an alien visit) would be much as when Columbus landed in America, which didn't turn out well for the Native Americans."

A true pessimist may also want to contemplate this other prospect, that there are no aliens whatsoever, and the human race is alone in this Universe. We would be safe from alien invasion, and that is good news. But we will also be utterly lonely, which some would find unbearable.

Soviet astrophysicist Nikolai Kardashev (1932-2019) proposed in 1964 an ascending scale to measure a civilization's level of technological advancement based on the amount of energy at its disposal, starting from the civilization's home planet, it's mother star, and through to the galaxy where its planetary system was situated. On this scale, the humanity has not even reached the level of a Type I civilization.

Technologically advanced civilizations across the Universe would be Type II (able to use all the energy of their mother star) or III (able to use all the energy of the galaxy) on the Kardashev scale, and as such we should be able to find telltale signs of their technological footprints (from various astro-engineering projects) via astronomical observations. To date, we have not found any. So, "where is everybody?" This was the question asked by Italian-American physicist Enrico Fermi (1901-1954) in 1950. If extraterrestrial intelligent life was so commonplace, why have we not found evidence of their presence already? This became known as the 'Fermi Paradox.'

Attempts have been made over the years to resolve this paradox. One answer is that just as indigenous people living in the Amazon rainforest may not be aware of radio waves around them, we are too backward to have detected any signs of their presence. Alternatively, alien civilizations may have deliberately concealed their presence, lest any inadvertent contact interfere with the natural development of other semi-intelligent species. This latter argument forms the 'Prime Directive' running through the *Star Trek* series, as a form of a cosmic 'non-interference' policy.

There is yet another plausible response to the Fermi Paradox. For some reason, humanity is the only species in the Universe to have evolved higher intelligence. There may be countless worlds out there harbouring all sorts of life forms, but none of these have evolved either intelligence or advanced technology or both. We are a one-off - one can even say freak - occurrence.

This may not sound as unthinkable as it seems. Dinosaurs dominated the Earth for 150 million years, yet they remained lizards. Even if that asteroid impact 65 million years ago causing worldwide extinction did not happen, and dinosaurs thus spared the fate of extinction, they would have gone on to thrive happily as before.

If intelligence only arose once in this Universe, and we are that lucky one, that would explain why we have not found any signs of other advanced extraterrestrial civilizations, Type I, II, III or otherwise, because there is none. Fermi Paradox solved.

Or we might well be the only *surviving* intelligent species in the entire Universe, for now. Extraterrestrial intelligence may well be commonplace in the Universe, but they never made it past the point where their technological prowess exceeded their moral growth. Their advanced technology *would have* destroyed them before they knew it was too late. In short, there is a self-destruct bottleneck which no intelligent species is able to pass through.

I wish I knew which way the truth lies. But for wishful thinking, I would love to believe that, somewhere in this vast expanse of time and space, there exists one or more technologically advanced civilization, and that - even more wishful thinking - a handful if not most of them would be wise enough not to let madness mangle their minds and end up annihilating themselves and their worlds. If only this was true for humanity as well.

Assuming humanity came into contact with extraterrestrial intelligence. Are we sufficiently similar to allow us to communicate and understand one another? Terrestrial life forms are as varied and diverse as the environments they inhabit, imagine an alien life form which has evolved in an environment so different from ours, so strange to us, that our scientists might not even know it is alive, let alone intelligent. How do they live? How would they look? What would they think? What about their beliefs and values? In short, how different are they from us? Once again we are reminded of the famous saying of British biologist J.B.S Haldane, that "the Universe is not only queerer than we suppose, but queerer than we can suppose," but in this case, replace Universe with Aliens. We all are prone to the failure of nerve when it comes to the question of extraterrestrial life. I would heartily recommend two works of science fiction about communicating with aliens: *The Black Cloud* (1957) by British astronomer Fred Hoyle (1915-2001) and *Solaris* (1961) by Polish writer Stanislaw Lem (1921-2006), the latter twice made into a movie.

There is this mind-boggling equation which is not in any science textbook: solve for X where

$$X : \text{human} = \text{human} : \text{ant.}$$

To make it more mind-boggling still, simply substitute 'ant' with 'virus.'

It used to be the domain of gods, deities and spirits in which X resides. Evolution, however, opens up another possibility. Give it another 50,000, or 500,000 even 5,000,000 years, we might find a humanity whose physical and spiritual realms have become totally incomprehensible, even unknowable, just as ours are incomprehensible to humans from 50,000, 500,000 or 5,000,000 years ago. It is my belief that given time, and plenty of it, 'X' in the equation above no longer has to be something requiring faith. It can be something born of and evolved in nature.

How would we find out? Well if we merely set our sights here on Earth, we would need to somehow go into hibernation and wake ourselves up in 5 million or 50 million years' time and see for ourselves. But if we cast our net far and wide, there might be plenty of surprise in store out there in the Universe. To a Universe 13.8 billion years old, 1 or 10 million years is merely an instant, but that instant, long enough for a lemur-like animal to evolve to an intelligent human being, surely would be long enough for biological beings to evolve into a level of sophistication and intelligence that would be god-like.

And in principle, these god-like super intelligent extraterrestrials might call on us anytime!

Encountering an alien will be a watershed moment in the history of humanity. It matters not that these aliens turned out to be less advanced than us. Their very existence, and the way we perceive, receive, and interact with them - or shall I say 'it' - will be the real test of our moral standards. Humanity has been there and done that, countless times in our history, and failed miserably. To find out, watch the movie *Avatar* (2009) for a sanitized rendition instead of a history documentary.

Another perceptive observation made by Arthur C. Clarke is also highly thought-provoking: "Sooner or later, we will meet types of intelligent life much advanced than our own, yet in forms completely alien. And when that time comes, the treatment man receives from his superiors may well depend upon the way he behaved toward the other creatures on his own world." Not very encouraging indeed.

There is yet another perspective on the whole matter. Even if we encountered a perfectly benign but far more advanced alien race, humanity may just the same be at risk - the risk of feeling inferior and beaten in the face of vast superiority, and the risk of losing our zest in exploring the mysteries of the Universe and pushing the boundaries of our knowledge and technology. Why put up with such sacrifice to reach the South Pole in Antarctica, if one knows that it has already been reached a month ago?

Goethe once said, "If God were to reveal all the mysteries of the Universe to us tomorrow, that would have put us in a most awkward situation, for knowing all the secrets of nature, we would not know what to do next, and would descend into utter despair and boredom." We may be in this position following an "encounter of the third kind."

So it all boils down to: If we received a call from an alien, and it could be as soon as tomorrow, should we answer it or not?

What remains a fantasy now could very well have become a fact by 2520, and hopefully by then, humanity is much better equipped, and prepared, to face that fact.

British science fiction writer Arthur C. Clarke once said in relation to the existence or otherwise of aliens, "Two possibilities exist: either we are alone in the Universe, or we are not. Both are equally terrifying." A terrifying 500 year travail indeed.

10.8 The Questions
We Don't Know…

This then is the end of our journey to a world 500 years in the future. Or to be honest, this is the end to the limit of my own imagination.

Remember the words of J.B.S. Haldane, "that the Universe is not only queerer than we suppose, but queerer than we *can* suppose"? Insight from history will show that there are many crucial questions missing. That's because there are questions we simply don't know how to ask.

In the best-selling satirical science fiction novel *The Hitchhikers' Guide to the Galaxy* written by British writer Douglas Adams in 1979, intelligent species across the Galaxy collaborated on the construction of a gargantuan super-computer. When asked to provide the answer to the ultimate question concerning "Life, the Universe and Everything", the computer entered a deep trance which lasted for 7.5 million years. At last, the computer announced it had succeeded, and the answer is 42. When asked what was the question to which the answer applies, the computer said it would be an even more stupendous – and hence more time-consuming - task to find out.

While this is just one of the many jokes in the novel, it does contain a deep insight i.e. it is often much more difficult to come up with the right question than seeking the right answer. Imagine we invited the most learned people with the most fertile imagination and the broadest of vision, all from 500 years ago in 1520, and asked them to predict what the world would be like in 500 years' time. Would they have asked the following questions?

By 2020,

• How many automobiles will there be in the world?

• How many flights and air passengers will there be each day?

• What are the number of countries possessing nuclear weapons?

• Which is the most powerful country in the world?

• Which are the top ten banks in the world?

• What is the percentage of the population connected to the Internet, and the percentage in possession of a smart phone?

• How many countries have conferred voting rights to their female population?

I can go on listing similar questions, but these already show the limitation imposed by the changing times on one's power to predict. Intellectuals in the year 1520 simply could not have forecast a world five centuries hence in any realistic terms, as automobiles, aeroplanes, nuclear weapons, banks, universal suffrage, smart phones, the Internet, and the United States of America did noy exist at that time. The highly imaginative might have predicted the automobiles and aeroplanes, as chariots that run by themselves, and men flying like birds. As for the others, it would be totally beyond their cognitive horizon. From a logical perspective, if they were able to forecast the emergence of the banking system, then banks would have come into existence in the 16th century, instead of the beginning of the 17th century.

Likewise, for us in 2020 (year of the Chinese edition of this book; English edition in 2023), predictions about a world in 2520 would most likely be laughable and totally off the mark. The truly pertinent questions to ask would be something like

• Will A be in condition X?

• Will B be in condition Y?

• Will C be in conditions Z?

Where A, B, C and X, Y, Z are things which at present are beyond our imagination.

Therein lies the allure of the future. The only thing we could be certain of is that there will be surprises. Still, it would not prevent us from making guesses. It costs nothing and it's a lot of fun. What more could we ask for?

Concluding Thoughts:

The End of Childhood, or
The End?

Our journey has come to an end. Whether it be 50 or 500 years into the future, the most important question is whether we would witness the decline of humanity? Or is it really the beginning of the grand adventure of humankind? Nobody knows. What we know for sure is that the human race is still rather young in evolutionary terms. Ants have been around for 140 million years. *Homo sapiens*, at a mere 200,000 years or so, are the new kid on the block.

Dinosaurs have long been ridiculed as an evolutionary failure, and yet they have lasted 24 times longer than us. Humankind would have to outlive the dinosaurs by at least 150 million years before we are qualified to make fun of them.

The Universe is still young, and our Sun younger still. Scientific research has shown that our Sun, formed about 4.6 billion years ago, can expect to shine for another 5 billion years. But no amount of scientific research has been able to, or indeed can, foretell how much longer humankind would exist. Palaeontologists tell us that since the rise of mammals at 65 million years ago, after the demise of the dinosaurs, the average lifespan of a mammalian species is around one million years or more. It would be a great irony if humankind, considered the Crown of Creation, turns out to be much more short-lived.

In 1960, American astronomer Frank Drake made the first attempt to detect radio signals coming from alien civilisations. Although no such signal was detected, Drake's effort inspired him and other scientists to look deeper into question, resulting in the formulation of the famous Drake Equation in 1961. An important part of the equation turns out to have not so much to do with aliens, but rather to do with us, or more specifically, how long would the human race as an intelligent species exist before we destroy ourselves.

The Drake Equation runs like this:

$$N = R_* f_p n_e f_l f_i f_c L.$$

where

N = the number of civilizations currently in the Milky Way Galaxy with which communication might be possible;

and

R_* = the average rate of star formation in our Galaxy;

f_p = the fraction of those stars that have planets;

n_e = the average number of planets that can potentially support life per star that has planets;

f_l = for planets that could potentially support life, the fraction that actually develop life;

f_i = the fraction of planets with life that actually go on to develop intelligent life with civilizations;

f_c = the fraction of civilizations that develop advanced technology and emit detectable signs of their existence into space;

L = the average longevity of such signal-emitting technological civilizations.

Decades long research has given us a much better understanding of the first three factors: R_*, f_p, and ne. However, the other factors from f_l onward remain very much a matter of speculation. The full exploration of the equation would fall outside the purview of this book. The most salient point that concerns us here is the last factor L, for it is as much about the lifespan of alien civilisations as it is about our own.

Humankind has only been a technological civilisation capable of interstellar communication for a few decades, and if, in the decades or centuries that follow, our civilisation is unfortunate enough to collapse or even destroy itself altogether, L will prove to be very short (close to zero in the cosmic timescale).

As mentioned before, this may well be *the* answer to the Fermi Paradox. It is not that civilisations possessing high degree of technology are rare. It is that all of them also possess a strong tendency to destroy themselves over time. Such a civilisation will blossom only briefly, before descending into oblivion (the Great Filter hypothesis). It will be therefore be very unlikely for us to catch one such technologically advanced alien civilisation in its heyday. If that was true, it is no surprise that so far we have not detected any signals from an alien civilisation.

What is the value of *L* for humanity? Ten thousand years? Ten million years? Or, like the dinosaurs, measured in hundreds of millions of years? I have shown how difficult it is predicting a future 500 years hence. Imagining one a hundred even thousands of times further into the future is almost impossible. What I am certain is this: if humankind can last that long, what we are going through now will just be humankind's childhood, or at most adolescence.

If we could survive the throes of adolescence, I am quite confident that humankind will spread out to the stars. Konstantin Tsiolkovsky (1857-1935), widely considered as the Father of Spaceflight, once said "The Earth is the cradle of humanity, but one cannot stay in the cradle forever." Yes, the challenge of space is tremendous, but if we fail to meet it, the story of our race will be humdrum and bounded. The choice, as British writer H.G. Wells once put it, is the Universe – or nothing! Writing in 1933, he continued: "For Man, there could be no rest and no ending. He must go on, conquest beyond conquest. First this little planet, its winds and ways and all the laws of mind and matter that restrain him. Then the planets about him, and at last out across the immensity to the stars. And when he has conquered all the deeps of space and all the mysteries of time – still he will be but beginning...."

Of course there is this other possibility, that as highly intelligent species gain mastery over matter, energy or even their own mind, they would have lost interest in interstellar communication, not to say interstellar exploration. They might become, in the words of the Irish poet W.B. Yeats 'Oh who would have foretold. That the heart grows old', or that worldly affairs would no longer be worthy of their concern. Such a situation was described by science fiction writer John W. Campbell in his 1937 story 'Forgetfulness'.

Which outcome will it be? No one can tell. And here, what Isaac Newton said centuries ago is as pertinent to himself as to the entire human race:

'I may not know what I appear to the world, but to myself I seem to have been only like a boy playing on the seashore, and diverting myself in now and then finding a smoother pebble or prettier shell than ordinary, whilst the great ocean of truth lay undiscovered before me.'

Yes, when faced with the immensity of the Universe, a sense of awe and humility is a most natural reaction. Science fiction writer Ray Bradbury captures the essence of the human condition most beautifully with these words: "The thing that drives me most often is an immense gratitude that I was given this one chance to live, to be alive the one time round in a miraculous experience that never ceases to be glorious and dismaying. I accept the whole damn thing. It is neither all beautiful nor all terrible, but a wash of multitudinous despairs and exhilarations about which we know nothing. Our history is so small, our experience so limited, our science so inadequate, our theologies so crammed in mere matchboxes, that we know we stand at the outer edge of a beginning and our greatest history lies before us, frightening and lovely, much darkness and much light...... In order to survive, we have to forgo asking that one question any longer: Why live? Life was its own answer. Life was the propagation of more life and the living of as good a life as possible."

Although it may seem arrogant, I was motivated to write this book to ensure that "our greatest history lies before us". By pointing out that we are all in dire strait, hopefully we will do our best to navigate through the roaring rapids ahead and arrive safely in calmer waters. Only then are we in a position to embark on a New Renaissance, and bring forth a new Golden Age.

Eddy Lee Wai-choi

3rd July 2023

Sydney

(Chinese edition: 31st October 2019

University of Hong Kong Library)

Further Reading

Since this is not an academic treatise, this section will not follow the formal citation styles. Instead, books will be recommended under different topical headings. Under each heading, classic works will be listed first, with the rest presented in the following order: (1) scope and breadth of treatment, from general to specific; (2) from less technical to more technical, and (3) year of publication, from less recent to more recent. For each book, the title will come first, followed by year of publication and author. Information on the publisher is omitted, as this is readily available from the internet.

A. On the Origin and Evolution of Humankind

1. *Man's Place in Nature* (1863) Thomas Huxley

2. *Seven Million Years* (2007) Douglas Palmer

3. *Your Inner Fish: A Journey into the 3.5-Billion Year History of the Human Body* (rev ed. 2009) Neil Shubin

4. *Master of the Planet: the Search for Our Human Origins* (2012) Ian Tattersall

5. *Lone Survivors* (2012) Chris Stringer

6. *Last Ape Standing* (2013) Chip Walter

7. *Evolution - The Human Story* (rev ed., 2018) Alice Roberts

8. *Our Human Story* (2018) Louise Humphrey and Chris Stringer.

9. *Human Origins - 7 Million Years and Counting* (2018) "New Scientist"

10. *Humans: From the Beginning* (2018) Christopher Seddon

11. *The Neanderthals Rediscovered: How A Scientific Revolution Is Rewriting Their Story* (2022) Dimitra Papagianni

12. *Cro-Magnons - How the Ice Age Gave Birth to the First Modern Humans* (2010) Brian Fagan

13. *Who We Are and How We Got Here: Ancient DNA and the New Science of the Human Past* (2019) David Reich

B. On the Logic of Evolution and Human Nature

1. *Sociobiology: The New Synthesis* (1975) Edward O. Wilson

2. *The Selfish Gene* (1976) Richard Dawkins

3. *The Evolution of Cooperation* (1984) Robert Axelrod

4. *Genome - Autobiography of a Species in 23 Chapters* (2013) Matt Ridley

5. *The Naked Ape* (1967) Desmond Morris

6. *On Human Nature* (1978) Edward O. Wilson

7. *The Third Chimpanzee* (1991) Jared Diamond

8. *The Human Touch* (2006) Michael Frayn

9. *The Ethical Primate: Humans, Freedom and Morality* (1994) Mary Midgley

10. *The Moral Animal* (1995) Robert Wright

11. *Our Inner Ape* (2005) Frans de Waals

12. *Primates and Philosophers - How Morality Evolved* (2006) Frans de Waal

13. *The Moral Landscape* (2010) Sam Harris

14. *The Social Conquest of Earth* (2012) Edward O. Wilson

15. *Moral Origins: The Evolution of Virtue, Altruism and Shame* (2012) Christopher Boehm

16. *The Language Instinct* (1994) Steven Pinker

17. *How the Mind Works* (1997) Steven Pinker

18. *The Blank Slate - the Modern Denial of Human Nature* (2002) Steven Pinker

19. *The Meme Machine* (2000) Susan Blackmore

20. *The Origins of Virtue* (1996) Matt Ridley

21. *Nature Via Nurture* (2003) Matt Ridley

22. *The Agile Gene - How Nature turns on Nurture* (2012) Matt Ridley

23. *The Human Condition* (1958) by Hannah Arendt

24. *The Nature of Man* (1968) Eric Fromm

25. *The Sovereignty of Good* (1970) Iris Murdoch

26. *The Lucifer Effect* (2007) Philip Zimbardo

27. *The Better Angels of our Nature* (2011) Steven Pinker

28. *Behave: the Biology of Humans at Our Best and Worst* (2017) Robert M. Sapolsky

29. *Humankind: A Hopeful History* (2021) Rutger Bregman

30. *Thirteen Theories of Human Nature* (2017) Leslie Stevenson

31. *Philosophy and the Human Condition: An Anthology* (2017) Brain R. Clack & Tyler Hower (eds)

C. On the Origin and Evolution of Civilizations

1. *Ancient Society* (1877) Lewis Henry Morgan

2. *The Philosophy of Civilization* (1923) Albert Schweitzer

3. *A Study of History (Abridged and Illustrated)* (1972) Arnold Toynbee

4. *Mankind and Mother Earth: A Narrative History of the World* (1976) Arnold Toynbee

5. *Origins of the State and Civilization* (1975) Elman Service

6. *Plough, Sword and Book* (1988) Ernest Gellner

7. *The Horse, the Wheel, and Language* (2010) David W. Anthony

8. *The Intimate Bond: How Animals Shaped Human History* (2015) Brian Fagan

9. *The Human Web: A Bird's Eye View of History* (2003) John R. McNeill & William H. McNeill

10. *Maps of Time* (2011) David Christian

11. *Big History* (2012) Cynthia Stokes Brown

12. *Sapiens: A Brief History of Humankind* (2015) Yuval Noah Harari

13. *The Story of Mankind (Updated)* (rev. ed.2013)Hendrik W. van Loon

14. *The Outline of History (Annotated & Illustrated): The Whole Story of Man* (rev. ed. 2017) H.G. Wells

15. *Guns, Germs and Steel* (1997) Jared Diamond

16. *The World Until Yesterday: What We Can Learn from Traditional Societies* (2012) Jared Diamond

17. *A Short History of Progress* (2004) Ronald Wright

18. *The Human Swarm: How Our Societies Arise, Thrive, and Fail* (2019) Mark W. Moffett

19. *A New Green History of the World* (new ed. 2007) Clive Ponting

20. *Collapse: How Societies Choose to Fail or Succeed* (2004) Jared Diamond

21. *A People's History of the World* (1999) Chris Harman

22. *Debt: the First 5,000 Years* (2011) David Graeber

23. *The Ascent of Money* (2009) Niall Ferguson

24. *A People's History of Civilization* (2018) John Zerzan

25. *The Square and the Tower* (2015) Niall Ferguson

26. *Energy and Civilization: A History* (2018) Vaclav Smil

27. *1001 Ideas that Changed the World* (2013) Robert Arp

D. Civilization in the Last 500 Years

1. *The Ascent of Man* (1973) Jacob Bronowski

2. *The Discoverers* (1991) Daniel J. Boorstin

3. *The Scientific Revolution* (1996) Steven Shapin

4. *The Age of Wonder* (2008) Richard Holmes

5. *The Dream of Enlightenment: the Rise of Modern Philosophy* (2017) Anthony Gottlieb

6. *Capitalism, Socialism and Democracy* (1942) Joseph Schumpeter

7. *The Great Transformation: the Political and Economic Origins of Our Time* (1944) Karl Polanyi

8. *The Social Origin of Dictatorship and Democracy* (1966) Barrington Moore

9. T*he Origins of Political Order* (2012) Francis Fukuyama

10. *Political Order and Political Decay* (2015) Francis Fukuyama

11. *Europe and the People without History* (1982) Eric Wolf

12. *Roads to Xanadu: East and West in the Making of the Modern World* (1989) John Merson

13. *Voltaire's Bastards: The Dictatorship of Reason in the West* (1992) John Ralston Saul

14. *The Origin of Capitalism: A Longer View* (1999) Ellen Meiksins Wood

15. *The Dynamics of Capitalism* (1985) Fernand Braudel

16. *The Nature and Logic of Capitalism* (1985) Robert Heilbroner

17. *The Limits to Capital* (1982) David Harvey

18. *The Great Divergence* (2000) Kenneth Pomeranz

19. *Before European Hegemony: the World System A.D. 1250 - 1350* (1991) Janet L. Abu-Lughod

20. *Sea Power: the History and Politics of the World's Oceans* (2017) Admiral James Stavridis

21. *Spaces of Capital: Towards a Critical Geography* (2001) David Harvey

22. *Why the West Rules - For Now* (2010) Ian Morris

23. *Civilization: the West and the Rest* (2011) Niall Ferguson

24. *The World System: Five Hundred Years or Five Thousand?* (1996) (eds) Andre Gunner Frank & Barry K. Gills

25. *World-Systems Analysis - An Introduction* (2004) Immanuel Wallerstein

26. *The Long Twentieth Century: Money, Power and the Origins of our Times* (1994) Giovanni Arrighi

27. *The Rise and Fall of the Great Powers* (1989) Paul Kennedy

28. *The Age of Extremes: the Short Twentieth Century 1914-1991* (1994) Eric Hobsbawm

29. *The New Imperialism* (2003) David Harvey

30. *The Enigma of Capital* (2010) David Harvey

31. *Upheaval: Turning Points for Nations in Crisis* (2019) Jared Diamond

32. *The Nutmeg's Curse: Parables for a Planet in Crisis* (2022) Amitav Ghosh

E. Humankind's Predicament in the Modern World

1. *Civilization and Its Discontents* (1930) Sigmund Freud

2. *Science and the Modern World* (1925) Alfred N. Whitehead

3. *The Scientific Outlook* (1931) Bertrand Russell

4. *The Social Function of Science* (1942) J.D. Bernal

5. *The Open Society and Its Enemies* (Vol I-III, 1945; one volume ed. 2013) Karl Popper

6. *Two Cultures: A Second Look* (1963) C.P. Snow

7. *Technopolis: Social Control of the Uses of Science* (1969) Nigel Calder

8. *Morality and Modernity* (1991) Ross Poole

9. *The Consequences of Modernity* (1991) Anthony Giddens

10. *The End of History and the Last Man* (1992) Francis Fukuyama

11. *The Clash of Civilization and the Remaking of World Order* (1996) Samuel P. Huntington

12. *The World Is Flat* (2005) Thomas Friedman

13. *Thank You for Being Late* (2016) Thomas Friedman

14. *The Meaning of the 21ˢᵗ Century* (2006) James Martin

15. *Globalization and its Discontents Revisited : Anti-Globalization in the Era of Trump* (2002, rev. ed. 2018) Joseph Stiglitz

16. *Falling Off the Edge: Globalization, World Peace and Other Lies* (2008) Alex Perry

17. *When Corporations Ruled the World* (2005) David Korten

18. *Expulsions: Brutality and Complexity in the Global Economy* (2014) Saskia Sassen

19. *Talking to My Daughter About the Economy : A Brief History of Capitalism* (2019) Yanis Varoufakis

20. *The Dilemmas of Domination* (2005) Walden Bello

21. *Secret History of the American Empire* (2008) John Perkins

22. *The Limits of Power: The End of American Capitalism* (2009) Andrew J. Bacevich

23. *No Logo* (1999) Naomi Klein

24. *The Collapse of Globalism and the Reinvention of the World* (2005) John Ralston Saul

25. *Capitalism and Freedom* (2007) Peter Nolan

26. *Bad Money* (2008) Kevin Philips

27. *How to Rule the World* (2008) Mark Engler

28. *The Globalization Paradox* (2010) Dani Rodrik

29. *Is Globalization Over?* (2019) Jeremy Green

30. *The Price of Civilization* (2011) Jeffrey Sachs

31. *Mismeasuring Our Lives: Why GDP Doesn't Add Up* (2011) Jean Paul Fitouss, Joseph Stiglitz & Amartya Sen

32. *The Global Minotaur* (2011) Yanis Varoufakis

33. *Currency Wars* (2011) James Rickards

34. *The Road to Ruin* (2016) James Rickards

35. *The Dollar Trap: How the US Dollar Tighten its Grip on Global Finance* (2015) Eswar S. Prasad

36. *The US Dollar and Global Hegemony* (2019) Thomas Costigan & Drew Cottle

37. *Capital in the 21st Century* (2013) Thomas Picketty

38. *The Urge of Capital: Root Cause of the World's Deep Contradictions* (2015) Eddy Wai Choi Lee

39. *Capitalism's Last Stand: Deglobalization in the Age of Austerity* (2013) Walden Bello

40. *The Revenge of Geography* (2012) Robert D. Kaplan

41. *Prisoners of Geography* (2015) Tim Marshall

42. *World Order* (2014) Henry Kissinger

43. *How the World Works* (2011) Noam Chomsky

44. *Hegemony or Survival* (2014) Noam Chomsky

45. *Who Rules the World?* (2017) Noam Chomsky

46. *Superclass: The Global Power Elite and the World They Are Making* (2009) David Rothkopf

47. *Winners Take All: The Elite Charade of Changing the World* (2018) Anand Giridharadas

48. *No is Not Enough* (2017) Naomi Klein

49. *On Tyranny: 21 Lessons from the 21st Century* (2017) Timothy Snyder

50. *The Power of the Powerless* (1985) Vaclav Havel

51. *The Parliament of Man: the Past, Present and Future of the United Nations* (2007) Paul Kennedy

52. *The Life and Death of Democracy* (2010) John Keane

53. *How Democracies Die* (2018) Steven Levitsky & Daniel Ziblatt

54. *Fascism: A Warning* (2019) Madeleine Albright

55. *How To Stop Fascism: History, Ideology, Resistance* (2022) Paul Mason

56. T*he Age of Surveillance Capitalism* (2019) Shoshana Zuboff

57. *We Have Been Harmonized: Life in China's Surveillance State* (2018) Kai Strittmatter

58. *The Hundred-Year Marathon - China's Secret Strategy to Replace America as the Global Superpower* (2016) Michael Pillsbury

59. *Destined for War - Can America and China Escape the Thucydides Trap?* (2017) Graham Allison

60. *Ill Winds: Saving Democracy from Russian Rage, Chinese Ambition and American Complaceny* (2019) Larry Diamond

61. *The Good State: The Principles of Democracy* (2020) A.C. Grayling

62. *Empty Planet: the Shock of Global Population Decline* (2019) Darrell Bricker & John Ibbitson

63. *The Space Barons: Elon Musk, Jeff Bezos and the Quest to Colonize the Cosmos* (2018) Christian Davenport

64. *Survival of the Richest: Escape Fantasies of the Tech Elite* (2022) Douglas Rushkoff

F. Neoliberalism and Managerialism

28. *The Road to Serfdom* (1944) F.A. Hayek

29. *Capitalism and Freedom* (1962) Milton Friedman

30. *Free to Choose* (1980) Milton & Rose Friedman

31. *Anarchy, State and Utopia* (1974) Robert Nozick

32. *The Commanding Heights: the Battle for the World Economy* (2002) Daniel Yergin & Joseph Stanislaw

33. *The Conscience of a Liberal* (2007) Paul Krugman

34. *A Brief History of Neoliberalism* (2007) David Harvey

35. *The Shock Doctrine: the Rise of Disaster Capitalism* (2007) Naomi Klein

36. *The Assault on Reason* (2007) Al Gore

37. *The Neoliberal State* (2009) Raymond Plant

38. *The Man Who Sold the World* (2010) William Kleinknecht

39. *Why the Third Way Failed* (2010) Jill Jordan

40. *Profit Over People: Neoliberalism and Global Order* (2011) Noam Chomsky

41. *The Precariat: the New Dangerous Class* (2011) Guy Standing

42. *What Money Can't Buy: the Moral Limits of Markets* (2013) Michael J. Sandel

43. *Plutocrats: the Rise of the Global Super-Rich and the Fall of Everyone Else* (2013) Chrystia Freeland

44. *Undoing the Demos: Neoliberalism's Stealth Revolution* (2015) Wendy Brown

45. *In the Ruins of Neoliberalism: the Rise of Anti-democratic Politics in the West* (2019) Wendy Brown

46. *Water Wars: Privatization, Pollution and Profits* (2015) Vandana Shiva

47. *Contesting Neoliberal Education* (2011) David Hill (ed.)

48. *Managerialism: A Critique of an Ideology* (2013) Thomas Klikuaer

49. *Neoliberal Culture* (2016) Jeremy Gilbert

50. *Cutting School: Privatization, Segregation and the End of Public Education* (2017) Roliwe Rooks

51. *Privatization* (2018) James Sherwood

52. *The Unconscious Civilization* (1999) John Ralston Saul

53. *At Any Cost: Jack Welch, General Electric and the Pursuit of Profit* (1999) Thomas F. O'Boyle

54. *Money and Power: How Goldman Sachs Came to Rule the World* (2011) William D. Cohan

55. *Gigged: the Gig Economy, the End of Job & the Future of Work* (2018) Sarah Kessler

56. *Will the Gig Economy Prevail?* (2019) Colin Crouch

57. *Confronting Managerialism* (2011) Robert R. Locke & J-C Spender

58. *Overcoming Managerialism* (2022) Robert Spillane and Jean-Etienne Joullié

G. On the Environmental Crisis

1. *The Limits to Growth* (1972) Donella H. Meadows

2. *Limits to Growth: the 30-Year Update* (2002) Donella H. Meadows etal

3. *The Ages of Gaia* (1988) James Lovelock

4. *The Revenge of Gaia* (2000) James Lovelock

5. *The End of Nature* (1989) Bill McKibben

6. *The Sixth Extinction* (1995) Richard E. Leakey & Roger Lewin

7. *The Story of Stuff* (2010) Annie Leonard

8. *Earth in the Balance* (1992) Al Gore

9. *An Inconvenient Truth* (2007) Al Gore

10. *The Long Emergency* (2006) James Howard Hunstler

11. *The Last Generation: How Nature will take her Revenge for Climate Change* (2006) Fred Pearce

12. *The Bridge at the Edge of the World* (2008) James Gustave Speth

13. *The Long Thaw* (2008) David Archer

14. *Storms of My Grandchildren* (2009) James Hansen

15. *Six Degrees: Our Future on a Hotter Planet* (2009) Mark Lynas

16. *Our Final Warning: Six Degrees of Climate Emergency* (2020) Mark Lynas

17. *Hell and High Water* (2009) Joe Room

18. *Hot, Flat and Crowded* (2009) Thomas L. Friedman

19. *Requiem for a Species* (2010) Clive Hamilton

20. *Our Dying Planet* (2011) Peter Sale

21. *The Ecological Rift: Capitalism's War on the Earth* (2011) John Bellamy Foster

22. *The Great Disruption* (2011) Paul Gilding

23. *The End of Growth* (2011) Richard Heinberg

24. *Field Notes from a Catastrophe* (2004) Elizabeth Kolbert

25. *The Sixth Extinction* (2014) Elizabeth Kolbert

26. *This Changes Everything* (2015) Naomi Klein

27. *Learning to Die in the Anthropocene* (2015) Roy Scranton

28. *The Coming Famine* (2010) Julian Cribb

29. *When the Rivers Run Dry* (2006) Fred Pearce

30. *Full Planet, Empty Plates* (2012) Lester R. Brown

31. *Food Wars* (2015) Tim Lang & Michael Heasman

32. *Climate Wars* (2015) Harald Welzer & Patrick Camilla

33. *Half-Earth: Our Planet's Fight for Life* (2017) Edward O. Wilson

34. *The Water Will Come* (2017) Jeff Goodell

35. *Rising Tides: Climate Refugees in the 21st Century* (2017) John R. Wennersten & Denise Robbins

36. *The Uninhabitable Earth* (2019) David Wallace-Wells

37. *What Every Environmentalist Needs to Know about Capitalism* (2011) Fred Magdoff & John Bellamy Foster

H. On the Threat of Big Data & AI

1. *World Without Mind: the Existential Threat of Big Tech* (2017) Franklin Foer
2. *Weapons of Math Destruction: How Big Data Increases Inequality and Threatens Democracy* (2018) Cathy O'Neil
3. *The People Vs Tech: How the Internet is Killing Democracy* (2018) Jamie Barlett
4. *Don't Be Evil: The Case Against Big Tech* (2019) Rana Foroohar
5. *Our Final Invention: Artificial Intelligence and the End of the Human Era* (2013) James Barrat
6. *Superintelligence: Paths, Dangers, Strategies* (2014) Nick Bostrom
7. *Surviving AI* (2015) Calum Chace
8. *The Economic Singularity: AI and the Death of Capitalism* (2016) Calum Chace
9. *Thinking Machines* (2016) Luke Dormeh
10. *Life 3.0: Being Human in the Age of Artificial Intelligence* (2017) Max Tegmark
11. *The Fourth Age: Smart Robots, Conscious Computers, and the Future of Humanity* (2018) Byron Reese
12. *Artificial Intelligence: A Guide for Thinking Humans* (2019) Melanie Mitchell
13. *A Human Algorithm* (2019) Flynn Coleman
14. *Artificial You* (2019) Susan Schneider
15. *Human Compatible: AI and the Problem of Control* (2019) Stuart Russell
16. *The AI Economy: Work, Wealth and Welfare in the Age of Robots* (2019) Roger Bootle
17. *Killer Robots: Lethal Autonomous Weapon Systems Legal, Ethical and Moral Challenges* (2016) Dr. U.C. Jha
18. *Should We Ban Killer Robots?* (2022) Deane Baker
19. *Fantastic Voyage: Live Long Enough to Live Forever* (2004) Ray Kurzweil & Terry Grossman
20. *The Singularity is Near* (2005) Ray Kurzweil
21. *Transhumanism: the History of a Dangerous Idea* (2015) David Livingstone

I. Predicting the Future

1. *The Poverty of Historicism* (1957) Karl Popper

2. *Profiles of the Future* (1962) Arthur C. Clarke

3. *Future Shock* (1970) Alvin Toffler

4. *The Third Wave* (1980) Alvin Toffler

5. *Power Shift* (1990) Alvin Toffler

6. *Megatrends* (1982) John Naisbitt

7. *Searching for Certainty: What Science Can Know About the Future* (1991) John L. Casti

8. *Why Things Bite Back?* (1996) Edward Tenner

9. *Superforecasting: The Art and Science of Predicting the Future* (2015) Philip Tetlock and Dan Gardner

10. *Blockchain Revolution* (2018) Don Tapscott & Alex Tapscott

11. *The Truth Machine: Blockchain and the Future of Everything* (2018) Michael J. Casey & Paul Vigna

12. *What Next? Surviving the Twenty-First Century* (2008) Chris Patten

13. *The Next 100 Years* (2009) George Friedman

14. *The World in 2050* (2010) Laurence C. Smith

15. *2052: A Global Forecast for the Next 40 Years* (2012) Jorgen Randers

16. *The Future: Six Drivers of Global Change* (2012) Al Gore

17. *The Collapse of Western Civilization: A View from the Future* (2014) Naomi Oreskes

18. *The Economic Singularity: Artificial Intelligence and the Death of Capitalism* (2016) Calum Chace

19. *Physics of the Future* (2011) Michio Kaku

20. *Tomorrow's People* (2009) Susan Greenfield

21. *Homo Deus* (2016) Yuval Noah Harari

22. *New Dark Age: Technology & the End of the Future* (2018) James Bridle

23. *The Future of Humanity* (2018) Michio Kaku

24. *On the Future: Prospects for Humanity* (2022) Martin Rees

25. *The Next 500 Years: Life in the Coming Millenium* (1996) Adrian Berry

26. *The Next Ten Thousand Years* (1975) Adrian Berry

27. *Deep Future* (2001) Stephen Baxter

28. *Deep Future: the Next 100,000 Years of Life on Earth* (2011) Curt Stager

29. *The Eerie Silence: Are We Alone in the Universe?* (2010) Paul Davies

30. *The Great Filter: Where Is Everybody?* (rev ed 2023) Gerard Alexander Willighagen

31. *Black Swan: the Impact of the Highly Improbable* (2008) Nassim Nicholas Taleb

J. The Way Forward

1. *Scientific Humanism* (1926) Lothrop Stoddard

2. *The Expanding Circle* (1981) Peter Singer

3. *One World - Now* (2004; rev. ed. 2016) Peter Singer

4. *Steady-State Economics* (1977, rev. ed. 1991) Herman E. Daly

5. *The Future of Life* (2002) Edward O. Wilson

6. *Manifesto for a New World Order* (2003) George Monboit

7. *Deep Economy* (2007) Bill McKibben

8. *Development as Freedom* (1999) Amartya Sen

9. *The Idea of Justice* (2009) Amartya Sen

10. *Plan B 4.0: Mobilizing to Save Civilization* (2009) Lester R. Brown

11. *The Global Deal* (2009) Nicholas Stern

12. *Agenda for a New Economy* (2010) David Korten

13. *The Green Collar Economy* (2009) Van Jones

14. *The Monfort Plan: the New Architecture of Capitalism* (2010) Jamie Pozuelo Monfort

15. *Prosperity Without Growth* (2008, rev. ed. 2016) Tim Jackson

16. *Post-Growth: Life After Capitalism* (2021) Tim Jackson

17. *Our Choice* (2009) Al Gore

18. *Beyond Capitalism & Socialism* (2008) Tobias J. Lanz (ed.)

19. *The Global New Deal* (2010) William F. Felice

20. *Anti-Capitalism* (2011) Ezequiel Adamovsky

21. *After Capitalism (new ed.* 2011) David Schweickart

22. *The Zeronauts: Breaking the Sustainability Barrier* (2012) John Elkington

23. *Of the People, By the People* (2012) Robin Hahnel

24. *Occupy the Economy: Challenging Capitalism* (2012) Richard D. Wolff & David Barsamian

25. *Democracy at Work: A Cure for Capitalism* (2012) Richard D. Wolff

26. *Alternatives to Capitalism* (2014) Robin Hahnel & Erik Olin Wright

27. T*he Zeitgeist Movement Defined: Realizing a New Train of Thought* (2014) Tzm Lecture Team

28. Here Comes Everybody: the Power of Organizing without Orgnizations (2008) Clay Shirky

29. *The Democracy Project: A History, a Crisis, a Movement* (2014) David Graeber

30. *The Age of Sustainable Development* (2015) Jeffrey Sachs

31. *Out of the Wreckage: A New Politics for An Age of Crisis* (2017) George Monboit

32. *Drawdown: The Most Comprehensive Plan Ever Proposed to Reverse Global Warming* (2017) Paul Hawken

33. *Net Zero: How We Stop Causing Climate Change* (2022) Dieter Helm

34. *How To Avoid a Climate Disaster* (2022) Bill Gates

35. *Humanity's Moment: A Scientist's Case for Hope* (2022) Joelle Gergis

36. *The Global Green New Deal* (2010) Edward Barbier

37. *The Green New Deal* (2019) Jeremy Rifkin

38. *The Green New Deal* (2019) Larry Jordan

39. *The Case for the Green New Deal* (2019) Ann Pettifor

40. *On Fire: the (Burning) Case for a Green New Deal* (2019) Naomi Klein

41. *Climate Crisis and the Global Green New Deal: the Political Economy of Saving the Planet* (2020) Noam Chomsky et al

42. *Sustainable Nation: Urban Design Patterns for the Future* (2018) Douglas Farr

43. *The Big Switch: Australia's Electric Future* (2022) Saul Griffith

44. *The Superpower Transformation: Making Australia's Zero-Carbon Future* (2022) Ross Garnaut

45. *The Spirit Level: Why Equality is Better for Everyone* (2008) Kate Pickett & Richard Wilkinson

46. *New Rules for Global Justice: Structural Redistribution in the Global Economy* (2016) ed. Jan A. Scholte etal

47. *People, Power and Profits: Progressive Capitalism for an Age of Discontent* (2019) Joseph Stiglitz

48. *In Defence of Democracy* (2019) Roslyn Fuller

49. *In Defence of the Open Society* (2019) George Soros

50. *Unfree Speech: The Threat to Global Democracy and Why We Must Act Now* (2020) Joshua Wong & Jason Ng

51. *The Great Turning* (2005) David Korten

52. *Change the Story, Change the Future* (2015) David Korten

53. *The Empathic Civilization* (2010) Jeremy Rifkin

54. *Enlightenment Now* (2018) Steven Pinker

55. *Fully Automated Luxury Communism: A Manifesto* (2019) Aaron Bastani

56. *Clear, Bright Future: A Radical Defence of the Human Being* (2019) Paul Mason

57. *Interest and Inflation Free Money* (1995) Margrit Kennedy & Declan Kennedy

58. *The Deficit Myth: How to Build a Better Economy* (2020) Stephanie Kelton

59. *Raising the Floor* (2016) Andy Stern & Lee Kravitz

60. *Basic Income: A Guide for the Open-Minded* (2017) Guy Standing

61. *The Case for Universal Basic Income* (2019) Louise Haagh

62. *Plunder of the Commons: How to Take Back Our Shared Wealth* (2019) Guy Standing

63. *Feral: Rewilding the Land, Sea and Human Life* (2013) George Monboit

64. *Regenesis: Feeding the World without Devouring the Planet* (2022) George Monboit

65. *What We Owe the Future: A Million-Year View* (2022) William Macaskill

66. *Envisioning Real Utopias* (2010) Erik Olin Wright

67. *Utopia for Realists: and How We Can Get There* (2014) Rutger Bregman